THE HOUSING POLICY
REVOLUTION
NETWORKS AND NEIGHBORHOODS

Also of interest from the Urban Institute Press:

Public Housing and the Legacy of Segregation,
by Margery Austin Turner, Susan J. Popkin,
and Lynette Rawlings

Subprime Mortgages: America's Latest Boom and Bust,
by Edward M. Gramlich

THE URBAN INSTITUTE PRESS
WASHINGTON, DC

THE HOUSING POLICY REVOLUTION

NETWORKS AND NEIGHBORHOODS

David J. Erickson

THE URBAN INSTITUTE PRESS
2100 M Street, N.W.
Washington, D.C. 20037

Library of Congress Cataloging-in-Publication Data

Erickson, David James.
 The housing policy revolution : networks and neighborhoods / David J. Erickson.
  p. cm.
 Includes bibliographical references and index.
 ISBN 978-0-87766-760-5
 1. Housing policy—United States—History—20th century. I. Urban Institute.
II. Title.
  HD7293.E75 2009
  333.33'8—dc22

2009019202

Printed in the United States of America
11 10 09   1 2 3 4 5

THE URBAN INSTITUTE is a nonprofit, nonpartisan policy research and educational organization established in Washington, D.C., in 1968. Its staff investigates the social, economic, and governance problems confronting the nation and evaluates the public and private means to alleviate them. The Institute disseminates its research findings through publications, its web site, the media, seminars, and forums.

Through work that ranges from broad conceptual studies to administrative and technical assistance, Institute researchers contribute to the stock of knowledge available to guide decisionmaking in the public interest.

Conclusions or opinions expressed in Institute publications are those of the authors and do not necessarily reflect the views of officers or trustees of the Institute, advisory groups, or any organizations that provide financial support to the Institute.

for Doug

Contents

Acknowledgments

A project as long as this leaves one in debt to a great many people. This book draws many ideas and insights from friends and colleagues in my work as the director of the Center for Community Development Investments at the Federal Reserve Bank of San Francisco. I would like to express my gratitude to the members of our advisory committee and the many community development practitioners and academics who have collaborated with us over the past four years on research projects, conferences, and conversations about community development.

While the Federal Reserve System gets headlines for supporting the financial system and setting interest rates, it also has a small group dedicated to researching and sharing best practices in community development. My colleagues at the Federal Reserve have given me valuable advice; they include Naomi Cytron, Ian Galloway, John Olson, Carolina Reid, and Scott Turner. I also had considerable help from Pat Rhea in our research library. While I am grateful for the input and suggestions from work colleagues, the views represented in this book are my own and do not reflect the views of the Federal Reserve.

The core aspects of this book were part of my dissertation in U.S. history at the University of California, Berkeley. I was fortunate to have a dissertation committee with expertise and patience. My thanks go to the chair of my dissertation committee, Richard Abrams, who taught me how to study U.S. history and guided this project for years. Robin

Einhorn provided many insightful critiques; her clear thinking is astonishing. John Quigley also gave valuable advice. He is one of the leading housing economists in the country, and as the I. Don Terner Chair of Housing Economics at Berkeley, has proved a statesman of affordable housing policy. David Kirp has also been an important advisor on this project and this project would not have been possible without his help. An influential early advisor was Langley Keyes at MIT who got this project started through informal conversations many years ago.

It has been difficult to cover such a vast terrain—30 years of housing policy history that bears witness to a significant shift in practice, from centralized bureaucracy to local policy networks. If there were an archive for this transition, it would be the Environmental Design Library at the University of California, Berkeley. The library has an amazing collection of government documents, industry journals, activist newsletters, and pamphlets. This is the case in part thanks to Berkeley professors, like Don Terner, who were on the cutting edge of all these program eras, from the 1960s to the 1990s. The foresight of these individuals, along with committed librarians, was instrumental in preserving so many government sources and documents from the larger affordable housing movement.

While I was at Berkeley, I had the good fortune to receive the advice and encouragement from several friends. Two served above the call of duty and offered many comments on early drafts—thanks to D. Bradford Hunt and Michelle Hoffman. Another important colleague with many helpful insights and contacts has been Margaret Pugh O'Mara at the University of Washington, Seattle, who shares a belief that historians have important lessons for policymakers.

Many friends helped this project by listening to my ramblings and, more painfully, reading early drafts. My thanks go to Brendan Barth, Mollyann Brodie, Suzzane Delbanco, Steve and Irene Juniper, and Michele Mozelsio. My father, James Erickson, also lent his considerable editing talent to this project. Janet Falk, a tireless housing developer and activist, not only helped shape and present the ideas contained in this book, but took the time to teach me about affordable housing policy and development.

I'm grateful to the Urban Institute Press staff who helped move this project along, including Kathy Courrier, Scott Forrey, and William Bradbury. I am also in debt to two anonymous reviewers who pushed me to provide more information and fill gaps in my arguments.

My husband Doug Jutte has read every page of this book many times. That alone is enough for special commendation. More than that, he has made the last nine years an adventure, and for that, I am ever grateful.

Introduction
Revolutionary Change in Housing Policy, 1964–2006

I n the public imagination, the idea of government-subsidized housing conjures up thoughts of a hopelessly inefficient Department of
Housing and Urban Development (HUD) or high-rise "projects" where
crime and drugs are rampant. That impression, however, bears little
resemblance to subsidized housing today. As a practical matter, HUD
has been out of the housing construction business since 1978. While it
plays a big role in providing Section 8 housing vouchers, it does not
build much housing other than small projects for senior citizens and
people living in rural areas.[1] Few people, however, are aware of HUD's
current role, even those who care deeply about low-income communities. In a recent op-ed article in the New York Times (July 2008), for
example, Columbia Professor Sudhir Venkatesh criticized HUD as an
ineffective tool for alleviating poverty and advocated its elimination.[2]
The reality is that for more than 20 years HUD has taken a back seat to
the new network of players now driving affordable housing policy; the
network includes HUD but also local advocacy organizations, nonprofits, and for-profit corporations, as well as local, state, and federal
government agencies and others. This network builds well-designed,
high-quality homes.

A Flexible, Decentralized, and Well-Integrated System

The recent history of government-subsidized housing should bring to mind architecturally significant apartment buildings that add value to their neighborhoods. These new government-subsidized programs have helped empower thousands of local communities through new institutions such as community development corporations (CDCs) and have helped revitalize many places that seemed hopeless a generation ago. Benson Roberts, senior vice president for policy and program development for the Local Initiatives Support Corporation, describes the current state of affordable housing production:

> Over the past 20 years, a cluster of federal policies has supported a flexible, decentralized, and well-integrated production system. The system is distinctively market driven, locally controlled, and performance based. It builds sustainable partnerships among nonprofit and for-profit developers, private lenders and investors, as well as among all levels of government. (Roberts 2008b, 36)

While the current approach to housing policy in America is producing better homes for low-income individuals and families than ever before, it is doing more than that: it is in the vanguard of how government delivers social services. This new approach to building housing demonstrates that multiple, disparate groups can form problem-solving networks and deliver high-quality housing and services. This change has contributed significantly to the much-acclaimed "comeback" of the American city. The influence of this model, first developed in the delivery of affordable housing, is even greater, however, because it is now providing an inspiration for policy areas as diverse as economic development, education, health, and the environment.

At first glance, this volume might appear to be another book on how public policy today often involves contracting outside of government and relying on public-private partnerships. That approach first captured widespread attention with David Osborne and Ted Gaebler's *Reinventing Government* (1992) and much of the so-called third-way literature that was inspired by the Bill Clinton–era policy changes. This literature also includes more recent works such as Stephen Goldsmith and William Eggers's *Governing by Network* (2004). But what these other books do not do is follow closely the formation of these partnerships—how they operate, cooperate, and execute over time. Brief treatments of public-private partnerships do not capture the complexities of these new policy-implementing structures.

The Housing Policy Revolution chronicles, through a historical analysis of political debates and detailed case studies, how a network approach to policy implementation developed in the 1970s, 1980s, and 1990s. It provides an in-depth history of who was involved, how they worked together, and what they built.

Evolution of Federal Housing Programs

In 1996, the *New York Times Magazine* ran an article that described affordable housing as a political issue that had "evaporated" (DeParle 1996, 52). The *Washington Post* reported that HUD was seen as a "scandal-ridden, regulatory rat's nest."[3] HUD survived calls for its dismantling, but only barely. HUD, which had once spearheaded all production of low-income housing, saw its production programs whither. HUD produced 248,000 housing units in 1977, but by 1996 that number had dropped to 18,000 and has remained low since. Housing scholar and advocate Peter Dreier concluded in 1997 that recent history was a period of political retreat for low-income housing programs: "The political constituency for housing policy is weaker and more fragmented now than it has been in decades." Dreier (1997, 273) lamented the loss of the old housing coalition that pushed access to housing as "part of the broad social contract." Other studies on recent housing policy, including Mara Sidney's *Unfair Housing: How National Policy Shapes Community Action* (2003), were severely critical of the federal government's abdication of responsibility for providing housing for low-income Americans. These critiques were published against the backdrop of significant need for affordable housing. The U.S. Census Bureau's "American Communities Survey" indicates that in 2006, 46 percent of all renters were paying more than 30 percent of their gross income on housing—a level generally considered a severe burden.[4]

The decline of federally built affordable housing closely follows the commonly accepted story about the U.S. welfare state generally—that it developed between the 1930s and the late 1960s and then suffered a series of setbacks during the 1970s, which triggered a political backlash. According to this interpretation, conservative politicians from Richard Nixon to Ronald Reagan successfully harnessed white middle-class anger over government programs to roll back the welfare state. At first glance, the fate of federal programs that subsidize apartments for low-income tenants confirms this narrative: the federal government created housing programs during the New Deal, added to them significantly during the 1960s, and in the 1980s cut them back in the wake of bad press, conservative attacks, and policy mistakes of the late 1960s and 1970s. The problem with this story is that you might have trouble hearing it over the din of construction of the more than 2 million federally subsidized apartments for low-income tenants built between 1986 and 2006 (NCSHA 2008). These units were built by for-profit and nonprofit housing developers and funded largely with tax credits and federal block grants.[5] The number of subsidized apartments met only a fraction of the need, but by 2008 there were nearly 33 percent more homes built under new government low-income housing finance programs (after 1986) than there were subsidized apartments built by all the HUD-sponsored programs dating back to the 1960s.[6] In fact, the number of homes built by the post-1986 programs compare favorably with *all* the existing subsidized apartments built since the beginning of federal programs in 1937 (2.0 million versus 2.7 million).[7]

The Rise of a Stealth Housing Program

Despite the lofty rhetoric of housing programs like the Housing Act of 1949, which promised every American family a "decent home and a suitable living environment," the federal government never built many low-income apartments.[8] In fact, in some years, it destroyed more units than it built. Before the creation of the Department of Housing and Urban Development in 1965, the peak annual production of affordable housing through the public housing program was 71,000 units in 1954 (Orlebeke 2000). During the Great Society, the production numbers skyrocketed for a four-year period to nearly half a million units annually. This pace was short-lived, however.

In 1973, Richard Nixon imposed a moratorium on new construction, in part because there were many complaints that bad design and shoddy workmanship created instant slums. HUD had one more burst of building during the Carter administration, but since then the number of units it builds has remained low.

As HUD building programs fizzled, funding for low-income housing was on the rise. While a new housing finance program, the 1986 Low Income Housing Tax Credit (LIHTC), churned out fewer units than the peak HUD production years, it did so at a rate that was higher than the historic average and consistent for over 20 years. By 2005, the program was funding more than 130,000 apartments annually (NCSHA 2008). To say that the federal government has been out of the affordable housing business since the Reagan administration is simply wrong.

During the 1980s two simultaneous policy revolutions took place (or perhaps a revolution and a counterrevolution). Reagan dramatically eliminated funding for low-income housing and cut back the role of the federal government in housing. At the local level, though, a revolution from below pulled together community groups, local and state governments, and elements of the private sector to find ways to build housing for low-income tenants without federal help. In 1988, housing advocate Paul Grogan testified before Congress that

> the brute force of the federal cutbacks in housing in the last seven or eight years, while doing undeniable harm to many, have produced an unprecedented response in the housing arena at the state and local levels and have activated a staggering array of new involvements on the part of state and local government, the nonprofit sector, the private sector, labor unions, churches, and the list goes on. (U.S. Congress 1988b, 332)

The local effort started small but demonstrated how a decentralized housing network might work. The 1980s were a period of tremendous institution building, although it took place at the local level and often went unnoticed. In time, the network grew in sophistication, became politically active, and lobbied successfully for more federal resources. The most important new funding programs were the Community Development Block Grant (1974), the Low Income Housing Tax Credit (1986), and HOME funds from the National Affordable Housing Act in 1990 (see figure I.1).[9]

The housing built through these programs was of higher quality than earlier low-income housing and was politically popular (a significant improvement over the old policies), but these programs did not solve the housing problem. The new network lacked the resources to build what was necessary for most of America's lowest-income families. The units built since 1986 were not for tenants who were as poor as those in projects built during the Great Society but instead targeted the working poor (tenants who earned less than 50 or 60 percent of the median income in their area).[10] Even so, the new programs managed to serve tenants who were poorer than the statutes required. A 1997 Government Accountability Office (GAO) report that surveyed projects built with funding from the 1986 LIHTC program—the largest of the new programs for subsidizing low-income housing—found that three-quarters

Figure I.1. Funds from CDBG (Land and Housing), HOME, and the Low Income Housing Tax Credit

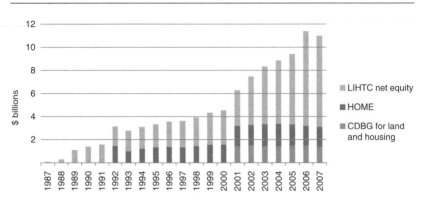

Notes: The data on the HOME Investment Partnership Program (HOME) and the Community Development Block Grant (CDBG) Program come from the U.S. Department of Housing and Urban Development's Office of Policy Development and Research. The CDBG program has been around since 1974; it is a large program with many goals. I have only counted the CDBG dollars allocated to land acquisition and preparation for development (e.g., demolition or environmental remediation) and housing. Those figures are broken out for CDBG budgets back to 2001.

   Data on net LIHTC equity are based on an estimate from Richard Floreani, senior manager at Ernst & Young's Tax Credit Investment Advisory Services. It is based on a combination of published data (e.g., the total amount of tax credit authority), statistical data (e.g., median tax credit pricing by year), and estimates (e.g., the percentage of the market invested on a guaranteed versus unguaranteed basis).

of the households earned less than 50 percent of the median income in their area (U.S. GAO 1997).

What Happened to the Welfare State

While the evolution of the decentralized housing network is important in its own right, it also sheds light on a larger story about recent public policy history, especially the history of the welfare state.[11] Historical scholarship on the welfare state maintains that this institution shrank in the face of deft attack and weak defense (Katznelson 1989; Edsall and Edsall 1991).[12] But what has happened to the welfare state since the 1970s and 1980s is more complicated. In subsidized housing programs, both liberals and conservatives were frustrated with the programs of the Great Society, and while they disagreed on emphasis, both looked to change the delivery of social services.

Some aspects of the welfare state have been weakened since the 1970s, but others innovated and grew. At the same time that the *Washington Post* was reporting that "HUD is about as popular as smallpox," billions of federal dollars began to flow into new subsidized housing programs.[13] Liberals like House Ways and Means Committee Chairman Charles Rangel joined with conservatives to increase block grants and tax expenditures for affordable housing at the same time they were cutting HUD's budget authority. Even more interesting, increased funding to subsidized housing through programs such as tax credits were enormously popular. These political debates lacked the sharp edge of prior eras and appeared to demonstrate a "willingness to walk away from ideology," in the words of Jack Kemp, George H.W. Bush's HUD Secretary (U.S. Congress 1989, 6).

This paradox in affordable housing policy illustrates many of the recent changes within the welfare state. The most dramatic change from the 1970s was not scaled-back funding—although that certainly affected key programs for the very poor—but a shift in how the federal government delivered welfare state services and who was served.[14] The federal government used an array of new policy tools (tax policy, regulation, loans, and loan guarantees) to induce nongovernment players (nonprofit corporations and for-profit firms) to participate in shaping new programs to deliver social services. Lester Salamon (2002), Steven Rathgeb Smith and Michael Lipsky (1993), Jacob Hacker (2002), Christopher Howard (1999), Julian Zelizer (1998), and Jennifer Klein (2003) have shown that when these other funding mechanisms are taken into account, the U.S. welfare state is larger and more comprehensive than one would conclude by looking only at the bureaucracy-led, and direct expenditure-funded, programs. The government used incentives for social services with increasing frequency in the 1980s and 1990s, challenging the popular conception of a withering welfare state.

Revolutionary Change in Housing Policy

To illuminate the revolutionary change in housing policy from the 1960s to the present, this book traces the historical events and larger forces that have shaped the options for politicians and activists over the past 40 years. The history is important because it shows that sometimes policymakers had few choices and that larger forces and trends often shaped the terrain on which this battle was fought. The history also demonstrates that many decisions and policies have had unintended consequences. What I lay out here suggests that for many years a current of many streams had been carrying us toward the policy we now have. The current was fed in part by history, in part by ideology, and in part by technology, but in all cases it was brought to life by policy actors—decisions made and not made along the way by individuals. Some of those decisions were made by powerful people on Capitol Hill and in corporate board rooms. Many of them were made by people who were less powerful—local activists and advocates hoping to improve communities. Together, they developed a new approach to building affordable housing.

Plan of the Book

To be clear, this book does not cover all housing issues. It focuses on how affordable rental housing has been built over the past 40 years, with a particular emphasis on subsidized multifamily development because since the War on Poverty, the effort to revitalize low-income communities has centered almost exclusively on developing safe and decent affordable rental housing.[15] In fact, in recent years, the terms *affordable housing* and *community development* are often used interchangeably. Lately, there has been an effort to broaden the strategies used to revitalize communities, an effort motivated partly by the re-recognition that all well-functioning communities need many ingredients to thrive, including jobs, good schools, safe streets, and the like.

In addition, programs that target individuals—including housing vouchers and income support programs (especially the earned income tax credit)—are crucial to helping low-income individuals and families afford shelter. While some important programs help low-income people buy homes, these programs are not within the scope of this book.

Directions in Housing Policy from Johnson to Reagan

Chapter 1 examines housing policy history from the mid-1960s to the mid-1980s over two distinct periods: (1) the rise and fall of federal bureaucracies, 1964–81; and (2) federal cutbacks 1981–86. The chapter outlines these broad policy shifts by examining two seminal reports that framed the debates and subsequent policies on housing and urban renewal programs. The first report was the voice of the Great Society in "A Decent Home: The Report of the President's Committee on Urban Housing" (U.S. President's Committee on Urban Housing 1969). The Kaiser Report, so named for the chairman of the committee Edgar Kaiser, was an analysis concurrent with, and in the spirit of, the Kerner Commission report on race. It sounded a warning and called for a spirited government response to solve social problems that affected the inner city and low-income citizens. It called for dramatically increased funding for affordable housing, coordinated by the federal government. Yet in practice, federal efforts experienced real and perceived difficulties.

The public and policymakers alike had become disillusioned with the government's inability to meet the goals the Kaiser report had set out. After the first era—the rise and fall of federal housing bureaucracies, 1964–81, came the second, in which conservatives now in power tested their strong beliefs that market forces and not government would solve the nation's affordable housing problem. "The Report of the President's Commission on Housing" (U.S. President's Commission on Housing 1982), a study conducted by a committee headed by William McKenna, was a direct attack on the housing programs of the late 1960s and trumpeted free markets as the solution to the housing problem. This second era, lasting only from 1981 to 1986, was a social welfare experiment in shock therapy. What is particularly interesting about this era was the energetic local responses where communities—local government, businesses, advocates, and nonprofits—sought new ways to meet the needs of local low-income tenants without federal help.

Building the Decentralized Housing Network

Chapter 2 takes a detailed look at the components of what later became the decentralized housing network, which include CDCs, new government entities at the state and local levels, capacity-building intermediaries, new private sector participants, and other institutions, such as foundations and the government-sponsored enterprises, Fannie Mae and Freddie Mac. This chapter documents how elements in all these different areas grew in sophistication over the 1980s; a service delivery approach that started out in church basements and city council chambers grew in capacity. In the words of one observer at the time, "The movement has matured into an industry" (Vidal 1997, 429).

Fighting for Federal Resources

Once established, this network needed more resources if it were to become more than a skirmish in a new war on poverty. Chapter 3 outlines how this network advocated for, and won, new resources. It describes a third era, which starts in 1987, that appeared to be a synthesis of previous periods.[16] A third report, "A Decent Place to Live: The Report of the National Housing Task Force" (1988), was the work of a committee chaired by David Maxwell and Jim Rouse. It argued for the federal government to get back into the subsidized housing business but in a different mode: as the funder of a new network of decentralized service providers. The new synthesis was a marriage of local networks of community development corporations, local and state government, nonprofits, and private businesses with financial resources from the federal government. In this latest stage, the network had matured and secured more funding, influence, and production capacity. As it came into its own, the network not only built more housing than the Great Society programs did but also defended itself politically. The decentralized housing network built on the conclusions of the Maxwell-Rouse report and helped pass the National Affordable Housing Act of 1990.

The affordable housing network was also behind a major push to establish the housing tax credit in 1986 and keep it alive through a series of challenges in the 1990s and early 2000s. Congress increased funding to housing tax credits by 40 percent in 2000 and indexed future increases to inflation (U.S. Congress 2000).

Lessons Learned

Chapter 4 focuses on individual low-income apartments built by the new approach to affordable housing. The chapter outlines how the different participants in the network—CDCs, banks, local government, and the private sector—worked together to build housing, even in the face of fierce opposition by neighbors and other local organized interests. Every project was different, showing how diverse and eclectic the decentralized program could be. The approach also illustrated how participants developed expertise and relationships within the network that enhanced their capabilities over time.

Consider the example of the Frank G. Mar low-income apartments in the Chinatown area of downtown Oakland, California. Built in 1988, the 119-unit project catered to young families and elderly tenants. It also included commercial space and public parking. Instead of HUD financing a single private real estate developer, as was typical, these apartments were built by a coalition of actors led by a community development corporation (East Bay Asian Local Development Corporation) and a regional nonprofit housing developer (BRIDGE Housing). In addition, the project had two local government partners—the city redevelopment agency and the city parking authority. Seven separate sources provided the financing, which included a conventional mortgage from a bank, federal block grants, and equity contributed by a corporation in exchange for federal tax credits.

What appeared to be a confusion of too many players and too many sources of funds proved to be one of the great assets of this new approach to developing affordable housing. The multiple financing programs were strings that brought the different players into a web of mutual support and supervision. Each lender and equity partner in the Frank G. Mar project had to underwrite the project separately. While it was difficult to coordinate so many players, all participants were able to vet critical development decisions. With so many people checking each other's work and decisions, the likelihood of a mistake diminished. When the project did encounter trouble—toxic contamination found on the site, for example—the same group worked together to find solutions because they were all at risk if the project failed. In the end, the project was a spectacular success; it had an award-winning design and helped bring new life to Oakland's Chinatown, providing homes for seniors citizens and families (mostly Asian Americans), commercial spaces for new businesses and social service providers (childcare, counseling), and desperately needed parking for downtown.

This web of players, or network, built higher-quality housing that was better suited to clients' needs than the affordable housing that had been built in prior eras. The network proved to be nimble in overcoming local obstacles to development—whether they were related to market problems, construction difficulties, or local political opposition.

The Rise of a New Institution

Chapter 5 explores the significance of a new type of decentralized institution that developed to supply low-income housing. Despite the fact that this institution was an amalgam of participants from the private sector, nonprofit corporations, and all levels of government (federal, state, and local), it managed to share an ideology and a culture, complete with its own practices, terminology, and mores in a way that resembles the policy communities Julian Zelizer writes about in *Taxing America*.[17] The decentralized housing network saw itself as an institution with shared interests and over the years has demonstrated considerable political acumen in organizing and promoting itself.

Because elements of this institution combined for certain projects and then disassembled only to regroup later in a different configuration for another project, it displayed an amazing capacity for adaptation. It also aggressively disseminated best practices. As a matter of course, technical problems were solved, and bad actors were weeded out. As a result, it had the ability to self-correct, self-police, and learn. In this regard, the actions of the decentralized institution have a flexibility somewhat like the market. It also policed itself in ways that were more efficient than older approaches to government regulation. And now that it is established, the decentralized housing network seems to demonstrate some time-honored characteristics of institutions, including path-dependent development, policy feedback, and expanding access to resources.[18]

Changing Our Approach to Housing Policy

Chapter 6 raises questions about where housing policy should now head to be effective. Housing policies from prior eras, were criticized because they were too slow to adapt to changing circumstances. As this book shows, however, more recent housing policies did not create programs per se but rather a decentralized institution made up of a network of service providers with the ability to anticipate and correct problems. In other words, the "program" adapts. Housing developers' use of transportation subsidies for transit-oriented development, the early adoption of "green" building techniques, and a number of innovations that tap world capital markets to fund affordable housing mortgages are examples of such adaptations.[19]

Here I argue for a new perspective on how we analyze the success or failure of a decentralized institution. Simply measuring the number of apartments built, for example, is not sufficient to determine if this network is functioning to its potential. Despite the steady drumbeat for "outcome measures" for different programs and policies, measuring what is important is difficult with such a complicated web of players. Simply examining the outcomes of each participant of the network one by one is not helpful; in some ways, exploring the space between participants (the sinews of the decentralized institution) may be what counts.

As we go forward, how will we use this network to help solve current and future problems? Even now as the country is experiencing a housing downturn that is a catastrophe for low-income home buyers and their neighborhoods, we see that the decentralized housing network is being called upon to find solutions to these new problems. Consider the testimony of the CEO of Enterprise Community Partners to the Senate Banking Committee on January 31, 2008:

> By leveraging the capacity of local governments and highly capable nonprofit organizations as well as proven programs and models—in this case, Community Development Block Grants, the ACA [HUD's Asset Control Area] program and New Markets Tax Credits—we will stem the tide of foreclosures that threatens the stability and viability of neighborhoods nationwide.[20]

And several community development intermediaries described in chapter 2 will be the lead organizations to implement the federal government's National Community Stabilization Trust to help low-income communities caught in the foreclosure crisis (Tingerthal 2009).

This chapter also looks at the blind spots and weaknesses of the decentralized housing network. One of its most serious flaws, for example, is that some communities are incapable of generating a problem-solving network, leaving them unrepresented in this new policy order. Recent research on communities of concentrated poverty by the community affairs function of the Federal Reserve System and Brookings' Metropolitan Policy Program, for example, shows that poor neighborhoods lack access to community development networks. How will such communities advance in this new era?

Among other issues, this chapter tackles a number of questions facing the community development field in light of a network perspective:

- In a decentralized network, who provides the oversight to make sure the network operates as efficiently and equitably as possible?
- Should nonprofits "scale up" to become larger and more effective institutions, or should they become more specialized?
- Should nonprofits use for-profit activities to subsidize their nonprofit work?
- Is the network equipped to handle the changing demographics of its constituencies (such as aging or newly arrived immigrant tenants)?
- How might new technology (especially web-based social network and collaboration software) enhance network outcomes?

Finally, this chapter examines how the decentralized housing network provides an example for other policy fields, such as education, economic development, and the environment.

Conclusion

The Housing Policy Revolution weaves the politics and policy into one story; it shows how national policies generate a matrix of government subsidy and information, and how some communities manage to nurture a network within that matrix to solve local problems. Understanding how these networks come together and evolve is essential to understanding how this new policy regime operates, whether it is effective and fair, and what its potential is in the future.

NOTES

1. Since the late 1970s, HUD's major programs included a small production effort for low-income elderly and rural tenants, a large housing voucher program (Section 8), an effort to undo past design and management disasters (HOPE VI), and a variety of insurance and grant programs.

2. Sudhir Venkatesh, "To Fight Poverty, Tear Down HUD," *The New York Times,* July 25, 2008.

3. Guy Gugliotta, "Report Suggests HUD Be Junked," *The Washington Post,* August 5, 1994, A19.

4. According to HUD's definition of worst-case needs, in 1978, 5.1 percent of all households fell in this category; in 2001, it was also 5.1 percent (HUD 2003, xix, 7). Another examination of how low-income renters were struggling during the economic boom years of the 1990s can be found in Nelson, Treskon, and Pelletiere (2004).

5. The Low Income Housing Tax Credit can be thought of as a tax coupon to corporate investors who put equity capital in apartment buildings rented to low-income tenants. To be considered "low income" one must earn less than 50 or 60 percent of the local area median income as measured by an annual survey by HUD. Since income is tied to local wages, it varies from county to county. The Internal Revenue Service (IRS) distributes the tax credits to state allocating agencies (typically each state's housing finance agency). They are distributed on a per capita basis—$1.25 per person from 1986 to 2001 when they were increased to $1.75 per person and indexed to inflation. In 2008, the credit was $2 per person (http://www.ncsha.org/uploads/Housing_Credit_Fact_Sheet.pdf).

6. I am comparing the two major prior building programs, public housing and HUD-assisted projects (such as 221(d)(3), 236 and Section 8) to Low Income Housing Tax Credits only. There were other subsidized homes built in the later period without tax credits, but it is nearly impossible to track them all.

Public housing is about 1.2 million units. "Since 1937, the public housing program has been one of the major federal vehicles for improving the housing conditions of low-income households, currently aiding 1.2 million households or about one-third of all those receiving assistance" (U.S. Congress 1983, 1).

HUD-assisted units total 1.5 million.

The U.S. Department of Housing and Urban Development's (HUD's) assisted project-based multifamily properties are privately owned properties representing a significant component of federally assisted housing for low-income families. This is in contrast to the public housing stock, which is publicly owned and operated. The HUD-assisted project-based multifamily housing stock includes more than 22,000 properties with more than 1.5 million units. They were developed under programs that were created in the 1960s and 1970s to supplement the public housing program, as part of a policy change that aimed to promote more privately owned development of affordable housing. (Finkel et al. 2006, vii)

7. See appendix table 5A.1 in chapter 5.

8. Housing Act PL 81-171. See also U.S. Housing and Home Finance Agency (1950). For a good background on the 1949 Housing Act, see Hoffman (2000).

9. CDBG funds are block grants to localities (counties and cities primarily) and local governments decide how to spend the money; therefore, how CDBG money is spent can vary considerably from locality to locality. CDBG money has been spent on affordable housing since the beginning of the program in 1975, but it has only been tracked as a separate category since 2001. (Reports on national disbursements of CDBG by program area are available at http://www.hud.gov/offices/cpd/communitydevelopment/budget/disbursementreports/.)

Richardson (2005, 12) notes that "The Housing and Community Development Act of 1974, as amended, established as the primary objective of the CDBG program 'the development of viable urban communities, by providing decent housing and suitable living environment and expanding economic opportunities, principally for persons of low and moderate income.'"

10. To be fair, the old system also lacked the resources to fix the problem of housing low-income Americans, and the focus on very low-income residents was a relatively brief period of the housing program. "In 1950, the median income of public housing tenants was over 60 percent of the U.S. median; by 1975, it was only 30 percent of the U.S. median" (U.S. Congressional Budget Office 1983, 2).

11. The welfare state is a term that often summarizes the set of social services that provide citizens with a social "safety net" from their governments. Many types of social services can be considered part of the welfare state, including government-sponsored health care, education, unemployment and disability insurance, and retirement benefits. Some welfare states are extensive, such as the "cradle to grave" type we often associate with Scandinavia. Others are less comprehensive. For a good overview of the different types of welfare states, see Esping-Andersen (1990).

12. For the Edsalls, the labor-dominated Democratic Party reached a political high point with the Civil Rights Act of 1964, but the increased focus on minority rights pushed it too far to the political left while the Republicans moved to the political center. However, Arnold Hirsch in *Making the Second Ghetto: Race and Housing in Chicago, 1940–1960* (1998) and Thomas Sugrue in *The Origins of the Urban Crisis: Race and Inequality in Postwar Detroit* (1996) argue convincingly that the divisions in the liberal ranks were already apparent before the Civil Rights Movement.

Many authors claim that the welfare state has withered since the 1970s, including Berkowitz and McQuaid (1988), Gilbert (2002), Levine (1988), Katz (1986, 2002), Patterson (1981), Trattner (1989).

13. Guy Gugliotta, "HUD Mans Its Lifeboats," *Washington Post National Weekly Edition*, February 13–19, 1995.

Table I.1. Federal Spending on Welfare State Services as a Percentage of GDP

	1970–75	1976–80	1981–85	1986–90	1991–96
Human Resources	9.1	11.2	11.8	10.7	12.3

Source: 2002 Federal Budget, Historic Tables (table 3.1).

14. The federal budget numbers also challenge the standard story. Direct expenditure spending did dip in the 1980s (see table I.1) and some programs—especially for the poor—have been eliminated or scaled back since the Great Society. But overall tax expenditures and direct expenditures continued to grow throughout the 1980s, albeit at a slower rate than the preceding 20 years. On this point, see Christopher Howard (1997, 35).

15. While the War on Poverty was more holistic in its approaches to community revitalization (job training, infrastructure improvements, community organizing), efforts since the 1970s have almost all focused on housing. Only in the past several years has that begun to change with such programs as the New Markets Tax Credit (small business) and efforts to promote community development financial institutions (which fund a range of community needs including homeless shelters and charter schools). In fact, I think an argument can be made that it is time to bring back the 1960s approach in a more deliberate way, combining it with the new institutions that have been built over the past 40 years—something I call Model Cities 2.0.

16. An interesting subtheme of these three presidential reports is that their chairmen reflect their zeitgeist. Kaiser was the master builder of prefab wartime housing (Greg Hise's book *Magnetic Los Angeles* has a good chapter on Kaiser Family Homes). McKenna was an ideologue who pushed the market as the solution for everything. And James Rouse and David Maxwell represented the decentralized approach to housing. Rouse founded the Enterprise Foundation, a capacity-building nonprofit intermediary and Maxwell was the CEO of Fannie Mae, another important facilitator of the decentralized housing network—especially through its purchases of low-income housing tax credits.

17. Zelizer (1988, 8) describes the tax policy community that included "political party officials, leaders and experts from umbrella business and financial associations (such as the Chamber of Commerce), staff members of the executive and congressional branch, bureaucrats and administrators, university professors, independent specialists, editors and writers of the specialized policy media, and participants in think tanks."

18. On path dependency and policy feedback, see Pierson (2004); Steinmo, Thelen, and Longstreth (1992); and Skocpol (1992).

19. Securitization was one tool to tap capital markets, but as the recent calamity in world financial markets suggest, it has significant problems in how it distributes risk.

20. Testimony of Doris W. Koo, president and chief executive officer, Enterprise Community Partners, Inc., before the Senate Banking Committee, January 31, 2008, http://banking.senate.gov/_files/Kootestimony13108.pdf.

1

Directions in Housing Policy from Lyndon Johnson to Ronald Reagan, 1964–86

Before the urban riots, before the Tet Offensive, before the strong showing of the racist presidential candidate George Wallace, the federal government had a historic moment when it combined authority with optimism and money with new ideas to mount an attack on poverty.[1] In 1964, with Lyndon Johnson's Great Society, the federal government was building on its New Deal successes in such areas as Social Security and stabilizing the agricultural economy, in addition to such economic development efforts as building the interstate highway system, underwriting the expansion of the home mortgage market, and massively increasing defense spending for the cold war.

With the fast-growing economy of the early-to-mid-1960s, the federal government had the wind at its back economically. And even though the government was taking in more revenue in taxes and spending more on the cold war military and social services, family income rose almost 75 percent in real terms from 1945 to the mid-1960s (Glyn et al. 1990). It appeared that the country could have both "guns and butter."

During this time, opposition to the welfare state was weakening. Corporations enjoyed the profits of the postwar economy, were happy with lucrative military contracts, and benefited from Keynesian-inspired fiscal growth policies such as the 1962 Kennedy-Johnson tax cut. The South, for its part, was also scaling back its fierce opposition to federal intervention in its labor market, thanks to increasing mechanization of its agriculture (Quadagno 1988, 268). While old allies withdrew from the fight against the welfare state, the conservative wing of the Republican Party promoted an ultraconservative candidate in Barry Goldwater for the 1964 election. Goldwater's extreme views on foreign and domestic policies appeared out of step with mainstream voters.[2] Moreover, in intellectual debates as well there were few remaining detractors of the welfare state. Lionel Trilling summed it up this way: "In the United States at this time liberalism is not only the dominant but even the sole intellectual tradition" (Trilling 1950, 6).

Meanwhile, a pro–welfare state political coalition waxed with new energy. An outpouring of support for liberal causes followed John Kennedy's assassination in 1963, for example, and a heightened sense of what poverty meant in the midst of prosperity was highlighted by writers such as Michael Harrington in his book *The Other America* (1962). In addition to public support, in 1964 strong institutions like organized labor and the articulate and effective civil rights movement helped elect the most liberal Congress since 1936. The new president and Congress launched a reform program that Lyndon Johnson labeled the Great Society.[3] Central to this effort were passing the Civil Rights Act of 1964 and the Voting Rights Act of 1965 and extending aid for medical expenses to the elderly (Medicare) and to the indigent of all ages (Medicaid). There was also new federal spending on education (the Elementary and Secondary Education Act of 1965 and the Higher Education Act of 1965), housing and urban development, transportation, environmental programs, and arts and humanities (Brinkley 1991, 471).

Another essential element of the Great Society was an effort to eradicate poverty. The lead agency was the Office of Economic Opportunity (OEO), which was responsible for multiple programs in health, employment, education, and housing (Brinkley 2004). Johnson said, "We are just not willing to accept the necessity of poverty." He added that his administration had "declared war on poverty in all its forms, in all its causes, and we intend to drive it underground and win that war."[4] Specific War on Poverty programs ranged from job training, Head Start (a subsidized early education program), Volunteers in Service to America (a domestic peace corps), and grants for community development and community action programs designed to help poor people organize and help themselves.

Affordable Housing and Johnson's War on Poverty

The spirit of optimism and determination in 1964 inspired new affordable housing and urban policy. The Johnson administration, for example, re-invigorated federal housing efforts by consolidating existing programs and adding new ones to create the Department of Housing and Urban Development (HUD) in 1965 (Katz 1986). HUD's first secretary, Robert Weaver, beamed with confidence as he explained HUD's mission to the delegates of a 1966 National League of Cities conference:

> I would hope that you are always aware that this Department was established by the president and the Congress in response to the needs of our urban and urbanizing areas. We are involved in the exciting and creative business of bringing all our resources and energies to bear in solving the problems of your cities.[5]

The Need for New Institutions

An important theme throughout many of the War on Poverty programs, but especially housing, was the poor helping themselves. In the debates over the Equal Opportunity Act, Attorney General Robert Kennedy argued that communities needed new institutions in order to take control of their political and economic destinies.[6] Kennedy explained the need for community participation by reflecting on the limits of past policies. In his remarks to the House Committee on Education and Labor, he noted that the "institutions that affect the poor—education, welfare, recreation, business, labor—are huge, complex structures, operating far outside their control. They plan programs for the poor, not with them."[7] Kennedy's solution was the community action plan, a start at creating new institutions that would improve the local community and economy with the "maximum feasible participation" from local residents.[8] Local initiatives, however, would be backed by federal expertise and subsidies.

Conservatives such as Congressman Bob Taft (R-Ohio) challenged Kennedy's premise that federal funding and support were necessary:[9] "Why would federal participation bring humanity and understanding into the health and welfare, and connected programs?" he asked. "I will say frankly my experience has been directly to the contrary in communities in which I have lived and worked," he continued. "The more you get of federal programs the further you are likely to get away from humanity and understanding."[10] Critics of the administration, such as Taft and his allies in Congress, complained that an expanded federal role would be too expensive, would duplicate efforts, and would quash local initiative to solve local problems.[11] Such expansion also represented a federal power grab that would eclipse local government. Distant Washington bureaucrats would inevitably be out of touch with the needs of any given community, according to Taft.

Kennedy won this debate and got the votes he needed to include the community action plans (and subsequently community action agencies) in the 1964 Economic Opportunity Act.[12] These agencies, a prototype for the institutions Kennedy envisioned, were expected to coordinate services such as job training and education in addition to community economic development.[13] The OEO spent nearly $3 billion in its first two years on these programs (Brinkley 2004).

The community action agencies are of particular interest here because many of them became community development corporations (CDCs). In 1966, CDCs received a boost with an amendment to the Economic Opportunity Act known as the Special Impact Program. An official with the Center for Community Economic Development, a liberal policy group, wrote that it was urban riots and the frustrating experience the OEO had with local governments between 1964 and 1966 that "led Congress to realize that traditional political entities were insufficient for an effective war on poverty." Hence, Section 202(a) of the Economic Opportunity Act was amended in 1966 to permit community action agencies in "any neighborhood or other area (irrespective of boundaries or political subdivisions) which is sufficiently homogeneous in character to be an appropriate area for an attack on poverty under this part" (Kelly 1976, 76). Between 1964 and 1974, poor communities created nearly 100 CDCs that got their start as community action agencies. Most of their funding came from the Special Impact Program and the Ford Foundation (U.S. Office of Economic Development 1976; Sirianni and Friedland 2001).[14]

The effort to go around local government to create institutions that were controlled by local residents had limited success in the 1960s. Some community action agencies and CDCs were quite good at incorporating the contributions of local citizens and delivering services. But many were inefficient, plagued by patronage, and overly hostile to local government (Simon 2001; Fisher 1994).

The initial ineffectiveness of the CDCs, however, was not caused by a lack of vision or ambition. Consider the testimony of David Lizarraga, president of the East Los Angeles Community Union (TELACU). This CDC planned to control and develop the local economy in a way that would have made J.P. Morgan blush. Through its venture financing, and by placing its members on the boards of new affiliates, it would exercise considerable control over a number of businesses and the local economy:

> TELACU's approach envisions having influence [through TELACU-created financial institutions] on many of the basic investment and development decisions that will determine the future of the economy; through its subsidiaries it aims to generate substantial employment opportunities for many of its residents. It is going beyond catalyzation of the economy; it intends to alter the structure.[15]

Even famously successful CDCs such as the Bedford Stuyvesant Redevelopment Corporation in Brooklyn failed to achieve such grand schemes. Although CDC results were mixed, they were successful in establishing themselves as community institutions with substantial support from local citizens. More important, CDCs embodied a new way of thinking about community economic development and housing. Their example laid a foundation for a future institutional arrangement that would involve more local control.

From Kennedy's perspective, CDCs offered the federal government a chance to skip over state and local government and reach directly into struggling communities. Although this approach was an important intellectual development in the evolution toward a more decentralized approach to delivering housing, it did not build many houses in the early years. Washington-based government bureaucracies had been the leaders in federal efforts to house low-income Americans since the New Deal, and they remained so through the 1960s.

Public Housing and HUD

The federal government has had programs to help low-income renters since 1937.[16] The program, known as public housing, was both an effort to provide needed shelter and a post–Great Depression economic recovery program. It provoked tremendous opposition from the private sector, including the U.S. Chamber of Commerce, the National Association of Real Estate Boards, and the U.S. League of Building and Loans (Radford 1996). Under the public housing model created by the Housing Act of 1937, state-chartered municipal and county housing authorities originated municipal bonds, and the federal government funded the entire capital costs through "annual contribution contracts" (Orlebeke 2000, 492). Elected officials—often mayors—appointed boards to oversee the housing authorities' operations and management of the properties (Orlebeke 2000).[17] Tenant rents were to cover operating expenses.

Public housing had many design, construction, and management problems. By the early 1980s, very few new units were being built, and no funds have been allocated to the program since 1994 (Bratt 2007). Although the public housing program is inactive, it leaves behind nearly 1.2 million apartments in 3,500 communities across the country. Public housing tends to serve very low income tenants; the median household had an annual income of $8,788 in 2006. Two-thirds of public housing tenants are elderly or disabled (Sard and Fischer 2008).[18]

In another approach to create affordable rental housing, the federal government provided below-market loans to housing developers. The first program of this type, enacted in 1959, helped low-income senior citizens. Two years later, Congress added the Section 221(d)(3) program, which provided below-market loans to nonprofits or for-profits that were willing to take a limited return on investment (Case 1991). The subsidy was a below-market interest rate loan, known as a BMIR loan, at 3 percent. Developers passed on the savings to renters, resulting in a rent that was around 15 to 20 percent below market (Orlebeke 2000).

The 221(d)(3) program was replaced by the Section 235 and 236 programs in 1968 (see below). In that year, the HUD was poised to make some dramatic increases in affordable housing production through existing and new programs (see table 1.1). This effort was a response to urban riots and accelerating urban decay in many inner cities.

The Kaiser Report, 1969

The inspiration for the War on Poverty housing policy was a report titled *A Decent Home: The Report of the President's Committee on Urban Housing* (1968), written under the chairmanship of Edgar F. Kaiser. Perhaps the most striking feature of the 1968 Kaiser Report was the supreme confidence in government capabilities that pervaded nearly every page. President Lyndon Johnson charged the committee to

> find a way to harness the productive power of America—which has proved it can master space and create unmatched abundance in the market place—to the most pressing unfulfilled need of our society. That need is to provide the basic necessities of a decent home and healthy surroundings for every American family now imprisoned in the squalor of the slums. (U.S. President's Committee on Urban Housing 1969, 1)

Table 1.1. Subsidized Housing Units, 1961–72 (thousands of units)

Year	New construction	Existing/rehabilitated	Total
1961	33.8	4.0	37.8
1962	42.9	3.4	46.3
1963	60.3	5.1	65.3
1964	65.2	4.3	69.5
1965	54.1	9.4	63.5
1966	72.2	26.7	98.9
1967	107.8	40.5	148.3
1968	139.5	57.9	197.3
1969	184.3	65.2	249.5
1970	366.1	79.7	445.7
1971	367.3	63.4	430.7
1972	352.0	83.9	435.9

Source: U.S. Department of Housing and Urban Development (1974).

Notes: Includes units with mortgage insurance written for assistance under the HOME section 235(l), multifamily housing sections 236, 235(j), below market interest rate programs, and rent supplement programs not elsewhere counted; units financed by direct loans under section 202; low-rent public housing units with assistance contracts executed; units financed by initial loans or grants made under section 502 Low- and Moderate-Income Program, and sections 515, 521, 514, 516, Family Housing Programs. Units may not sum to totals because of rounding.

The committee analyzed the problem of the "squalor of the slums" and came to the conclusion that in the next 10 years the country must build 26 million new housing units, 6 million to be subsidized for low-income tenants. According to the report, "Attainment of this goal should eliminate the blight of substandard housing from the face of the nation's cities and should provide every American family with an affordable, decent home" (U.S. President's Committee on Urban Housing 1969, 3). Production of 600,000 units of subsidized housing in each year of this period, however, would have been quite an achievement, considering it was over five times the greatest number of units ever built in one year (71,000 units in 1954)(Orlebeke 2000, 495).

More than confidence, the report reflected a sense that the federal government had an obligation to lift up poor communities. Housing was considered an economic right, as well as an important national investment in the future. As the report stated,

We strongly believe that the goal is necessary and justified for these reasons:
[1] Decent housing is essential in helping lower-income families help themselves

achieve self fulfillment in a free and democratic society; [and 2] Public expenditures for decent housing for the nation's poor, like public expenditures for education and job training, are not so much expenditures as they are essential investments in the future of American society. (U.S. President's Committee on Urban Housing 1969, 3)

To fulfill this obligation, the report suggested that the federal government join "private enterprise, organized labor, and state and local governments in creative and affirmative partnerships." The report was unequivocal, however, on the point that the federal government should be the leader and coordinator of the effort to eradicate slums. The report warned that if the new partnerships failed to materialize, the federal government would have to become the "houser of last resort," using its resources, organizational capacity, and legal tools to build the millions of necessary housing units. "Unquestionably," the report concluded, "a direct federal program of land acquisition, public construction, and public ownership and management of subsidized housing would produce the millions of dwellings needed by low-income families within any determined time span" (U.S. President's Committee on Urban Housing 1969, 5). In other words, there was always the option of dramatically expanding the public housing model.

Kaiser's recommendations shaped the Housing Act of 1968, which both increased public housing production and created two new interest-rate subsidy programs for private developers to build affordable housing. For the latter programs, the federal government covered most of the mortgage payment for loans secured by private developers and local housing authorities.[19] The programs—Sections 235 (single-family home mortgages) and 236 (mortgages for apartments)—built on the innovation of earlier Section 202 and Section 221(d)(3) programs (Orlebeke 2000). Under the 236 program, the developer (nonprofit or for-profit) would get a mortgage at market rates, and HUD would pay the difference between the market finance cost and the finance costs of a steeply subsidized mortgage (at 1 percent interest). The savings were then to be passed along to the tenants. The advantage of these programs was that it induced a tremendous influx of mortgage capital into the market at a relatively low initial cost. While the government still covered most of the cost and carried the ultimate risk, it was a step away from the public housing program that came before it.

1969 Report to Congress.   In addition, the Housing Act of 1968 mandated annual reports by the president to Congress to explain the progress on the Kaiser goals. The first report from the Nixon administration in

1969 echoed and confirmed the report's definition of the problem and its remedies. The administration also emphasized the need to "obtain greater commitment by large corporations and provide business leadership in coping with urban housing and urban development programs" (U.S. Congress 1969, 46). While there was an added emphasis on the role of the private sector, entrepreneurs, and the use of the tax code to create incentives to build more housing, Nixon did not propose any new programs to that end. Overall, the 1969 report simply confirmed the goals of the Housing Act of 1968.

1970 Report to Congress. In 1970, the Nixon administration again submitted a report to Congress that supported existing programs: "The goals established by Congress in the Housing Act of 1968 still seem to be a reasonable expression of the magnitude of overall needs" (U.S. Congress 1970, 5). For the first time, however, the federal government was building a substantial number of houses for low-income tenants, over 400,000 subsidized units in that year. While the number was still shy of the Kaiser 600,000 annual target, it was an impressive achievement. In time, according to the administration, federal effort and organization would boost production to the 600,000 unit annual target. In what was primarily described as a shortage of capital, the administration claimed to have undertaken "extensive efforts to secure the needed mortgage financing for these programs on reasonable terms" (U.S. Congress 1970, 2). The report predicted that housing production in 1970 would be 50 percent higher than in 1969, with a further increase for 1971.

The report ended with a cautionary note, however. It called for a renewed national commitment to housing: "Meeting the [Kaiser] goals will . . . however, require that both the executive and the Congress— and, in a broader sense, the whole Nation—accord to the national housing effort the appropriate and necessary priority among the Nation's domestic concerns" (2). The report was casting a wide net in an effort to infuse new ideas, new funds, and new vitality into a program that was showing signs of strain. Without renewed commitment, the report predicted, "the prospects for success will be meager indeed" (5).

1971 Report to Congress. Any remaining optimism faded by 1971. Even with hundreds of thousands of newly built and rehabilitated housing units, federal efforts could not stop the deterioration of inner cities. In the third presidential report to Congress, the administration claimed that "the process of decay and obsolescence of basically sound housing units—and indeed of whole neighborhoods of units—seems to be proceeding at an excessive and accelerating pace" (U.S. Congress 1971, 20). The spectacle of tens of thousands of new apartments becoming available in central cities at the same time that an equal or greater number of houses were being abandoned in those same neighborhoods began to call into question the entire enterprise of federally subsidized housing production. "The rapid deterioration and abandonment of many existing housing units, if unchecked, could turn our new production efforts into a treadmill," warned the report (U.S. Congress 1971, 25).

Housing production appeared to be a one-step-forward-two-steps-back proposition because larger forces were at work, according to the administration: "The abandonment problem is largely an abandonment of the neighborhood out of fear of crime, social disintegration and other such factors rather than the result of something inherent in the particular building. This kind of problem can be dealt with, therefore, only on a broad-scale, neighborhood-wide basis" (U.S. Congress 1971, 20). This might sound like a call to action for a comprehensive government effort to reverse this disturbing trend, but the report cautioned against any grand gestures:

> The temptation, of course, is to attempt to solve this problem by immediately creating some new federal program funded with a large amount of budget resources. All too often, however, the result of past federal efforts has been either to benefit those who probably would have undertaken maintenance or repairs on their own anyway or—as in the case of the urban renewal program—to accelerate rather than slow deterioration of demarcated neighborhoods. (U.S. Congress 1971, 20)

Instead, the report called for "intensive dialogue" in an effort to determine what, if anything, could create new housing and stem the process of urban decay.

To make matters worse, any future policy also would have to tackle the growing problem of ever-increasing housing construction costs. Inflation in building material prices and construction wages combined with a tight mortgage capital market to increase housing costs dramatically. The administration continued to say it supported the Kaiser Report goals in principle, but the growing costs were alarming: "Clearly, the public interest demands that the federal government not stand impassively at the cash register and continue to pay out whatever is necessary to feed runaway inflation of housing costs" (U.S. Congress 1971, 22).

In addition to being ineffective and overly expensive, the existing housing programs were unfair, according to the report. The subsidized houses built by the government reached only a fraction of those who qualified and deserved them: "In spite of rapidly increasing production, the families receiving subsidies are among the fortunate few compared to the universe of families who are potentially eligible."[20]

1972 Report to Congress. By 1972, the president's fourth report to Congress no longer paid lip service to the goals of the Kaiser Report. There was now an open fight over the goals and objectives of the federal housing programs outlined in 1968. According to the report, "Congress, the housing industry, economists, social scientists, and others interested in housing have been actively debating the merits and flaws of both present programs and possible alternatives to them" (U.S. Congress 1972, 2).

The problem with the 235 and 236 loan subsidy programs was that over time, the cost of supporting the programs would grow dramatically as each year brought new mortgage subsidy commitments along with the commitments from prior years. The report asserted that "the federal government is already committed to about $12 billion in future subsidy payments for these two programs alone, based on the number of units approved through FY 1972, although the maximum payments legally permissible could reach as high as $36 billion" (U.S. Congress 1972, 29). That amount was nearly 16 percent of the overall federal budget in 1972 (U.S. Office of Management and Budget 2008).

The 1972 report reiterated the equity problems of a program that was essentially a lottery; only a few enjoyed new housing while the vast majority who qualified for subsidized housing were simply left out. The report asserted a need for "an improved" balance between the haves and have-nots. Federal production programs, according to the report, suffered from operational problems that stemmed from inadequate oversight by government. "HUD," the report noted, "has experienced operating problems in both the newer interest subsidy programs and the high risk inner city programs. Continuous surveillance over program operations has uncovered many instances of loose program processing, shoddy construction, excessive profits, and consumer victimization" (U.S. Congress 1972, 30). The report concluded that federal production programs were not the answer.

One potential solution was a shift to housing allowances to low-income tenants, also known as vouchers.[21] HUD, according to the report, was poised to start "a number of housing allowance experiments in a variety of localities to test the effects of direct housing aid to families including cash payments and housing voucher payments" (U.S. Congress 1972, 31). The Nixon administration argued that if low-income consumers had the power of choice, then market forces would impose greater discipline on low-income housing providers—more effective discipline than any federal oversight or regulation could provide.

Oversell and Underdeliver

The confidence and aggressive goal setting of 1968 were running into problems in implementation, which contributed to a sense of oversell and underdeliver. The Kaiser Report stated that "within urban slums, there are the knotty sociological relations between rundown housing, human behavior, environmental conditions of total neighborhoods, and the disadvantaged life of the poor" (U.S. President's Committee on Urban Housing 1969, 2). Linking housing to the "knotty" problems of slums made sense then. It makes sense today. But framing the problem in this way meant that a policy success required a triple win against the material, social, and economic conditions of urban poverty. As the subsequent Nixon reports conveyed, larger forces were making this goal harder to reach in the 1970s.

The general economic problems of the 1970s also made it harder to deliver on the goals of housing policy. The economic assumptions underlying the Kaiser Report were wildly optimistic. While the analysts assumed an annual GDP growth rate of 5.5 percent with a 4 percent unemployment rate, they admitted that the models did not hold if there was high inflation. In fact, the 10-year period from 1969 to1979 had an average unemployment rate of 6 percent and an average annual inflation of 7 percent (McCusker 2001). Economic growth too was sluggish.[22] From 1970 to 1976 the growth rate for real gross domestic product was 2.3 percent, picking up by the end of the decade to 4.7 percent in 1979 (Johnston and Williamson 2002). With the economic rug pulled out from under the Kaiser plan, it became increasingly difficult to sell the idea of a massive new investment in housing for the urban poor.

Another weak spot in the Kaiser plan was that the partners in local government and the private sector never quite materialized. It is one thing to invite everyone to a party but quite another for them to show up. This situation would be much different years later. Consider the four snapshots comparing 1969, 1991, 1998, and 2005 in table 1.2.

In the 1960s, the federal government invited participation from other levels of government and from the private and nonprofit sectors, but they were not ready. These partners lacked the staff, the experience, and the know-how to participate.

Meanwhile, the long-term trends that were transforming the inner cities into slums—suburbanization, deindustrialization—persisted, making matters worse. In this environment, liberal policies lost ground to growing public cynicism and doubt in government capabilities. The problems faced by subsidized housing reflected the problems faced generally by the welfare state. For example, the Nixon administration's repeated reference to the housing program as a "lottery" resonated with general complaints against the welfare state from the "near poor"—the mostly working class whites who made just too much to qualify for social programs. When the bulk of voters began to feel as though social welfare programs were a "bad deal" for them (i.e., they paid more than they got), the welfare state lost important support.

Table 1.2. Comparisons of the Decentralized Housing Network, 1969–2005

	1969	1991	1998	2005
States with housing finance agencies	0	48	50 + D.C., Puerto Rico, and Virgin Islands	50 + D.C., Puerto Rico, and Virgin Islands
CDCs building housing	112	2,000	3,600	4,600
Nationwide capacity-building nonprofit intermediaries	0	4	6	8

Sources: National Congress for Community Economic Development (1988, 1991).

Note: Capacity-building intermediaries include the Local Initiatives Support Corporation, Enterprise Foundation, The Community Builders, Housing Assistance Council, Neighborhood Reinvestment Corporation, Low Income Investment Fund, Mercy Loan Fund, and the Rural Community Assistance Corporation.

The Mixed Legacy of the Great Society

As with previous eras of reform, the Great Society has a mixed legacy. It ended in political failure—in part because of the gap between what was promised and what was delivered (Patterson 1996). It also struggled for funding at a time when the costs of the Vietnam War were rising rapidly (Brinkley 2004). In the end, the Great Society set the stage for a backlash against liberal policies in general and the welfare state in particular. But the programs of the 1960s did have their successes. Poverty, for example, dropped from 18.1 percent in 1960 to 10.1 percent in 1970.[23]

By the mid-1970s, however, opportunities to promote an old-style welfare state vanished, a shift partly explained by a growing cynicism over the government's ability to solve any problem at all.[24] Polling data on voters' trust in government showed a precipitous decline in the number of people who said they trusted the government "most of the time" from a high of almost 60 percent in 1966 to a low of nearly 25 percent in 1979 (National Election Studies 2000).

Cynicism also seems to have undermined Americans' belief that political activity was worth the effort of participation. Voting declined steadily from 1960 to the late 1980s, even though levels of education, the best predictor of political participation, had risen sharply throughout the period (Verba, Sholzman, and Brady 1995).[25] The decline in interest in politics hurt particularly the pro–welfare state coalition as more members of the working class withdrew. A historian of the 20th century, James Patterson, wrote that lower voting rates and political participation were "disproportionally serious among poor, working-class, and lower-middle-class people, most of whom had been Democrats" (Patterson 1996, 708).

A weakening economic outlook also became a liability for the welfare state as slower economic growth created more anxiety for individual families. For most of American history, but especially after the Second World War, incomes for American families had grown rapidly. Between 1947 and 1973, the typical family's income roughly doubled. From 1973 to 2008, however, median family income increased by only about 20 percent (Isaacs, Sawhill, and Haskins 2008).[26] Overall growth picked up again in the mid-1990s, but the benefits of this new growth disproportionately went to the top income earners.[27] In light of these economic circumstances, it was hard to call for bold new and expensive programs in what Jerry Brown called "an era of limits" in his 1976 bid for the presidency.[28]

During the 1970s, middle-class voters were losing ground in terms of real income but were often bumped up to higher tax brackets, thanks to inflation-fueled increases in nominal income. Even as they had less buying power, they were paying more in taxes, which set the stage for a tax revolt. Harold Wilensky sums up this period in his book *Rich Democracies:*

> If you combine slow growth, double-digit inflation, a large number of income-tested or means-tested benefits (targeted to the poor or near-poor), and heavy reliance on progressive income taxes, you will produce a large number of families whose real income deteriorates as they simultaneously move into higher tax brackets and lose income-tested benefits (such as social assistance, Medicaid, or rent supplements). Hardly a formula for political calm. (Wilensky 2002, 379)

Middle-class voters vented their frustration on "visible" taxes, spurring the tax revolt. While this famously played out with property taxes in California (Proposition 13) and in Massachusetts (Measure 2½), promises to cut income taxes also fueled Ronald Reagan's presidential win in 1980.[29]

Business interests also grew increasingly hostile to government, particularly after more aggressive regulation on a number of issues in the 1960s and 1970s, including the environment, workplace safety, consumer protection, and civil rights. Business leaders opposed social spending and labor market programs that threatened to raise taxes, boost wages, or limit managerial decisionmaking (Ferguson and Rogers 1986).

At a time when the welfare state was struggling against increasingly hostile social, political, and economic realities, it was also losing its intellectual force. Many liberal intellectuals left the Democratic Party because of a list of concerns, especially growing isolationism in international policy, the reintroduction of race in public policy, thanks to affirmative action programs, and the rising militancy of black nationalists, feminists, and the counterculture (Abrams 2006). This group of new conservatives, known as "neocons," went on to found some of the leading conservative institutions—think tanks such as the American Enterprise Institute and publications that included *Commentary* and *The Weekly Standard.*

Old-line liberals who continued to promote the welfare state had the neocons on their right flank, in addition to their traditional adversaries on the right, and a new challenge on their left with the emergence of a more aggressive liberal movement in the New Left. One of the early guiding documents for the New Left was the 1962 Port Huron Statement, which trumpeted a new approach to government that would encourage participatory democracy and empower those who had been left out of decisionmaking. It is not that this movement wanted to do away with the welfare state, but its adherents wanted to clip the wings of what they saw as overly powerful and insular federal bureaucracies.[30] New Deal and Great Society liberals were caught in a vise between those who, in the estimation of political scientist Aaron Wildavsky (1996, 76), "love government too little" and "those who love it too much."

These developments—the rising distrust of government, political apathy (particularly among likely Democratic voters), tough economic conditions, growing resentment toward taxation, and the lack of a clear ideology for government action—made any new welfare state policy politically infeasible. The federal government lacked the credibility to launch new programs or even to defend existing ones. Against this backdrop, affordable housing programs struggled, and in 1973, in a dramatic gesture, Nixon froze all housing production programs.

Pause and Reevaluation of Housing Policy, 1973

The political scientist Theodore Lowi commented once that Richard Nixon was the last Democratic president of the 20th century; the subsidized housing production numbers of his HUD secretary, George Romney, bear out his observation.[31] Between 1969 and 1973, for the first time in history, the federal government built a significant number of subsidized housing units. In 1970, HUD came as close as it ever did to the Kaiser Report's 600,000 unit-per-year goal, with nearly 446,000 subsidized homes built that year (Quadagno 1988, 268). But, as noted earlier, all was not well with the effort. These units were built by private developers with subsidies to help pay the mortgages. By 1975, so many projects were failing that HUD had to assume the mortgages for 282,000 units of housing and foreclose on 141,000 units (Struyk, Turner, and Ueno 1987). In 1973, Romney concluded that "time has come to pause, to re-evaluate and to seek out better ways."[32]

Nixon commissioned the National Housing Policy Review, which comprised more than 100 experts from various federal government departments to analyze the existing housing programs. Although their 500-page report, *Housing in the Seventies,* acknowledged achievements, it was ultimately critical of federal housing production programs. The report acknowledged that, to their credit, housing production programs provided assistance to 1.6 million families between 1969 and 1972, more subsidized housing than the previous 34-year history of national housing assistance. More than just numbers, federal programs were reaching into poor and neglected neighborhoods, "This administration, in response to the 1968 legislation, also has underwritten high-risk mortgages on more than 150,000 units in inner-city neighborhoods, another record achievement," noted the report (U.S. Department of Housing and Urban Development [HUD] 1974, 2).

Housing in the Seventies reiterated criticisms articulated in the administration's earlier reports to Congress. Federal housing programs operated like a lottery that treated some low-income tenants with a windfall of a new and cheap apartment, while many other low-income tenants got nothing. The report also noted growing resentment of the near poor: "Millions of people with incomes only slightly above those of program beneficiaries live in units older and poorer than those subsidized with their tax dollars" (HUD 1974, 2).

The report claimed that current federal housing policy was confusing because the "balancing of roles of the various levels of government is an ever-continuing process with no final resolution of how they should be balanced in sight" (U.S. Congress 1973, 1,940). The confusion over programs and roles discouraged the private sector and other nongovernmental players from helping solve the nation's affordable housing crisis. HUD Secretary Romney spoke of the problem as early as 1970 when addressing the Senate Committee on Banking and Currency:

> Even the most sophisticated and experienced builders, lenders and sponsors find it frustrating and costly to accommodate their operations to the red tape and delay occasioned by the maze of our confusing authorizations and the regulations, circulars, forms and processing procedures that have grown out of them. (U.S. Congress 1970, 1-34)

Communication among government organizations and between government and outside contractors was confused. *Housing in the Seventies* concluded that little could be done to fix the problems. In a voice that was a far cry from the confidence of the Kaiser Report, the administration seemed ready to throw in the towel: "Government subsidized housing programs contain structural problems that result in considerable program inequities and inefficiencies. Certain problems could be remedied through legislative changes. However, legislative correction of one problem would often tend to aggravate or create others."[33] Essentially, the administration identified a laundry list of problems while at the same time it discouraged doing anything about them.

While the political will to fix housing faltered, the need for decent housing continued to exist for millions of Americans. In fact, a joint study conducted by Harvard and MIT in 1973 claimed that the Kaiser Report had *underestimated* the need for affordable housing. The study reported that nearly 13 million low-income households were without adequate housing in 1970. Of this total number, 5.5 million overpaid for housing, spending more than 25–30 percent of their income. Nearly 7 million lived in housing that was structurally inadequate, and another 700,000 households were overcrowded.[34]

Two External Reports on Federal Housing Policy

Alongside *Housing in the Seventies,* two prominent outside reports also evaluated federal housing programs during Nixon's construction moratorium—one by the real estate industry and another by the Ford Foundation.

Real Estate Industry Report. The National Association of Home Builders, National Association of Mutual Savings Banks, and United States Savings and Loan League hired the Real Estate Research Corporation, headed by the prominent housing scholar Anthony Downs, to analyze the federal housing subsidy programs. The report, titled *Federal Housing Subsidies: Their Nature and Effectiveness and What We Should Do about Them,* challenged the numerous criticisms of federal programs (Downs 1972).

Among the complaints with which this report agreed were (1) that investors in affordable housing apartments did not have proper incentives to maintain their properties; (2) that the economic return was the same for building apartments in middle-class neighborhoods as it was for very poor neighborhoods; and (3) that operating costs were underestimated to get project approval and invariably went over budget, resulting in mandated rent increases from HUD that were passed on to the tenants (Downs 1972). Perhaps the most damaging criticism, however, was that HUD was unable to manage a large-scale housing production program. The report, though, went on to blame Congress for overburdening the agency with myriad new programs and greater responsibility without adequate staffing resources:

> In 1966 HUD's total permanent staff was about 14,000. It rose to 15,200 by the end of fiscal 1972. This is a net increase of about 8.5 percent in six years. From 1966 to

1971, the annual number of subsidized housing units produced in the United States rose 521 percent, and the annual number of housing units produced under FHA non-subsidized insurance programs increased 80 percent. (Downs 1972, 32)

The report concluded that inefficiencies and corruption were inevitable, given the rapid increase in production without a commensurate increase in department staff or resources. Past problems, however, were no reason to abandon subsidies for poor families. In fact, this report called for even greater subsidies to help low- and moderate-income individuals and families improve their housing situation.

Ford Foundation Report. In a seminal report, the Ford Foundation (1973) put much of the blame for federal housing policy failures on HUD's partners. Ford's criticism was that an influx of resources from the federal level overwhelmed local governments and other institutions. The report concluded that "the mismatch between society's capacity to provide resources and the limited ability of local communities to absorb and use them effectively" was responsible for the weak impact of the program (see Faux 1971). Because of this mismatch, two lessons were clear. First, "changing social problems cannot be best solved by narrowly focused 'crash' programs with large budgets." The report argued that "a greater impact on problems of distressed areas is likely to be made by a locally based, multipurpose institution—a community development corporation—than would result from government acting directly." Second, local institutions would need capacity-building development and strengthening.[35]

The Ford Report noted that communities of need required an "innovative problem-solving mechanism" that could leverage all available resources from inside and outside a community. This mechanism, or institution such as a community development corporation, would need the flexibility respond to the changing real estate market and dynamic needs of tenants. The Ford Foundation itself was on the cutting edge of experimenting with such a mechanism in its Gray Areas Program in 1961 and 1962 with grants to programs in Oakland, New Haven, Boston, Philadelphia, and Washington and throughout North Carolina. The program sought to develop local capacity to address local needs, including education, job training, and legal services (Wright 2001). "Some programs proved highly successful, most notably in New Haven and North Carolina; others had uneven records; still others languished," according to the Ford Foundation (1971, 6).

Yet if community development corporations were a potential answer to HUD's problems, there were too few of them. Despite the efforts at fostering these institutions, Ford estimated that there were between 60 and 100 of them in 1972. Of these, many did not have the capacity to complete a complicated project such as constructing an apartment building. "There is as yet no satisfactory institutional model with responsibility for the resurrection of depressed areas and the internal capacity to evolve new programs in response to changing problems," the report concluded (Ford Foundation 1973).

Nixon and Congress Wrestle over New Policy Directions

Nixon made three new housing policy proposals in his 1973 State of the Union speech. The first was an easing of multifamily mortgage credit through a series of measures ranging from creating incentives in the tax code to instructing secondary market investors to buy more mortgage capital. The second envisioned a cancellation of the federal production programs, replacing them with housing allowances (or vouchers) paid directly to low-income tenants. The third eliminated eight narrowly defined categorical programs for community infrastructure (lighting, sewer, parks, and the like) that had been awarded competitively under the Model Cities and urban renewal programs. Money would be distributed to state and local governments as block grants.

"As our housing study concludes" (referring to *Housing in the Seventies*), Nixon told Congress, "the forces which will do the most to shape the future of housing in America will be the forces of the marketplace: families with sufficient real income and sufficient confidence to create an effective demand for better housing on the one hand, and builders and credit institutions able to respond to that demand on the other."[36] The only way the market could work from the demand side of the equation, of course, was for the federal government to boost effective housing demand with subsidies to low-income consumers. Funds for this new approach would come from cutting all housing production programs.

Nixon's proposal to abandon all production programs was met with harsh initial responses. The U.S. Conference of Mayors and the National League of Cities savaged the proposal as insufficient to tackle the intractable problems facing cities. The president of the National Association of Home Builders, George C. Martin, agreed: "The nation's cities deserve a more comprehensive, unified housing proposal than was presented."[37]

A *New York Times* editorial joined this criticism: "A halt to housing subsidies, a revenue-sharing umbrella for urban renewal and Model Cities and an administrative realignment do not add up to a national program for the cities. On the contrary, they express President Nixon's determination to abandon the federal government's leadership role in coping with housing and urban problems." The editorial concluded that without federal leadership "too many communities across the nation can be expected to ignore the bad housing and other miseries of the impoverished who live across the tracks, in the next town or in the inner city. Only the national Government can assure the fulfillment of a national commitment."[38]

Congressional Democrats also criticized Nixon's proposal. Senator William Proxmire (D-Wis.) called it, for example, "cruel and brutal" and "a great disappointment."[39] Proxmire predicted that cash assistance would do little more than line the pockets of landlords and push rent inflation nationwide. The chairman of the Senate Subcommittee on Housing, Senator John Sparkman (D-Ala.), said that Congress and the administration were "far, far apart" in their thinking.[40]

Although Democrats and liberals were critical of Nixon's proposals, they were also disappointed in existing housing policies. A report sponsored by the Democrats on the Joint Economic Committee (a joint House and Senate committee with oversight over housing issues) charged that HUD failed to supervise adequately its many subsidy programs, which, according to an article in the *Wall Street Journal,* were "racked with kickback charges."[41] The report acknowledged that with improved systems and procedures "billions could be saved." At the same time, the report railed against "the administration's arrogant solution by elimination." Speaking for the group of senators who sponsored the report, Senator Proxmire said, "There is a better alternative than the meat-ax treatment." The existing problems "can be corrected by reforming existing programs."[42]

Even though congressional Democrats and liberals were critical of Nixon's plan, simply calling for better management and oversight of production programs was not a politically viable alternative. A *Wall Street Journal* editorial was even more pointed in its accusation that liberals lacked any real housing policy solutions: "Although they are still murmuring that the programs could have worked had they been properly managed, the failures of public housing have been so visibly profound that their most earnest early champions are embarrassed by them."[43] The

Wall Street Journal charged that liberals did not have "the slightest notion of what to put in place of the discredited programs. They are bankrupt of ideas, and when they go to the social planners who dreamed up the 1968 housing act, all they get are the same old schemes."[44]

So what was the right housing policy? That was a question Congressman Henry Reuss (D-Wis.) often asked himself as the chairman of Congress's Joint Economic Committee. Bruce Bartlett, a former staffer for the committee and an avowed conservative, praised Reuss's efforts to find fair and effective policies. Reuss "was no conservative nor even a moderate. Henry Reuss was an old fashioned New Deal/Great Society liberal," said Bartlett (2002). But when asked why HUD was ineffective and why the federal government had never developed a successful low-income housing program, Reuss responded, "We never could figure out how to do it" (Wood 1984, 67).

The frustration over ineffective policy extended beyond liberal policymakers. Even those who were supposedly benefiting from federal programs complained. Theodore Cross, author of *Black Capitalism* (1969), criticized government housing efforts, ultimately calling on poor people to develop their own programs. His message to the federal government: "Get out of our way and let us try something" (Cross 1969, 69).

An Urban Institute report titled *The Urban Predicament* (1976) also questioned government housing programs and the political will to make them work. According to the report, "a smaller percentage of the population care about cities, while even fewer have confidence that the federal government (or any other level of government for that matter) knows how to make things better." But what further undermined the confidence necessary to strike out on a new path was the fact that supporters of more federal involvement in housing distrusted any "imposition of a great plan from outside" (Gorham and Glazer 1976, 14).

The Debate over Community Development Block Grants

One program that seemed to sidestep the political acrimony over federal housing policy was the Community Development Block Grant (CDBG) program. In some respects, the CDBG program was born out of similar frustrations as those outlined above. It was also an experiment in providing federal funds to local government to accomplish broad community development goals. As the following debate shows, there was a growing consensus among liberals and conservatives that an experiment with decentralized funding through a block grant program was worth a try.

Nixon had proposed a block grant program, but as the Robert Kennedy debates over CDCs demonstrate, decentralization of federal authority was not an exclusively conservative approach. Block grants, or "revenue sharing" and "federalism," are associated with Nixon and conservative politics, but decentralization had bipartisan support. Nixon did push the program, but so did liberals who were disillusioned by earlier urban renewal programs and HUD inefficiencies.

David Garrison, who worked on the CDBG legislation in the early years as legislative counsel to the Office of Federal Relations for the National League of Cities and the U.S. Conference of Mayors and later as a budget analyst for the House Committee on the Budget, said that efficiency was a concern across the political spectrum: he noted that it "was hard to argue then that you get a better result if you had a HUD bureaucrat in some regional office hundreds of miles away making that [real estate development] decision instead."[45] Both Republicans and Democrats saw block grants as an improvement, Garrison said. "There was broad agreement to the basic idea" and the "concept of a block grant was not seen then as a device to do away with the program long term. No one suggested that at all—ever."[46]

Momentum for Change

Over the course of 1973 and 1974, Congress and the administration debated the shape that a decentralized grant program might take. In an argument that mirrored the Taft-Kennedy debates over CDCs a decade earlier, conservative and liberals struggled to define the right balance of federal versus local control over housing and community development programs. The Senate passed a bill that tilted control toward the federal government, setting clear priorities and objectives for the new block grant program. The administration, champion of maximum local control, threatened to veto it. In the meantime, the House tried to hammer out a compromise the president would accept.[47]

James Lynn, who succeeded George Romney as HUD secretary, argued the president's views in these debates. He lobbied for a reduced role for the federal government, with more participation from local government and the private sector. He also called for a roll back of overall building: "We don't plan to build each year as many projects as we did, for example, in 1971. But we are going to be part of far fewer white elephants" (U.S. Congress 1974, 202). As aggressive and combative as the rhetoric could get, Lynn, by his own admission, saw a substantial amount of overlap with the administration, Senate, and House versions of a block grant bill (U.S. Congress 1974).[48]

In October and November of 1973, the hearings of the subcommittee brought scores of witnesses ranging from civil rights activists and local government officials to academics. In the main, their testimony showed serious disappointment with the existing housing and community development programs.

Many of those who testified doubted whether state and local governments were up to the challenge of administering these programs. States that had housing finance agencies by this time—New York, Michigan, and Massachusetts—were often referred to as models. But as the research director of the Urban Land Institute concluded, most state and local governments lacked the capacity to run complex programs. "It is unrealistic," he said, "to assume that the majority of general purpose governments will develop such a capacity in the near future, even with the incentive of block grants."[49]

Some questioned whether those governments that were able would also be willing. National Association of Home Builders President George Martin explained that in his experience local governments often opposed new housing construction of any kind. Handing over the purse strings to local officials would only add to their existing power over zoning and land use controls. "Local officials are, of course, the closest to the people," he said, "but they are also those most susceptible to the momentary passions and pressures of those opposed to, or afraid of, subsidized housing, or new housing for any people at all" (U.S. Congress 1973, 862).

A few witnesses complained that the "hue and cry about the disaster in the subsidized market" was overblown, as did William J. White, executive director of the Massachusetts Housing Finance Agency (U.S. Congress 1973, 574). White explained to the committee that his agency had financed 20,000 units in three years and had another 20,000 in the pipeline, pending the outcome of the moratorium. "And I can assure this Committee," he said, "that this housing is the finest housing that has been built in our state in its history" (U.S. Congress 1973, 575).

Despite these doubts, even liberals and housing advocates, including HUD's first secretary, explained that the spirit of the 1968 Housing Act had faded and that new ideas and new approaches were needed. HUD's first secretary, Dr. Robert C. Weaver, who was now a professor and president of the National Committee Against Discrimination in Housing, agreed with the idea of moving resources and decisionmaking to the state and local level, provided there were safeguards against abuses. Weaver said that using state and local governments to help build housing was worth a try. While that new approach was not guaranteed to work, he noted that placing all the responsibility for building housing with the federal government had not yielded good results (U.S. Congress 1973, 455). A wide range of groups—from mayors to civil rights activists to Wall Street bankers—agreed with Weaver.

Mayors and a string of local government officials testified for a change in federal programs, including New York City Mayor John Lindsay. Lindsay said the existing programs had made cities pursue actions that "violated commonsense." By way of example, he explained that New York was forced to demolish existing buildings to provide space for 70,000 urban renewal apartments but that there was no construction money to finish the project. Meanwhile, rents were soaring because of a lack of housing supply, and the city was "forced to relocate families from homes where they could have continued to live" (U.S. Congress 1973, 481). When an apartment was built, it was often not worth having, according to Lindsay, because the city had to meet certain federal construction guidelines while constrained by building costs. "We in New York City," Lindsay continued, "over the years have cut corners, had inferior designs on all kinds of things to get in under cost limitations" (U.S. Congress 1973, 481). Many other mayors testified to similar challenges for large and small towns all across the country. A statement adopted by the International City Management Association preferred block grants to the earlier federal production programs.

African American Civil Rights Groups Weigh In. One part of the testimony that is particularly surprising was that many African American civil rights groups—just a few years after the assassination of Martin Luther King and with the civil rights struggles as fresh memories—had lost faith in HUD and supported Nixon's move to the block grant program. There also appeared to be a lessened concern, as Robert Kennedy argued in 1964, that local governments would be obstacles to reform.[50] James Harvey of the Leadership Conference on Civil Rights, a coalition of 132 national civil rights, labor, religious, and civic organizations, also supported the concept of block grants. Harvey saw them as an effective tool in creating housing options for the poor and minorities after acknowledging that past federal, state, and local policies and practices had created and perpetuated concentrations of these vulnerable populations in decaying ghettos (U.S. Congress 1973). Part of this motivation seemed to be based in the reality that housing was a desperate need for the minority poor.[51]

The director for national housing programs for the Urban League, Glenn A. Claytor, agreed with the opinions of the Leadership Council on Civil Rights. The Urban League urged "in the strongest possible terms to act on the proposed legislation on a priority basis. We have lost considerable momentum since the moratorium and the situation may get worse. Meanwhile the housing needs of millions of Americans go unmet" (U.S. Congress 1973, 1723). Civil rights leaders, who had good reason to distrust local government, decided to take their chances on decentralization in the hopes that a new approach would ease existing housing conditions.

Private Financial Institutions. Private financial institutions were largely divorced from housing policy in the past, but by the late 1960s and early 1970s that was beginning to change. Commercial banks began to develop community lending departments, and investment banks explored the business potential of managing mortgage capital for low-income housing. Scaled back federal programs reinforced this trend, according to Donald D. Kummerfeld, vice president of First Boston Corporation. Speaking of state and local government, he said, "I am impressed with the growing awareness on their part that they can no longer rely on the federal government to meet the housing needs of low- and moderate-income families in their communities. This may be the most positive result of the current freeze [referring to Nixon's moratorium]" (U.S. Congress 1973, 687).

Implementing the Community Development Block Grant Program. Congress and the Gerald Ford administration reached an agreement on housing programs in the Housing and Community Development Act of 1974. In the end, many agreed with the *New York Times* editorial's assessment that the final "conference report was a tilt toward the House." The *Wall Street Journal* wrote that the president signed the legislation at the White House with "a bevy of governors, mayors, and county officials looking on."[52] In a statement released before the signing ceremony, Ford said that "in a very real sense, this bill will help to return power from the banks of the Potomac to people in their own communities."[53] The act provided $8.4 billion over three years in community development grants, now known as the Community Development Block Grant program. The money would be distributed based on a new formula that weighted population, the percentage of housing units that were overcrowded, and the level of poverty for a particular community.[54]

In the end, CDBG was not a substitute for a housing production program. It had many restrictions on how the money could be spent, including prohibitions against using it for "brick and mortar" construction costs. It could be used, however, for land acquisition and preparation and other costs.[55] It has been a politically popular funding program because of its flexibility and, according to the Millennial Housing Commission's 2002 report, 28 percent of CDBG funds have gone to housing.[56]

More than simply providing new funds, though, the CDBG program started a trend in government finance that pointed to a new future. In the congressional debates over CDBG, there was a faint outline of a group that would later become an effective prohousing lobbying group. The many different players (state and local government, CDCs, banks, consultants, and advocates for the poor) would take nearly a decade to evolve into an effective network of service providers. In later years, however, they would speak with one voice and become the driving force in developing and protecting federal housing programs. [57]

The Housing and Community Development Act also created the Section 8 program that was designed to give localities more flexibility in using housing funds for new construction, substantial rehabilitation, or tenant-based assistance for occupancy of existing rental units. Section 8 housing vouchers made up the difference between what a low-income tenant could pay (at 30 percent of his or her income) and what the landlord charged in rent. The new construction and rehabilitation programs were canceled in 1983, but the voucher program remains an important housing resource to millions of low-income families (Bipartisan Millennial Housing Commission 2002).

Jimmy Carter's Vision for a Cooperative Housing Policy

In 1978, the President's Urban and Regional Policy Group issued a housing policy report titled *A New Partnership to Conserve America's Communities* (1978). In it, Jimmy Carter wrote, "The job of revitalizing America's communities cannot be done by the federal government alone; the national urban policy recognizes and encourages local initiative and leadership. I have been most encouraged by the positive responses from all levels and branches of government, the private sector, labor, and neighborhood and voluntary organizations." Carter's vision was that this new approach would bring the skills, energy, and resources from multiple participants to alleviate the housing problem.[58]

The president's optimistic view was not always shared by those charged with making the new approach work. In the same report, a business leader said that cooperative programs were a good idea but were flawed in practice: "Government agencies can't or won't deliver them on time. The bureaucracy and paperwork are just too much. Everyone talks coordination but very few do anything about it," he said (U.S. President's Urban and Regional Policy Group 1978, 5–6).

States were also having trouble playing their part. Massachusetts Governor Michael Dukakis, for example, said in a statement before the Senate Intergovernmental Relations Subcommittee in 1978 that the federal government was not clear on the state role "beyond the need to keep them [the states] from causing trouble." Dukakis explained to the committee that states had an important and unrealized contribution to make to housing: "State governments have both money and power which can be marshaled in the battle to bring stability and vitality to the cities," he said (U.S. President's Urban and Regional Policy Group 1978, 7–8).

Despite Carter's view, this new multiple-player approach to housing had not yet reached the point where all the partners were synergistically contributing to solving problems. Even the president's 1978 report admitted that current programs did not provide the appropriate incentives for the private sector or were too limited in scope and "governed by rigid ground rules" (U.S. President's Urban and Regional Policy Group 1978, 25).

The legislation that flowed from that report was the $4.4 billion New Urban Initiatives, which proposed the creation of a National Development Bank, providing $1.7 billion in tax incentives and loan guarantees for private industry to relocate in depressed urban areas. Other efforts included helping CDCs, developing Neighborhood Reinvestment Centers, and using the purchasing power of the federal government to encourage defense contractors to provide jobs in the inner city (Bauman 2000).

The late 1970s were a time of trial and error in efforts to find a cooperative strategy for building housing. But the experimentation looked as if it might come to an end when the conservative coalition led by Ronald Reagan came to power. In addition, the belief that markets were more effective in allocating resources than government planning gained ascendancy. Ronald Reagan campaigned on a message that government was not the solution to society's problems but the source. That thinking inspired a number of policy changes, retrenchments, and outright cancellation of long-standing government programs. Subsidized housing was not immune from this revolution in public policy.

Ronald Reagan's Approach to Subsidized Housing

The welfare state probably reached its nadir under the withering criticism of President Reagan. "Government is not the solution to our problem," the president stated in his 1981 inaugural address; it "is the problem." Citing the "unnecessary and excessive growth of government" as the cause of the country's troubles, the president proposed to "curb the size and influence of the federal establishment" (Campbell 1995, 224). Reagan's 1981 budget made multiple cuts in need-based programs such as food stamps, housing assistance, Medicaid, and public sector jobs; urban programs (especially mass transit and community development); and aid to local schools. Reagan also cut the federal bureaucracy by eliminating jobs in the Federal Trade Commission, the Food and Drug Administration, the antitrust division of the Justice Department, and other regulatory bodies (Campbell 1995). He did not, however, shrink the overall size of the federal government, not only because of "increased military outlays but also because of continued subsidies to important Republican Party constituencies in business and agriculture" (Abrams 2006, 299). Federal spending as a percentage of gross national product stayed steady at 22 percent in the 1980s (U.S. Congressional Budget Office 2002, 163).

The philosophy that government was not the solution to problems but the cause of them had predictable results in affordable housing policy. Reagan appointed a presidential commission, chaired by William F. McKenna, to analyze the current state of the housing problem and what could be done about it. The committee's report, *The Report of the President's Commission on Housing* (1982), criticized the Kaiser committee's approach to housing policy as one that contributed "to deterioration rather than renewal" (U.S. President's Commission on Housing 1982).

McKenna's report, rather than putting its faith in government, based its optimism "on an entirely different belief: that the genius of the market economy, freed of the distortions forced by government housing policies and regulations that swung erratically from loving to hostile, can provide for housing far better than federal programs." The fundamental conclusion to this report was that the market was the answer to the housing problem—a problem that was created by naïve government meddling: "The 1970s taught not only the limits of the good that can be done by government action, but also the depths of the harm that can be wrought by ill-thought or ill-coordinated government policy" (xvii).

McKenna's committee asserted that the "commission seeks to create a housing sector that functions in an open environment with minimal government participation" (U.S. President's Commission on Housing 1982, xvi). In this vein, the commission's report opposed new federally subsidized construction and vowed to shrink, or eliminate, the government housing bureaucracy. In its place, this commission envisioned unrestricted block grants to states and, more important, vouchers paid directly to low-income tenants who could exercise their consumer sovereignty in the housing marketplace. Moving to vouchers would be less expensive, according to the report, and "relatively simple and straightforward" (17).

Additional recommendations included deregulating the savings and loan industry, so that it would be "empowered to solve its own problems without legal handcuffs and regulatory restrictions." Such a system would "generate more money for housing than could be hoped for from institutions seeking to recapture a past that is gone forever" (xviii). In addition to giving private industry a free hand, the report recommended reducing federal oversight of housing authorities and making federal park land available to low-income housing developers (Government Accounting Office 1991).[59]

Anticipating the argument that the federal government could try to improve existing service delivery systems, the McKenna Report said the federal government was incapable of reform: "Officials in government agencies and organizations often perceive change as a threat to competing public concerns or to their own personal interests" (U.S. President's Commission on Housing 1982, 223). More bureaucracy could not solve the "knotty" problems of the inner-city slums the 1968 Kaiser Report had identified; only the market could do that. Entrepreneurs, aided by tax incentives and unleashed from government red tape, would rebuild slums. "In enterprise zones the approach is to relax governmental controls, reduce taxes, modify regulations, and remove other inhibitions on business investment," the report asserted (107).

The McKenna Report, like the Kaiser Report, saw a role for state and local governments in providing housing. Unlike Kaiser, however, McKenna could look back on a decade of innovation and institution building at the state level and affirm that states rather than the federal government *could* play a more important role in solving housing policy problems. The McKenna Report urged states to use both general obligation bonds and tax-exempt bonds to generate capital for subsidized apartment buildings, in addition to below-market interest rate mortgages for first-time home-buyers: "There is now in existence both a network of marketing channels for tax-exempt housing bonds and a corresponding set of institutional arrangements for using the bond proceeds in the production of multifamily housing for low- and moderate-income households and the financing of single-family homes" (171). It appeared that the partners that the Kaiser Report had hoped for were finally beginning to materialize.

The policies that flowed from the McKenna Report were fairly drastic changes from prior programs. From 1977 to 1980, HUD assisted on average more than 300,000 new households a year with vouchers or new apartments. Between 1981 and 1988 that number dropped to an average of 82,000 households per year (Leonard, Dolbeare, and Lazere 1989). HUD's budget authority plummeted during this period (see table 1.3).

While it is true that HUD's budget authority was shrinking substantially during this period, budget outlays were going up. The distinction is important though often lost in the debate over subsidized housing (Hunt 2006). In a complicated budgetary sleight of hand, Congress could "cut" the budget for HUD without reducing the actual number of subsidized households.[60] Still, the rate of growth of housing commitments slowed considerably from the pace of the Carter years, and the tone of Reagan's budget proposals was negative.

Conclusion

The dramatic shifts in affordable housing policy from Johnson to Reagan mirrored larger shifts in attitudes toward government and the welfare state. It was evident that a Washington-based "crash" program was insufficient to solve the affordable housing problem. It was also evident that no one program would be the answer to housing and community

Table 1.3. HUD Budget Authority Trends, 1976–89
(in billions of constant 2002 dollars)

Fiscal year	Total HUD budget authority	Subsidized housing programs	All other HUD programs
1976	83.6	55.9	27.8
1977	89.8	78.2	11.6
1978	94.4	81.9	12.4
1979	71.3	58.9	13.5
1980	74.1	59.5	14.6
1981	62.8	50.4	12.4
1982	35.3	25.4	9.9
1983	26.8	17.6	9.3
1984	28.7	21.6	7.1
1985	48.6	41.7	6.9
1986	24.1	18.3	5.8
1987	21.6	15.6	6.0
1988	21.3	14.7	6.6
1989	19.7	13.7	6.0

Sources: Compiled by National Low Income Housing Coalition; budget authority and outlay data from Office of Management and Budget, Budget of the United States Government, Fiscal Year 2003, tables 3.2 and 5.1.

development, since the problems each community faced were unique and changing over time. Throughout the period, however, there was almost always a sense that *something* had to be done to help crumbling communities across the nation. The question was, what? There was no definitive answer to this question, but increasingly there were themes and trends that pointed to the direction in which affordable housing policy was headed. Among these were more local control and reliance on public-private partnerships.

In the mid-1980s, the Harvard Law School professor and former HUD assistant secretary Charles Haar questioned whether public-private partnership was an honest and viable approach or simply a ruse to abandon housing subsidy for the poor. In an essay for the Lincoln Institute of Land Policy, he wrote that 1984 was a "crucial juncture in the history of American housing":

> Federal housing policy, more than at any time since 1930, appears to be drifting without direction. In the face of this uncertainty, it is possible to detect the philo-

sophical parameters that will shape that policy in the coming decade. The pendulum continues to swing up and to the right, away from heavy reliance upon government intervention in the areas of urban redevelopment and housing. Indeed, since the late 1970s, the public sector has assumed an increasingly auxiliary and passive role. Even within liberal camps, the focus has shifted toward the devising of new cooperative relationships between public and private actors.

Will the federal government's abandonment of its leading role in the low-income housing field be answered by innovative cooperative efforts on the part of local governments and local developers? (Haar 1984a, vii)

Haar acknowledged that public, private, and nonprofit players could bring different and essential expertise and energy to solve the problems that the War on Poverty could not. But, he wrote, "the question that hovers ominously in the background is whether 'sharing' will become just a euphemism for the mutual abdication of responsibility." So was it innovation or abdication? At the same time, it was not clear how, or if, the public-private model would develop. And if it did, would it have the resources to be effective?

2

Building the Decentralized
Housing Network

I n the early 1980s, the Reagan Revolution cut funding for building
affordable housing. In city halls and church basements across the
country, however, another revolution was taking place—a revolution
from below, where local groups began to take control of and improvise
new approaches to local affordable housing needs. The participants often
started small—in one state or one city or one neighborhood—but over
time, the seeds grew. The community organizer in Pittsburgh, Dorothy
Mae Richardson, for example, started a nationwide intermediary,
NeighborWorks America, in a rented trailer. And a group that became a
billion-dollar-a-year financial institution, Enterprise Community Partners, started out as a neighborhood response to local housing needs by
rehabilitating abandoned townhouses in Washington, D.C.

Overview

Between the dismantling of traditional housing production programs in
1981 and the flow of new federal housing funds from tax credits in 1987
(what some housing development veterans called the "starving time"),
there was a tremendous amount of innovation among state and local governments and groups in civic society. In 1981, local groups (community
development corporations or CDCs, city and state governments, and

local housing activists) were unsophisticated and shied away from ambitious building projects or complex financial transactions. They seemed to be an unlikely force for housing policy innovation. Yet by 1987 there was a new respect for these rag-tag local groups. A 1987 article in the journal of the National Association of Housing and Redevelopment Officials, *Journal of Housing*, praised local housing initiatives. According to the article, "The state-of-the-art among neighborhood organizations has grown so steadily that, individually and especially in the aggregate, they have become developers of scale of affordable housing" (Shabecoff 1987, 105). The article pointed to a growing list of local accomplishments by 1987:

- San Francisco's neighborhood housing developers had produced between 2,000 and 3,000 homes, according to an estimate from Daniel Liebsohn, executive director of the Low Income Housing Fund (a local housing finance intermediary).
- The Greater Boston Community Development Corporation estimated that neighborhood-based groups had built over 2,750 units in Eastern Massachusetts, with nearly 1,000 other units in the process of rehabilitation.
- Chicago's 15-member Chicago Rehab Network had 1,000 units in production.
- New York's neighborhood groups had developed nearly 3,000 units a year, according to the estimates of Brian Sullivan of the Pratt Center (a group that monitored the work of nonprofits) (Shabecoff 1987, 105)

Among the pack, Boston and Chicago were early leaders in developing affordable housing networks. Chicago had nearly 100 community-based groups, according to a 1987 Ford Foundation report on the growth of CDCs, *Corrective Capitalism: The Rise of America's Community Development Corporations*. The authors, Neal Pierce and Carol Steinbach, attributed this flowering to Chicago's history of neighborhood organizing and advocacy.[1] Chicago's housing activists were also particularly successful in getting support from city hall, private corporations, and especially banks (Zielenbach 2000).

Boston's success had a different genesis. The drive came from "the strong state support for CDCs initiated by Governor Michael Dukakis in the late 1970s." In the next decade, the number of CDCs grew from 12 to around 70, with about half in Boston, according to Pierce and Steinbach

(1987, 17). Other cities with a growing CDC network included Baltimore, Cincinnati, Cleveland, Denver, Hartford, Indianapolis, Kansas City, Los Angeles, Minneapolis, Oakland, Philadelphia, Pittsburgh, Providence, St. Louis, San Francisco, Seattle, and Washington, D.C.

Far away from the corridors of power in Washington, D.C., there was an army swelling with new recruits from all walks of life. They had in common a desire to do something about improving their neighborhoods, as Dorothy Mae Richardson in Pittsburgh said when she started a group that later became NeighborWorks: "I could see houses starting to lean, windows rotting away. The solution was not to tear down the whole neighborhood and move everybody into public housing," said Richardson. "The solution was to fix the houses."[2]

Individuals across the country refused to accept passively either community decline or the policy changes coming from the federal government; they were leading the revolution from below. In a burst of creativity, resourcefulness, and institution building, community groups, state and local governments, capacity-building intermediaries, and the private sector were forging new alliances and developing new strategies for housing low-income citizens. The following tells the story of key individuals and organizations that started small but over time built the backbone of what would eventually become a large and sophisticated decentralized network of affordable housing developers.

Community Development Corporations

Most CDCs date from one of three distinct periods: during the War on Poverty, after the passage of Community Development Block Grant (CDBG) program in 1974, or in the 1990s when funding had increased and become more stable.[3] As the Kennedy-Taft debates and groups like the East Los Angeles Community Union (TELACU) and others demonstrated in chapter 1, early CDCs were seen as rooted in and rooting for their communities. Although they were ambitious, only a few of the first wave of CDCs that came out of the War on Poverty programs survived. A survey of CDCs operating in 1990 found that only 27 percent were founded before 1973. "These groups were born of the activist spirit of the '60s— products of the War on Poverty and the civil rights movement, and reactions to the negative effects of the federal urban renewal program," according to affordable housing scholar Avis Vidal (1992, 2), who noted that "often these groups began as community service or community action agencies and later moved into community economic development."

The second act for CDCs came in 1974, thanks to the CDBG program. CDCs born in this era were more specifically oriented to affordable housing development. Over 50 percent of the CDCs in Vidal's study were created between 1973 and 1980 (Vidal 1992). Overall, of the CDCs in existence in 1990, nearly 80 percent had been founded before 1980, and their first efforts in affordable housing were almost entirely funded by the federal government. When HUD funds dried up after 1981, however, they were forced to branch out and create new alliances with other local organizations in a search for funding and new strategies to achieve their mission.

During the early 1980s, existing CDCs had to scramble for funds. A good example is an Indianapolis CDC, Eastside Community Investments (ECI). In 1980, nearly 90 percent of the funding for this nonprofit came from federal sources.[4] Six years later, ECI received only slightly more than 10 percent of its funding from the federal government. Rather than giving up, ECI had continued its mission. In those six years, it rehabilitated 1,000 units of housing, created a subsidized mortgage pool, started a small-business incubator program, and developed a 25-acre industrial park that attracted 300 jobs (Pierce and Steinbach 1987).

ECI President Dennis West explained how ECI managed to thrive in spite of its loss of federal dollars. "The cuts forced us to utilize our own resources better and extend our network," he said. "We turned to the larger community." ECI's 1986 annual report listed nearly 100 "partners" that had supplied financing and other assistance. The list included "city, state, and federal government, Indiana Power and Light, the Joyce Foundation, the Lilly Endowment, four church organizations, Goodwill Industries, Aetna Life and Casualty, local banks and realtors, the Local Initiatives Support Corporation, the Indiana School for the Deaf, accounting firms, law firms, and McDonalds" (Pierce and Steinbach 1987, 56).

As ECI's experience suggests, no CDC survived on its own. Behind every successful CDC were many supporters. Reaching out to all these groups may have had an air of desperation about it—ECI was clearly desperate—but it was increasingly plugged into many new institutions that could offer more than just money. The new network of partners also provided advice, information, and key contacts. This example demonstrates Friedrich Nietzsche's point that what does not kill us makes us stronger. The unintended consequences of trying to stay alive actually created a much stronger organization.

A final burst of CDC creation took place in the 1990s when federal funding became more diversified and stable, although most of the funding continued to be for projects rather than for core operations or organizational development. During this period, community development nonprofits diversified, too, with the advent of community development financial institutions (CDFIs), which began to finance a wider variety of community needs (e.g., small business loans and community facilities such as homeless shelters and charter school loans). And CDCs engaged in broader development activities as well, including construction of commercial space. In 1984, just under 20 percent of CDCs were building commercial space; by 2005 almost half were. Much of the commercial space was used for community-supporting social services, such as child care, health care, youth centers, and other social services (National Congress for Community Economic Development [NCCED] 1997).

By any measure, the 1990s represented a tremendous increase in the scale and scope of CDCs. Their influence, however, was extended through for-profit developers. [5] Nonprofits, for example, set benchmarks and standards for mission-critical issues such as reasonable developer fees or incorporating community involvement.[6] In other words, nonprofits set high standards for social impact. This process worked the other way as well. For-profits helped nonprofits work smarter. Nonprofits adopted many underwriting and accounting procedures from the private sector, and they also had to match the efficiency and building quality standards set by for-profit firms. This sort of mutually reinforcing dynamic extended the influence of CDCs through the entire affordable housing production system.

The Evolution of Community Development Corporations

CDCs were designed to be independent of local government, but, contrary to Robert Kennedy's suggestions a decade earlier, their independence did not always imply that they were to be rivals of local government. As late as 1975, federal guidelines on the CDBG program made it clear that independence for CDCs was necessary to make it "more difficult for local governments to preempt CDCs and incorporate them into their own organizations." The report went on to say that "one of the primary objectives of the Special Impact Program [part of CDBG] is the creation of new institutions and a change in the attitudes and behavior of existing institutions"

(U.S. Office of Economic Development 1975, 7). Competition with CDCs could be a valuable check on the behavior of local government.

But CDCs walked a tightrope; they were fostered and often funded by government but were independent and sometimes antagonistic toward it. In their ideal form, CDCs gave local residents an institution of their own, one that would make decisions based not just on the economic bottom line, or the strict guidance of some bureaucratic program, but on the needs and desires of the community in which they operated. The CDCs were to be responsive and flexible in relation to the community, but more than that, by their presence and nature, they were to build cooperation and cohesion in that community. More attractive still, this community building was to take place without the need for government regulation or oversight. Finally, multiple CDCs might compete in their efforts to deliver services. Presumably, CDCs would become more efficient by competing with one another.

Broad Political Support

CDCs had political support across the ideological spectrum. They were a sort of Rorschach test: when people looked at them, they saw different things. Conservatives, on the one hand, saw the corporate aspect of these organizations—independence, market discipline, and freedom from government interference. Intellectuals on the political right also saw a need to promote local community organizations. A 1977 book, *To Empower People,* called for a resurgence of community-based institutions that would maximize individual freedom by reasserting traditional roles that had been usurped by the state (Berger and Neuhaus 1996). It was an example of conservative hopes that churches, clubs, and local organizations would foster grassroots democracy and potentially create more effective solutions to social problems.

Liberals, on the other hand, saw the community development aspect of CDCs. Local communities could use these new institutions to challenge existing authority and empower themselves. The New Left, for example, often decried large-scale government intervention and championed more local responses and "participatory democracy." According to this view, big government bureaucracies, along with big corporations, squeezed the meaning out of daily life. Both were dehumanizing institutions.

The drive to use CDCs was more than just politically popular. Prevailing economic theory suggested that bureaucracies like HUD had inherent problems because (1) bureaucrats have weak incentives to innovate and work hard; and (2) decisionmaking power is at the top of the organizational pyramid, while much of the important information resides with the line staff at the bottom of the organization.[7] For economists, the answer to this problem is the market, or at least something that operates like a market, and CDCs could operate as market actors.

Of course, there was a potential problem with using the market to solve the market failure that created the problem of decaying neighborhoods in the first place. The trick, as the Ford Foundation stated in earlier reports, was to create an institution that could respond to signals as quickly as a market actor and at the same time remain committed to the improvement of a community. In other words, there was a need for an institution with a double bottom line, one demanding efficiency and one promoting social goals.

Double-Bottom-Line Mission

CDCs seemed to be a logical answer to the problem of the double bottom line. They had a commitment to their communities and were investing in social improvement. At the same time, they could be nimble in the marketplace. In a 20th Century Fund Report, *CDCs: New Hope for the Inner City* (1971), Gregory Faux wrote that the CDCs

> have been able to make decisions faster and commitments with more authority than have Model Cities organizations, Community Action Agencies and urban renewal authorities. Such freedom and flexibility are indispensable to a successful economic development program. Obtaining urban land without the two-to-three-year delay involved in urban renewal is a case in point. (14)

As an institution, CDCs also seemed to address effectively another vexing urban development problem—whether to focus on the physical place (as many of the urban renewal programs of the 1950s had done) or on the urban resident (as many of the job training and community empowerment programs of the War on Poverty did). CDCs did both. If they were well run, they could be effective real estate developers because they knew their markets. They often hired local residents who also had superior "on the ground" knowledge of what the real estate needs were in their community. CDCs could always be on the lookout for good deals on a construction site or on an apartment building and could acquire one without as much red tape as a government agency. They could also make snap decisions to take advantage of changing real estate market conditions.

CDCs built physical capital (apartment buildings), and, in the process, they also built human capital, often by employing local residents and providing valuable training and work experience. Many community development leaders of today got their start with low-level jobs at CDCs.

CDCs managed to build connections among different individuals and groups within a neighborhood and from the neighborhood to the outside world—local government, local business, and other institutions concerned with improving the city. It appeared that CDCs were effective catalysts for developing what Harvard professor Robert Putnam (2000) calls social capital.[8] According to Faux (1971, 9), "The development of marketable skills, the growing self-confidence and the increase in contacts on the basis of mutual respect can bridge the gap between the larger society" and "residents of the ghetto."

Detractors of the CDCs

CDCs were not without detractors. Randy Stoecker's assessment in a *Journal of Urban Affairs* article was that the CDCs' objectives and the community's objectives were diametrically opposed. The community's desire "is to preserve neighborhood space as a use value for the service of community members, while capital's tendency is to convert neighborhood space into exchange values that can be speculated on for a profit" (Stoecker 1997, 5). Stoecker complained that the results of a successful redevelopment effort would drive up rents, colonize open space, and attack existing neighborhood patterns of commerce and socialization. And even if the community's interests were aligned with those of the CDCs, their efforts were puny compared to the scale of the problem— CDCs were a "hodgepodge of small, scattered efforts" (Stoecker 1997, 11).

Harry Brendt, in his 1977 book *New Rulers of the Ghetto*, complained that CDCs' narrow focus—"designing programs for the benefit of discreet groups; i.e., the poor or the black"—was too limiting. "These programs are self-defeating," he said, "because of their failure to gain the support of the majority." According to Brendt (1977, 140), "The best approach would be to devise programs dealing with specific societal needs rather than specific societal groups."

To look at the company CDCs kept, one might agree with Stoecker and Brendt. In 1977, for example, the National Congress for Community Economic Development, a group that represented most CDCs, became a member of the National Association of Manufacturers, a group that often opposed welfare programs for the poor. Brendt also claimed that CDCs were joining local chambers of commerce and had more allegiance to the business community than to the poor (Stoecker 1997, 10).

In the debate over "whose side are you on?" that raged in the 1970s and 1980s, the question of how CDCs would play themselves—were they hard-nosed corporations or community advocacy institutions?—was always in the background. Furthermore, if they were a safety valve to release some of the simmering steam of discontent in low-income neighborhoods, then it might be said they were taking away an important tool of the poor, the ability to create some havoc. Francis Fox Piven and Richard Cloward (1993), in their book *Regulating the Poor* (first published in 1971), explain that the fear of disruption, whether by voter rebellion, strike, or riots, motivated elites in American history to provide poor relief (which happened to some extent with the Housing Act of 1968 after the urban riots of the 1960s). If that was true, then the work of CDCs co-opted the urban poor.

On the other hand, it was not clear what other options were available. By the 1970s, there was no political support for government intervention on the scale of the War on Poverty programs (see chapter 1). Indeed, many participants in the War on Poverty welcomed the shift to market-inspired programs. Bennett Harrison wrote from the perspective of someone who knew both sides of the corporate versus community debate for CDCs. A former Harlem community organizer, Harrison wrote in a Ford Foundation report that the 1960s were a time of "beautifully motivated mistakes." Over the 1970s and 1980s, CDCs became more businesslike in their orientation, and this development was positive, according to Harrison. As Faux had predicted in 1971, many Harlem groups created links with outside organizations and corporations—local government, small and big business, and the like. According to Harrison (1995, 24), "The built-in economic and political power that comes through links with outside organizations is a vital part of all the most successful CDCs, the ones that have survived and grown."

A Philadelphia CDC director who lived through the transition from the 1960s to the 1980s put it this way: "We may be tending now, with more Harvard and Wharton grads, to be approaching development with less 'political' sense. It may be creating a complacency among us," said West Oak Lane CDC Director Jan Rubin. It is "harder to fight with a Sun Oil or a Bell Tel when you want to look and act like them," she said (Pierce and Steinbach 1987, 34).

The CDC concept that had its birth in the Great Society underwent considerable changes through the 1970s and early 1980s. The model of the CDC as a challenger of local political and economic structures did not survive. CDCs did not transform traditional capitalism in their neighborhoods. Nor did they operate as a new type of governance outside the existing local government framework. In the end, CDCs continued to be based in neighborhoods; they drew many neighborhood members for their boards of directors. But they also became partners with local government and the private sector to accomplish housing and economic development goals. By the 1990s, this model seemed to dominate and enjoyed growing support from government.

New Government Bureaucracies at the State and Local Levels

At the same time that CDCs were innovating, state and local governments were experimenting and adding capabilities making them the partners that the Kaiser Report hoped for back in 1968.[9] In the 1970s, two developments in particular spurred administrative capacity in subnational government. First was more authority and discretion over federal monies that came with the CDBG program. Second was a need to innovate, thanks to a decline in federal funds for housing production programs.

A New Activism

In a 1986 conference on public-private partnerships in housing and urban development, Denver Mayor Frederico Peña claimed that federal housing programs were now virtually irrelevant to the housing needs of his city. "I don't care who becomes the next president of the United States," he said. "We in Denver accepted many years ago that the decentralization process was here." If cities were not going to get the funds they needed to build low-income housing, they would have to pool "our resources, our talents, our energies, and our ideas," to solve the problem (Davis 1986, 35).

Peña's attitude toward federal policy may have been cavalier, but it underscored a trend that gathered momentum under Reagan's presidency. In fact, one of the great ironies of the Reagan Revolution—the effort to slash funding for federal social programs—was that it triggered a flowering of state and local government programs. The effort to "starve the beast," in David Stockman's famous phrase, triggered a wave of new local government programs and new local bureaucracies (Stockman 1986).

Richard Nathan and Martha Derthick, in a 1987 op-ed for the *New York Times,* wrote that Reagan was successful in reducing federal aid to states and cities from a high in 1978 of 25 percent of state and local government outlays to a low of 17 percent in 1988. But, as they observed, if "decentralization was meant to promote retrenchment, it backfired." Their Brookings Institution study was based on the analyses of field researchers in 14 states. The study concluded that states "actually increased their activity during the Reagan years."[10] They noted that "increased activism of state governments is likely to be one of the most important legacies of the Reagan years."

A knowledgeable and interesting perspective on state contributions came from I. Don Terner, a legendary figure in affordable housing. He was a University of California, Berkeley, urban planning academic who also directed the California Housing and Community Development Department in the 1970s. Terner left state government to start a nonprofit real estate development firm, known as BRIDGE Housing. By the early 1990s, San Francisco–based BRIDGE was the largest nonprofit housing developer in the country and continues to rank among the top five nonprofit affordable housing owners in the country (Nixon 1994).[11] In a policy essay in 1990, Terner argued that state governments had to "replace the activism" of HUD and the federal government. Each state, he said, "needed to identify and research its own housing problems, devise policies and programs to address those problems, and then find ways to implement the policies and fund the programs." From 1983 to 1989, state governments developed more than 300 new housing programs that ranged from homeless shelters to rehabilitation and new construction subsidies (Terner and Cook 1990, 115).

Housing Finance Agencies

State governments used many approaches to compensate for the federal withdrawal of programs and resources, but the most effective strategy was the development of housing finance agencies (HFAs). These new bureaucracies were essentially mortgage banks that had the advantage of being able both to borrow money from capital markets in conventional ways and, because they were state-chartered, to issue tax-exempt bonds.[12] In 1968 there were no state housing finance agencies. By 1974 there were

30, and they had financed over 50,000 units for low-income families (Stegman 1974; Alexander 1973). By 1989, there were 48 state HFAs. Terner estimated that these HFAs collectively had financed more than 900,000 homes. State HFAs were making a significant contribution and doing so in many different ways. Solving problems and mastering complex financial underwriting techniques were "building capacity into the state bureaucracies," according to Terner (DiPasquale and Keyes 1990, 125). By 2007, all the states—as well as Washington, D.C., Puerto Rico, and the U.S. Virgin Islands—had HFAs, which by then had financed 3.1 million low- and moderate-income apartments (NCSHA 2008).

State HFAs did more than provide low-cost mortgage capital. They also organized themselves politically, founding their own trade association in 1972 (the National Council of State Housing Agencies). These agencies were significantly affected by federal actions, such as IRS interpretations of the uses of tax-exempt bonds. Michael Stegman, a housing scholar and later assistant secretary for policy development and research at HUD during the Clinton administration, wrote in the *Journal of Housing* in 1981 that state HFAs had made heavy investments and had become integral players in affordable housing.

HFAs aggressively incorporated new strategies to lower the cost of housing for low-income citizens, taking advantage of different programs ranging from below-market interest rates to new tax incentives and tax-exempt bonds. At a 1986 conference of the National Association of Housing and Redevelopment Officials, two HFA officials—one from Michigan and the other from Illinois—encouraged states to create "a new arsenal of techniques for housing production because every deal that comes to them in this new environment will be different" (*Journal of Housing* 1987, 30). The presenters encouraged states to follow the example of Illinois, which was experimenting with loans that were not subsidized but were insured by the Federal Housing Administration. In 1986, the Illinois Authority completed $540 million in loans for low-income apartments through this process.

Other weapons in the arsenal were different techniques to minimize the risk to investors for buying HFA-issued bonds. To this end, the presenters encouraged states to learn how to use Government National Mortgage Association credit enhancement along with credit enhancement programs through HUD (e.g., Federal Housing Administration coinsurance). These enhancements made the bonds, which were sold to investors through Wall Street banks, less risky.

Part of becoming a mortgage bank meant that each state HFA had to underwrite each apartment project the same way private sector banks did. Since the HFAs held these apartments as collateral for their loans, they would also have to be confident that they were constructed properly and were supervised and maintained well. This was critical early on-the-job training for organizations that were evolving into mortgage banks (*Journal of Housing* 1987, 31). HFAs staffed up with architects who could oversee construction, asset development professionals who understood how to manage apartment buildings, and underwriters who could analyze the sources and uses of construction funds and the operating performance of the buildings.

Grants

In addition to providing low-interest loans, state housing bureaucracies were experimenting with ways they could provide grants to projects. The Michigan State Housing Development Authority, for example, developed a pilot grant program and funded it with $1 million to make grants of up to $50,000 as seed money for affordable housing projects. In the first year, the Michigan authority awarded nine grants totaling $330,000 to 16 community groups (*Journal of Housing* 1987, 31). Massachusetts invested $4.4 million in 1987 for the Office of Community Economic Development to support the work of community-based organizations (Shabecoff 1987).

Support for CDCs

In terms of support for CDCs, Massachusetts was leading the field with a variety of strategies. In the 1970s, the state created the Community Development Finance Corporation, which provided small loans and venture capital to CDCs for housing and other projects. Next came the Community Economic Development and Assistance Corporation, which provided technical assistance and small, interest-free loans to help CDCs get their projects started. A third agency, created in 1978, was the Community Enterprise Economic Development program, which provided operating grants to CDCs. This was critically important because most funding was tied to construction project transactions, which put CDCs in a catch-22. They could not secure funding for a project without a strong organization, but they could not build a strong organization without the income from a funded project.[13] By 1987, New York, Minnesota, Wisconsin, Florida, and Ohio were also supporting their CDCs with state funding (Pierce and Steinbach 1987, 60).

Housing Trust Funds

Another state and local government-sponsored effort was housing trust funds. The Michigan Housing Coalition, a group comprising community leaders and housing advocates that incorporated under the sponsorship of the state HFA, launched a housing trust fund that sought to finance housing for tenants with very low incomes (lower than 50 percent of the area's median income). The trust fund was initially capitalized by social investments from foundations, insurance companies, religious organizations, and the state. All these groups committed to ongoing support of the trust fund. Other similar programs drew revenue from a variety of sources—fees for for-profit real estate development in San Francisco and Jersey City, contributions from developers for favorable development terms like higher density allowances (Seattle), interest on escrow accounts (Maryland), fees for converting apartments to condominiums (Montgomery County, Maryland), annual state budget appropriations (New York State), proceeds from sales of urban renewal land (Denver), and revenue from tideland oil revenue (California) (Shabecoff 1987).

A 1990 report by the Urban Institute, *Housing America: Learning from the Past, Planning for the Future,* explained that more than 15 states had developed housing trust funds to help offset the cost of building housing for low-income tenants (Turner and Reed 1990). The funds were "supported by a variety of sources, including surplus bond funds, real estate transfer taxes, and interest on escrow accounts. These trust funds have generated new reliable sources for support of housing production programs" (14). By 2002, the number of housing trust funds sponsored by state, county, and city governments had risen to 275 and had provided over $750 million per year for housing (Brooks 2002).

Local Government Efforts

Nathan and Derthick's conclusion about an explosion of new state government programs was also true for local government, according to a 1988 study by the National Association of Housing and Redevelopment Officials. Local housing and community development bureaucracies

Table 2.1. Average Annual Growth in Community Development Block Grant Appropriations, 1975–92

Administration	Years	Average real growth (%)
Ford	1975–77	4.1
Carter	1977–81	5.1
Reagan	1981–89	−6.5
Bush	1989–92	0.6

Source: Walker et al. 1994.

maintained their housing programs "despite severe cutbacks in financial resources," according to the report. Nearly 80 percent of city and county governments relied on CDBG funds, "the largest federal government funding source for neighborhood revitalization." While CDBG was critically important, those funds were dwindling, from 1981 to 1988 (see table 2.1), according to the study. In response, local governments tried to maintain services by "leveraging private investment, forming partnerships with nonprofits, and devising new financial mechanisms" (Matulef 1988, 239).

Zoning Approaches

Denver Mayor Peña was an important advocate for activist city government in an era of diminished federal resources for housing. "City governments are opening their doors. If you're a community activist and do your nuts-and-bolts work, you'll get a response from the city," he said. "We'd be foolish not to find alternative funds from city coffers to make CDC projects work. They're a wise investment for the future of the city" (Pierce and Steinbach 1987, 60).

The "nuts and bolts" that Peña referred to included new local incentives and programs to promote low-income housing production. One approach used land use and zoning authority to exact some low-income housing from for-profit real estate developments. This approach, called "inclusionary zoning," typically involved setting aside a small percentage of apartments or houses from large developments for low-income tenants. A 1984 report by the Rutgers University Center for Urban Policy Research claimed that "consideration was being given to inclusionary housing programs as an alternative to federal subsidy programs" (Mallach 1984, 247).

A similar program that started in San Francisco was called "linkage," which tied the zoning approval of profitable office and commercial developments to an accompanying obligation to provide some affordable housing. The rationale was that job-creating development had to add to existing housing to offset the greater demand new commercial development put on the existing housing stock (Turner and Reed 1990). The developer could build low-income housing or pay an "in lieu" fee to local government, which would use those funds for affordable housing development. The program got its start in San Francisco in 1980 and by 1986 was used in five other cities: Boston, Hartford, Miami, Santa Monica, and Seattle (Mallach 1984). Both inclusionary zoning and linkage programs produced results, but they were dependent on a booming real estate economy. The incentives to participate in these programs disappeared during real estate downturns.

Other Innovations and Partnerships

Other innovative local government programs during this time included Philadelphia's "land banking" scheme, where the city held tax-delinquent and abandoned properties for CDCs, allowing them enough time to arrange financing for purchase and rehabilitation (Pierce and Steinbach 1987). Cities also gave away city-owned land, gave local tax rebates, and provided loans and grants from their CDBG funds.

At the same time that New York City was experiencing a significant rise in homelessness, a shortage of affordable housing, and diminished federal assistance, Mayor Edward Koch launched an ambitious 10-year program to use municipal resources (mostly bonds) to acquire, rehabilitate, and build new apartments. The city had been managing a growing portfolio of tax-foreclosed properties during the late 1970s and early 1980s. While other cities were selling or demolishing these tax-foreclosed buildings, New York acquired them, and by 1986, it owned over 100,000 apartments. The city raised over $5 billion in bonds to pay for the program and in the end provided over 150,000 apartments (Schwartz 1999).

These new programs relied on partners in the community to help implement them. They could not work without close cooperation from local groups, especially CDCs and for-profit real estate developers. Partnerships during the period 1981–87 were also more collegial than before. In the War on Poverty era, when CDCs were seen as an alternative governance structure to local government, there was animosity between community groups and cities. These old antagonisms melted away in the 1980s when the only chance of success depended on cooperation and pooling resources. One example of these new relationships at the local level came in a 1986 report from the International City Management Association (Hershey 1986).[14] That report focused on the work of Metro-Dade County, Florida, and county government's close working relationship with CDCs in 11 low- and moderate-income neighborhoods. The director of Metro-Dade's Office of Community and Economic Development, Dr. Ernest Martin, said that the county was drawn to CDCs because they were an efficient way to connect local government to the private sector and the community. "The three-way partnership works because the neighborhood, the public sector, and the private sector each stands to benefit from it," according to Martin (Hershey 1986, 7).

Martin explained that neighborhoods benefited because CDCs provided new housing stock. The county government also benefited because it was more effective at involving the affected community. An additional advantage for the county was that CDCs were not as tightly regulated as county government. One example is that "Florida law," according to Martin, "requires that transfers of land owned by a local government to any entity other than a non-profit corporation must comply with a variety of bidding and appraisal requirements. If the land is transferred to a non-profit, this red tape can be eliminated." The private sector also benefited: "Local lenders and for-profit developers involved in the project stand to profit financially while also improving their community" (Hershey 1986, 7). These projects were also potentially less risky because CDCs were more likely to have public subsidy.

By 1988, state and local governments were light years ahead of where they had been two decades earlier. Not only were they now able partners in federal programs (such as they were), but also they brought new funds contacts, expertise, and creative problem solving.

Capacity-Building Intermediaries

Capacity-building organizations, known as intermediaries, were vital to the success of the housing revolution from below. Intermediaries were a sort of cross between a management consultant and a creative investment banker. They engaged in technical assistance and training for nonprofits and local governments and operated as bankers, making grants and loans for low-income housing projects. They mobilized capital from all levels of government and from philanthropies and private capital markets. Because they were seen as having "business sense," their involvement in a low-income housing project provided a sort of Good Housekeeping seal of approval for new and untried CDCs. Also because of their high profile, they were a respected voice in the housing policy debates of the 1980s. There were several nationwide intermediaries and many local ones by the end of the 1980s.[15]

The Importance of Intermediaries

As early as the Economic Opportunity Act debates of 1964 and 1966, people had recognized the need for organizations able to build the capacity of CDCs and others engaged in housing and urban development. But for all the talk, no such organizations appeared until much later. In 1974, Congress established what is arguably the first nationwide intermediary by providing Dorothy Mae Richardson's Neighborhood Reinvestment Corporation with new resources and expanded it dramatically in 1978. In 1979, the Ford Foundation helped launch the Local Initiatives Support Corporation (LISC), and the next year, philanthropist Jim Rouse started the Enterprise Foundation. All three organizations grew to provide capacity-building services nationwide.

Intermediaries helped spark a rapid increase in the number of CDCs. Avis Vidal (1997) considered them essential for a "take-off of the CDC movement." As she explained, referring to these intermediaries, "Collectively, their impact has been enormous: they have articulated a vision of community development, and have developed ways to set the vision into action." They created "new roles and financial tools that have both expanded dramatically the financial resources available for community development" at the same time drawing in "new stakeholders in the success of the work" (Vidal 1997, 433).

Neal Pierce and Carol Steinbach, in a 1990 report for the Council for Community-Based Development, wrote that veterans of affordable housing development considered the contributions from intermediaries to be "substantial," agreeing with a statement by Andrew Mott of the Center for Community Change:

> Good intermediaries create an environment which nurtures the growth of vital organizations. They devote time and skill to watching for the seeds of new organizations, help emerging groups get through their first few months and first crises,

assist in raising the crucial early money, connect people with others who have relevant experience, and help them find and break in their initial staff. One particular value is an ability to bring groups together to work in coalitions on larger issues or projects. (Pierce and Steinbach 1990, 26–27)

The intermediaries were catalysts—diffusing new ideas and best practices and knitting different groups together. They were a focal point for new CDCs and the wider government, philanthropic, and corporate community that wanted to do something about housing.

In later years, Bill Clinton's HUD Director Henry Cisneros recognized the value of intermediaries and began funneling some federal resources to them. HUD's Public Private Partnership Program funded four intermediaries: the Local Initiatives Support Corporation, the Enterprise Foundation, the Neighborhood Reinvestment Corporation, and Community Builders. Jim Rouse wrote a foreword for a HUD report on the program, claiming that intermediaries were necessary for "system building and system change." HUD's support, according to Rouse, was "a wonderful example of how national resources can be made available in a flexible manner that allows individual communities to determine an organizational and programmatic approach responsive to local needs and opportunities" (HUD 1996, iv).

The importance of intermediaries to CDCs appears only to have grown. In a 2005 survey by the National Congress for Community Economic Development, the percentage of CDCs receiving more than $50,000 in grants, investments, or loans from an intermediary rose from 27 percent in 1994 to 41 percent in 2005. For a breakdown of the percentage of CDCs receiving financial support from leading intermediaries, see table 2.2.

Table 2.2. Percentage of CDCs Receiving Financial Support from Six Intermediaries, 2005

Intermediary organization	Percentage of CDCs
Local Initiatives Support Corporation	24
Enterprise Community Partners, Inc.	11
Neighborhood Reinvestment Corporation	11
Housing Assistance Council	5
Rural Community Assistance Corporation	3
Local intermediaries/collaborations	9

Source: NCCED 1999, 21.

Local Initiatives Support Corporation

Part of the Ford Foundation's early interest in LISC came from Franklin Thomas, who became president of the foundation in 1979 after heading the Bedford Stuyvesant Redevelopment Corporation, one of the earliest CDCs in the model envisioned by Robert Kennedy (Lee 1986). Five other sponsors joined Ford in founding LISC, including Aetna Life and Casualty Company, Cigna Corporation, Metropolitan Life Insurance Company, Prudential Insurance Company of America, and the MacArthur Foundation. Together, they donated nearly $10 million. From 1980 to 1991, the Ford Foundation contributed more than $44 million to LISC (Ford Foundation 1991).

According to its 1986 *Annual Report,* LISC operated under two principles: first, to raise corporate and foundation funds for the support of locally created, locally executed community development projects in cities across the country; and, second, to work in communities where there was evidence of existing local initiative. As the second principle suggests, LISC's approach changed based on the needs and resources of a given community:

> In Los Angeles, LISC started a training program to teach 17 community organizations and social service agencies how to become developers of affordable housing. In Washington, D.C., a city that had been weak in public-private partnerships, LISC helped unite community groups, local government, banks, and the Federal National Mortgage Association behind the HomeSight initiative, an effort to produce 1,600 units of low-income housing in 36 months. And in Chicago, LISC joined with the LaSalle National Bank and the Illinois Housing Development Authority to create the country's first "predevelopment" loan fund for community organizations. (Pierce and Steinback 1990, 28)

Paul Grogan, who led LISC from 1986 to 1998, characterized the organization as a unifying force holding together the many participants of the decentralized housing network. In agreement with that view, Avis Vidal wrote in a 1986 *Wall Street Journal* article that "LISC has provided the glue in a mosaic of neighborhood revitalization efforts"(Lee 1986, 1).

In the same *Wall Street Journal* article, Chicago's Mayor Harold Washington explained that his city had lost 90 percent of its federal housing funds in the previous six years but that LISC-funded housing projects replaced nearly half that amount. "This kind of public-private partnership is more than just a glimpse of the future," he said. "Some good has come out of the attrition of federal funds, and that's been the growth of these creative and effective local initiatives." Boston's Mayor

Raymond Flynn also praised LISC and the decentralized network it fostered. "Clearly," he said, "urban policy for the remainder of this century and beyond will be collaboration of community groups, local government and business" (Lee 1986, 1).

In spite of all the praise, some saw LISC as a distraction. In the same article, Robert Reischauer, then a senior fellow and economist at the Brookings Institution, said the LISC approach was too little, too late. George Sternlieb, director of the Rutgers University Center for Urban Policy, added to the criticism that LISC and groups like it were not up to the daunting challenges of solving urban housing problems. He complained that this approach was palliation and good only "for the psyches of the boards of directors of foundations" (Lee 1986, 1).

Despite criticisms of the LISC approach, Grogan said in a 1998 interview published in *U.S. Banker* that while he was not prepared to declare victory over substandard housing, the environment for building affordable housing was better than ever before, thanks to organizations like his. He spoke of the role of intermediaries and the decentralized approach to housing development in an interview after he retired from LISC in 1998:

> **Grogan:** We have what I consider the legacy of 40 years of urban decline that went on: virulent poverty, this isolation between city and suburbs, a lot of racial isolation that's come with that. If you look at the statistics, they still look bad. But if you go into these neighborhoods, they're changing very rapidly for the better, and they look better than they have since the Fifties.
>
> This stuff takes a while; you've got to stay with it. This business of small successes, the fact that private capital has been at work—government has been important, but it hasn't been a government program. Government has been pulled in along with banks and other private sources.
>
> **U.S. Banker:** Government didn't have the resources?
>
> **Grogan:** It didn't. We believe we [LISC] put out the first corporate [Low Income Housing Tax Credit] equity fund. We raised $12 million, with enormous effort, and the corporations that gave us that money were convinced that that's what they were doing—giving us the money. LISC had a good reputation—many of these institutions had provided grants to us, or loans—so they said, "All right, we'll give this a try." And, of course, they've enjoyed tremendous returns [on their initial investments]. (Marshall 1999, 62–68)

LISC was successful in building capacity into the decentralized housing network, and the numbers speak for themselves. From 1980 to 2007, LISC worked with thousands of CDCs, raised more than $8.6 billion to build or rehab nearly 230,000 affordable homes and develop 32 million square feet of retail, community, and educational space nationwide.[16] While LISC was perhaps the best known, other intermediaries resembled the successful LISC model; the rival that most closely matched it was the Enterprise Foundation.

The Enterprise Foundation

The Enterprise Foundation (now known as Enterprise Community Partners) was founded by James Rouse, a real estate developer whose successful career as a builder of suburban shopping malls and master-planned cities began in the 1940s.[17] In later years, he turned his focus to the decaying downtowns that he helped depopulate. With developments like Faneuil Hall in Boston and Harborplace in Baltimore, Rouse tried to recreate a dynamic city center that would bring people back to old downtowns.

With his extensive real estate background and profit from real estate investments, he created the Enterprise Foundation in 1980 and worked to provide technical assistance and loans to community-based groups (Zoglin 1996).[18]

He was inspired to create the foundation after working with a Washington, D.C., church that started a group called Jubilee Housing to acquire and rehabilitate housing in its neighborhood. Some of the proceeds of his for-profit business were earmarked for the foundation. In addition, Enterprise used its business acumen to help nonprofits work more efficiently, after the model of for-profit businesses. In the early years, there was also a plan for the foundation to engage in some profit-making activity that would further subsidize its work in low-income communities. In Rouse's words, "Enterprise is a resourceful application of the free enterprise system to the solution of an important national problem involving deep human needs" (Enterprise Foundation 1983, 3).

The idea of a profit-fueled foundation, however, did not work. Rouse also tried to recreate his successful formula of downtown revitalization in second-tier cities such as Toledo, Flint, and Richmond. These were financial failures ("Current Topic Award" 1989). By contrast, the foundation was quite successful at earning support from philanthropies such as the Ford Foundation and from government and corporate sources in ways that mirrored LISC's approach. Like LISC, Enterprise enjoyed a surprisingly favorable return on its investments in low-income housing projects.

Even though the plan to use for-profit activity to fund nonprofit work never quite materialized, Enterprise never strayed far from its business mindset. F. Barton Harvey III, an early employee who became CEO, always spoke of Enterprise as bringing business sense to social problems. Harvey, a Harvard-trained MBA, wrote that the "Enterprise Foundation, like a well-run business, must find the best solutions given its scant resources" (Harvey 1989, 15). Integral to this cost-saving strategy was leveraging support from local organizations, bringing "together churches, banks, foundations, nonprofit organizations, cities, and the business sector to target resources and coordinate efforts" (Harvey 1989, 38).

As much as Harvey extolled the values of business and the pluck and energy of local organizations, he never envisioned that urban renewal could happen without the federal government. Organizations like his, he said, "cannot replace the federal government's necessary involvement." He went on to explain that, in his view, "the federal government should stimulate with funding efforts to states, localities, and the private sector to live up to their community responsibilities: to creatively address the problems, to release the efforts of caring, compassionate people, and to involve self-help to the greatest extent possible." He thought that Enterprise could lead the way by experimenting with new approaches and new models and that its successes could set examples and "raise new convictions about the cities and generate a new state of discontent with the way poor people are living and how neighborhoods are deteriorating" (Harvey 1989, 38).

Again, like LISC, Enterprise was racking up an impressive list of accomplishments. From 1982 to 2003, for example, Enterprise (2003) helped finance 160,000 affordable homes and invested nearly $5 billion in affordable housing and community development. In 2006 alone, Enterprise raised and invested $1.2 billion in equity, loans and grants and built or rehabilitated more than 23,000 affordable homes and apartments (Koo and Donaue 2006).

Neighborhood Reinvestment Corporation/Neighborhood Housing Services

Although the Neighborhood Reinvestment Corporation (later called NeighborWorks) was similar to LISC and Enterprise, it was a national public nonprofit supported by annual grants from Congress. It had started, however, as a local organizing effort in Pittsburgh. In 1968, Dorothy Mae Richardson organized her Central North Side neighborhood and was successful in attracting new loans for the community from local banks. With a grant from a local foundation, the organization "rented a trailer, hired staff, and named the effort Neighborhood Housing Services."[19]

Over time, the Neighborhood Housing Services approach gained attention from HUD and received additional funding and help from the federal government. In 1978, Congress passed the Neighborhood Reinvestment Corporation Act, which provided funding and charged the organization to promote "reinvestment in older neighborhoods by local financial institutions in cooperation with the community, residents and local governments."[20]

In an article in *Mortgage Banking* magazine, a sales manager for the First National Bank of Chicago explained that working with Neighbor-Works made his job of lending in low-income communities easier. "They're a proven entity," he said. "They can deliver" (Gottschall and Justa 1997, 38). In a 1996 article in the same magazine, NRC's executive director, George Wright, wrote,

> For nearly 20 years, Neighborhood Reinvestment Corporation has concentrated on providing affordable housing as a key to community revitalization. Through the 178 local affiliates making up our national NeighborWorks network, more than 300 municipalities across the country and in Puerto Rico are being served. In the last five years alone, the supply of safe, affordable housing has increased by 35,000 units, stimulating $1.2 billion in direct and indirect reinvestment. (68)

Wright was quick to point out that his organization went into communities that were otherwise too risky or intimidating for conventional mortgage lenders. "Most of the production," he wrote, "has occurred in communities on the edge, many rife with boarded-up, hazardous or unsightly housing." NRC (later, NeighborWorks) created local boards that brought residents together with local government and private sector participants. Together, they tried to find ways to bring investments to these neighborhoods. Undergirding these investments, however, were federal resources. The local boards were able to combine private capital with federal block grants and tax credits. Because the boards were able to coordinate so many players, there was "a marked increase in market-generated investment," according to Wright (Neighborhood Reinvestment Corporation 1979, 51).

Local Intermediaries and Housing Partnerships

Another important type of intermediary is the one that is more local or regional in its scope. In nearly all the nation's major cities, housing partnerships were organized: Thirty-seven such partnerships were in operation by 1993, and local intermediaries existed in nearly all areas of the country by 1998 (Walker 1993).

One of the most prominent local intermediaries, and the only one in HUD's Private Partnership Program (in addition to LISC, Enterprise, and NRC), was the New England and mid-Atlantic–based group, Community Builders. This organization was founded by a leader in the community development and affordable housing industry, Patrick Clancy.

Community Builders offered expertise and technical assistance for affordable housing developers. "We make ourselves available as a resource to enable local nonprofits to effectively control and manage the development and operation of projects which are critical to their neighborhoods," said Clancy. "To create affordable housing today, it is absolutely crucial to know how to tap into the complex network of available sources and how to knit these together to make a project work" (Pierce and Steinbach 1990, 32).

Like the other intermediaries, Community Builders got its start in a small, local way—restoring 83 townhouses in Boston's South End. It was a HUD-funded project for the group then known as South End Community Development.[21] By 1990, Community Builders had assisted in the development of housing for more than 26,000 New Englanders in addition to the development of several hundred thousand square feet of commercial space (Pierce and Steinbach 1990).

Housing partnerships operated like intermediaries and were usually located in one city or state. They provided technical assistance and worked as a catalyst to bring together local government officials and community-based organizations to get housing projects built. The standard definition of a housing partnership came from Diane Suchman (1990, 5), who described them as "formalized, permanent arrangements among local and sometimes state governments, private funding sources, and private (usually nonprofit) development entities designed to increase production of low-income housing . . . achieved by systematizing and centralizing the functions common to low-income housing projects." By 1990, nearly every large city in the country had a housing partnership.

The Private Sector

> Only if business learns to convert the major social challenges facing developed
> societies today into novel and profitable business opportunities can we hope to
> surmount these challenges in the future. (Drucker 1984, 287)

In many ways, the private sector was the dark matter of the decentralized
housing network. By many measures, its role was larger than that of any
other player. The private sector was involved in almost every aspect of
housing development: as real estate developers (building more subsidized housing than CDCs), as consultants (lawyers, accountants, architects, contractors, financial analysts, real estate agents) that made the
projects work, and as financial service providers who underwrote the individual mortgages, sold the Low Income Housing Tax Credits (LIHTCs),
and connected investors to mortgage revenue bonds, tax-exempt bonds,
and investments in the secondary mortgage market.

Private sector actors were also an important source of funding to
CDCs. By 2005, the depth and scope of funding from private institutions
for CDCs were impressive. Table 2.3 shows the percentage of CDCs
receiving $50,000 or more from private sources.

The effort to get the private sector involved in building affordable
housing predates the War on Poverty. As former HUD official Charles
Haar explained, "The epitome of New Frontier legislation, Model Cities,

Table 2.3. CDCs Receiving $50,000 or More from Private Sources

Private sources of funding	Percentage of CDCs
Banks	55
Foundations	55
Corporations	34
Insurance companies	7
Religious institutions	14
United Way	15
Fannie Mae	13
Freddie Mac	3
Federal Home Loan Bank Affordable Housing Program	26
Other Federal Home Loan Bank programs	3
Fee income	30

Source: NCCED (2005, 22).

aimed strongly at private participation, both in the formulation of the plan for a distressed urban neighborhood and its implementation. The legislative history abounds with references to private industry." In the end, however, he noted that "the involvement of the private sector proved minimal in practice" (Haar 1984, 64).[22]

The private sector has attracted less scholarly interest that other participants in affordable housing, partly because it appeared to play a supporting role to what was going on with CDCs, intermediaries, and state and local governments. The private sector has also been slow to organize itself politically. While there are some longstanding trade associations of groups such as mortgage bankers or real estate agents, these groups did not focus on subsidized housing issues. One exception was the National Association of Home Builders, which had been lobbying federal housing policy for a generation. This politically powerful organization has hundreds of chapters across the country (Bryan 1993). Private for-profit individuals and organizations became a much more important political force for affordable housing in the late 1980s with influential lobbying groups such as the National Association of Affordable Housing Lenders.[23]

Among the services provided by private industry, mortgage lending is in a category by itself. As the testimony of Donald Kummerfeld from First Boston in chapter 1 demonstrated, private banks were just beginning to get into the affordable housing business in the late 1960s, mainly through high-finance bond transactions, not by underwriting individual apartment buildings. This aspect of affordable housing grew during the 1970s. Mortgage lending, however, took off with the Community Reinvestment Act of 1977 (CRA).

This legislation was an anti-redlining effort that required banks to develop lending programs to reach out to underserved areas of the geographic areas in which they did business. CRA is Title VIII of the Housing and Community Development Act of 1977, whose underlying premise was (and is) that although banks are privately capitalized, they enjoy government rights and services and thus have a special obligation[24]:

> This obligation grew out of the depository charter, which requires banks (and thrifts) to serve the "convenience and needs" of the local communities in which they are allowed to do business. Senator [William] Proxmire argued that this public obligation was the quid pro quo for the substantial economic benefits conveyed on chartered depositories: a franchise to do business in a geographic area, federal deposit insurance, access to the payments system, and access to low-cost credit through the Federal Reserve Banks or the Federal Home Loan Banks. (Litan et al. 2000, 13)

In return, the government asks banks to be more comprehensive and fair in serving the credit needs of their local communities (Fishbein 1992). During routine examinations, federal regulators determine whether the bank is meeting the needs of low- and moderate-income borrowers and neighborhoods. Specifically, regulators look to see if sufficient lending, investment, and services are provided to the low-income geographies where the bank or thrift conducts its business (its "assessment area" in the parlance of the regulation).[25]

The two main enforcement mechanisms are public shame, since CRA ratings are publicized, and withholding regulatory approval for expansions. A bank cannot open new branches or engage in a merger or acquisition with another bank without a good CRA record. The need for a good record became an extremely effective motivator during the wave of bank consolidations in the 1980s and 1990s (Apgar and Duda 2003; Matasar and Pavelka 1998).

Advocates have been effective in using the CRA to pressure banks to provide more capital and services to low-income communities. The model for this type of activism was established by community organizers, such as National People's Action Director Gail Cincotta in Chicago in the early 1980s. Activists used data collected by the Federal Reserve (Home Mortgage Disclosure Act data) to demonstrate that poorer areas of Chicago were capital starved. They went further, by marching, protesting in front of banks, and even covering one banker's house with red paper to dramatize the effects of "redlining" (Zielenbach 2000, 79).

Isolating and measuring the effects of the CRA are extremely difficult, but one of the most ambitious efforts, led by Michael Barr, formerly at the U.S. Treasury Department, involved researchers from the Brookings Institution and the Joint Center for Housing Studies at Harvard University. The study found that between 1993 and 1998 "depository institutions covered by the CRA and their affiliates made nearly $620 billion in home mortgage, small business, and community development loans to low- and moderate-income borrowers and communities" (Barr 2005, 151).[26] Since CRA regulations were rewritten in 1995, the inclusion of an "investment" test has also been a boon to low-income communities.[27] Motivated to score well on this part of the test, banks compete for tax credits (thereby pushing up their price) and support community development finance institutions. In addition, banks are now a major source of contributions (considered investments under CRA) to community development corporations and community development finance institutions.

The investment requirements of the CRA have also led banks to purchase Low Income Housing Tax Credits, which have benefited affordable housing real estate developers. By one estimate, two-thirds of all corporations purchasing tax credits in 2007 were banks and thrifts motivated by the CRA (Moss 2008).

The CRA-motivated banking community also began to experiment with loan consortia as a new way to pool risk and underwriting expertise. Multiple regional banks contributed funds and staff to a sort of clearinghouse that specialized in low-income housing mortgages. For example, the California Community Reinvestment Corporation, which was the product of multiple banks, provided the mortgage on several projects in the case studies featured in chapter 4 of this book. The consortia model provided both good investment opportunities and CRA credit. As a 1994 article in *American Banker* magazine explained, "The theory [with consortia] is to spread risk, spread cost, and concentrate expertise," according to Andrew Gordon, president of the Arizona MultiBank Community Development Corporation. "Our job is to be on our toes, and [be] creative and flexible" (Henry 1994, 48).

Finally, the CRA has encouraged banks to provide human capital to the decentralized housing network as well. The "service" test of the CRA generally requires that bank services from branches and ATMs must be made available to low-income areas. But it also credits other services, such as serving on the boards of directors of local CDCs.

In total, it is hard to overestimate the role that the CRA has played in promoting the decentralized housing network. At every turn in the process of developing affordable housing—site acquisition, construction, long-term mortgage financing, repair, and rehabilitation—there is a need for financing, and banks and thrifts have provided that credit to CDCs and to for-profit real estate developers. Banks have also been good advisers and political allies in funding battles, as the next chapter will show.

Other Institutions

The revolution from below also brought in other participants, particularly public-minded institutions anchored to specific neighborhoods. These included corporations, universities, hospitals, and churches. A Conference Board report, for example, explained that "business is a stakeholder in the success or failure of an entire urban region. A corporation's headquarters can be jeopardized by deterioration of surrounding neighborhoods, and the productivity of its work force threatened" (Peterson and Dana Sundblad 1994, 7).

A 1986 Conference Board survey indicated that corporate contributions to community development had doubled since 1975. Gifts to housing increased fivefold during that time. In addition to giving, corporations such as Aetna Life and Casualty, Prudential Insurance Company, CIGNA, and the Equitable Assurance Society became investors and partners in affordable housing projects. Pierce and Steinbach, in *Corrective Capitalism,* wrote that since the late 1960s, "insurance companies [have] set an industry-wide goal of investing some $2 billion in low- and moderate-income housing, job creation, and improved social services for inner-city residents. The industry later went on to establish its own organization to promote social investing—the Center for Corporate Public Involvement" (Pierce and Steinbach 1990, 67). Today, insurance companies—and increasingly other financial institutions such as mortgage lenders and private equity and hedge funds—are considering more community development investments as a way of heading off future CRA-inspired regulations.

Religious institutions (local congregations in a given community in addition to larger umbrella organizations) have made substantial contributions to the decentralized housing network. The Catholic Church's Campaign for Human Development provided more than $100 million in grants and interest-free loans to some 2,500 self-help projects from 1970 to 1990. And the Presbyterian Self-Development of People's Fund committed millions of dollars to support housing projects (Pierce and Steinbach 1990). The Methodists, through their pension program, have been a leader in financing novel community development investment strategies.[28]

Philanthropic foundations, too, have played an important role. Housing and community development rarely received more than 1 percent of total foundation giving in any one year. Nevertheless, at various times, their support has been crucial. Enough has been written in this study about the Ford Foundation to make it clear that it was an essential catalyst for the decentralized housing network. In addition to Ford, local foundations have been critical in getting certain CDCs and area-wide initiatives off the ground. The Cleveland Foundation and the Lilly Endowment, for example, were the prime movers in Cleveland and Indianapolis in bringing along early CDCs. Other foundations that supported low-income housing and community development included the Charles Stewart Mott Foundation, Levi Strauss Foundation, ARCO Foundation, McKnight Foundation, Standard Oil Foundation, Joyce Foundation, Northwest Area Foundation, Honeywell Foundation, Dayton-Hudson Foundation, Hewlett Foundation, Mary Reynolds Babcock Foundation, and MacArthur Foundation (Pierce and Steinbach 1990; Dreier 1997).

Fannie Mae and Freddie Mac have also been significant promoters of the decentralized housing network by both buying more affordable multifamily mortgages (thereby driving down their price to developers) and purchasing LIHTCs. Fannie Mae and Freddie Mac stepped up their purchases of multifamily mortgages after Congress passed the Federal Housing Enterprise Financial Safety and Soundness Act of 1992. In 1990, the two government-sponsored entities owned 9 percent of those mortgages, but by 2000, they had increased their purchases to 17 percent (Schnare 2001).

Conclusion

By the mid-1980s, building subsidized housing was more complicated than it had been in the 1960s. New actors, new tools, and new programs had proliferated. Don Terner of BRIDGE Housing explained that the new approach to housing made each transaction more complicated than the old system. "In the past," he said, "affordable housing development consisted primarily of negotiating the terms of a single federal program with a designated subsidy program at the center of the transaction." And that project often had very little community input. Under the decentralized network, by contrast, building low-income housing combined "a wide variety of resources such as local land use concessions, predevelopment loans, low interest construction and permanent financing, federal block grant funds, and private investment and contributions." What some saw as an overly complicated approach to policy implementation, however, was a great advantage, according to Terner. He wrote that these new programs forced "nonprofit organizations, local governments, and private builders to be skillful real estate and political entrepreneurs. State governments must be equally knowledgeable in designing housing programs that maximize the leverage of these funds, and that help creative [real estate] developers coordinate the necessary pieces" (DiPasquale and Keyes 1990, 119). The multiple-player decentralized housing network, as confusing as it could be, had potential synergies with more actors scrutinizing and invested in a development, resulting in improved outcomes. In this case, more was more.

The different players introduced in this chapter were not participants in a grand design. Instead, policy entrepreneurs like Paul Grogan, Patrick Clancy, and Don Terner, through trial and error, built up their organizations, taking advantage of opportunities as they came along. And community activists, like Dorothy Mae Richardson, took a stand to improve their neighborhoods. Activists and entrepreneurs, residents and advocates grew together, influencing each other's development. The models that these innovators created were replicated elsewhere and thus amplified their innovations across the nationwide network.

Even as the federal government was pulling back from traditional funding programs, it was experimenting with new funding and regulatory approaches. Funding was parsimonious in the early years of the evolving network, but it grew more generous over time. In the early years, federal involvement meant community development block grants, tax-exempt bonds, and CRA-motivated funding. The federal government augmented funds in 1986 with its LIHTCs and again in 1990 with the federal block-grant program known as HOME. In 1994, there was the addition of the New Markets Tax Credit. Meager as it was in the 1980s, federal funding was always necessary to community development corporations, new state and local government bureaucracies, intermediaries, and the participation of private capital.

Growing Trust among Players

Over time, the multiple players in the network began to overcome their distrust of each other. As Paul Grogan put it, "You find that community leaders are sophisticated and talented, government leaders are entrepreneurial, and bankers have hearts and care about social problems" (Pierce and Steinbach 1990, 57). A chief executive officer of the Miami-based Knight Ridder newspaper chain, James Batten, worked with and praised CDCs and the fledgling network of affordable housing providers in his city. "It's our extraordinary good fortune as a community that people [nonprofit CDCs] this savvy are doing the things they are doing," he said. "The attitude here is much more than 'these folks are not so bad.' It's 'God we are fortunate to have people like this in our community.'" Community leaders like Batten were overcoming decades of cynicism about what could be done to improve cities. He said, "A lot of people I know came out of the '60s with lowered sights and disillusionment about whether anything works." Working with CDCs and local government, however, made him realize that he was in an effective and important coalition that was making a difference (Pierce and Steinbach 1990). By the mid-1980s, the various components of the decentralized housing network were in place, and, as Batten's comments indicate, they had begun to see themselves as a group with common cause.

A testament to this sense of connectedness was that in later years, the participants in the decentralized network often traded jobs. It was not uncommon for someone to get a start at a CDC and then switch over to a city redevelopment agency or a community lending department of a local bank. Because almost all players in the network had to know at least something about the job of their counterparts with other organizations, the network created an important job ladder in many communities. In fact, the resumes of those now running government departments or private corporations show a fair amount of such movement, solidifying the formal and informal personal ties have kept this network together.

A Dynamic, Adaptive Process

The fact that the network never developed in exactly the same way from place to place also indicated that it was spurred on by a robust and adaptive process. A variety of strategies got communities to similar places. In a pattern of development that bears out Alexander Gerschenkron's theories of national industrial development, communities were able to substitute different attributes or characteristics in their effort to develop a network of housing developers (Gerschenkron 1965). Chicago, for example, had a strong tradition of neighborhood groups that acted as development entrepreneurs. These entrepreneurs were effective in marshaling the energy of city and state government and local business to build housing. Massachusetts, in contrast, had a strong state government presence that fostered the development of CDCs and other members of the network. Foundations led efforts in Indianapolis and Cleveland.

Taking advantage of local opportunities, the decentralized housing network was also able to overwhelm problems with overlapping efforts and multiple strategies. Perhaps the only truly consistent aspect of the decentralized housing network was that it always involved collaboration. In the end, these interactions began to create something more than a complex coalition of organizations to improve housing. These early, often feeble, efforts were changing the policy paradigm. The decentralized housing network generated new ideas and invented new approaches, new programs, and ultimately a new institution for developing and implementing social policy.

The Next Step in Building the Decentralized Network

Perhaps the best way to view this paradigm is to see how the decentralized institution evolved and began to advocate for itself. Creativity is powerful, but it does not build millions of homes. To create a system capable of that required more resources than were available locally, which meant petitioning the federal government. The following chapter explores how the fledgling decentralized housing network locked into place and began to secure its own resources through federal programs such as the Low Income Housing Tax Credit in 1986 and the HOME block grant program in 1990. These programs were efforts at funding the "revolution from below" housing production system, rather than the public housing and other HUD programs—such as 221(d)(3), Section 236, and Section 8—that were largely "top down."

3

Fighting for Federal Resources for the Decentralized Housing Network

At the beginning of the 1990s, the pro–affordable housing coalition seemed to be cautiously optimistic. The coalition took a great deal of pride in what it had accomplished without much in the way of federal resources. And, increasingly, political wins matched growing confidence that a decentralized affordable housing network might make a difference in the nation's low-income communities. A 1990 Council for Community-Based Development report, *Enterprising Communities,* captured this spirit:

> There is no doubt that community development has matured rapidly and substantially widened its impact. By 1989, the movement had demonstrated that a diverse array of community groups, working on behalf of residents in America's poorest places, could successfully carry out development projects and mobilize residents to exert control over their lives and communities. (Pierce and Steinbach 1990, 11)

The problem, according to the report, was that this model, while promising, had only just begun to deal with the housing crisis. "As the 1980s drew to a close," the report concluded, "community development more closely resembled a guerrilla war against poverty than a large-scale invasion" (Pierce and Steinbach 1990, 12).

Small operators proved they could do something to help low-income tenants and neighborhoods, but could they grow to become a more effective force, "a large-scale invasion"? Success on a large scale would require a rethinking of how the federal government provided social services. In fact, it would necessitate a rethinking of what was once considered the welfare state.

The Rise of the Decentralized Welfare State

When scholars try to explain the radical departure of the two approaches to public policy that are typified by the Kaiser Report's government-intervention optimism and the distrust of government in the McKenna Report, they often paint the story as a failure of liberalism and an example of the political backlash against the welfare state in the 1970s and 1980s. To some degree, the welfare state is used interchangeably with its champion, the Democratic Party. The historian Alan Matusow (1984), for example, wrote that the War on Poverty was a failure for the welfare state in *The Unraveling of America: A History of Liberalism.*[1] Ira Katznelson (1991), in "Was the Great Society a Lost Opportunity?" argues that by the early 1970s, the Democrats' New Deal-Great Society coalition, which sought to use the state to address social ills of poverty, poor health, and inadequate housing, had lost its force.

Thomas and Mary Edsall echo many of the same arguments as Katznelson in their book *Chain Reaction.* For the Edsalls, the Democratic Party's increased focus on minority rights pushed it too far to the left. The Republicans moved to occupy the abandoned center, tarring the Democrats as the party that defended "criminal defendants, women, the poor, non-European ethnic minorities, students, homosexuals, prisoners, the handicapped, and the mentally ill" (Edsall and Edsall 1991, 4). The programs for so-called special interest groups, like the War on Poverty, were expensive. Increasingly, many white voters saw "their rising tax burdens going to finance programs disproportionately serving black and Hispanic constituencies" (17).

Even more recent books on the welfare state—including Michael Katz, *The Price of Citizenship* (2002) and Neil Gilbert, *Transformation of the Welfare State* (2003)—argue that the spirit of the McKenna Report was transcendent and hegemonic; critics successfully shrank the welfare state in favor of allowing markets to have a greater sway in distributing goods and services.[2] To Katz, this development is in stark contrast with British sociologist T.H. Marshall's classic 1950 characterization of the welfare state as "the subordination of market price to social justice." Katz (2002, 1) writes,

"While the tension between capitalism and equality remains as powerful as ever, today it is social justice that is subordinate to market price."[3]

It is true that the former champion of the welfare state, the Democratic Party, was weakening in 1970s and 1980s; its coalition was in tatters. Organized labor, which had been a pillar of the party, was on the decline. Union membership dropped from a high of 37 percent of the labor force in 1954 to 22 percent in 1980 (Neumann and Rissman 1984). The urban political machines failed to keep working-class whites in the party. And what was once the "solid South" for the Democrats became solidly Republican (Katznelson 1989).

But too much focus on the travails of the Democratic Party, or on events in Washington, can obfuscate what the last chapter demonstrates— welfare state innovation was taking place at the state and local levels. New institutions were using new tools to tackle old problems. It is true that the United States failed to adopt a Scandinavian-style welfare state, but a growing literature highlights how the federal government did create incentives for nonprofits, subnational government (state, county, and city), and the private sector to provide social services.

New Tools for the Welfare State

Understanding what Lester Salamon calls "the new governance and the new tools of public action" is essential for making sense of the evolution of affordable housing policy specifically and the welfare state generally. Among these tools is the use of for-profit and nonprofit corporations for social service delivery and decentralized funding mechanisms, especially those embedded in the tax code (Salamon 2002). "What is most distinctive about American social welfare practice," Jacob Hacker explains in his book *The Divided Welfare State*, "is not the *level* of spending but the *source*." The United States ranks last among the nations of the Organisation for Economic Co-operation and Development (OECD) in traditional welfare spending but scores higher when other forms of public subsidy such as tax incentives are included. According to this more comprehensive measure (counting both direct expenditure and tax benefits), the "net public and private spending, at 24.5 percent of GDP, is above the average for all eleven [OECD] nations (24 percent)" (Hacker 2002, 13–16).

Tax Expenditures versus Appropriations

Important incentives for welfare state services are now embedded in U.S. tax law. Christopher Howard's *Hidden Welfare State* (1997) was an important early study that pulled back the veil from social welfare policy funded through the tax code. He shows 56 separate federal tax expenditure programs (most created in the 1970s and 1980s) in income security, health, employment and job training, housing, education, and veterans' benefits. The bulk of tax expenditures go to subsidizing employer-provided health care, retirement plans, and the mortgage interest deduction, very little of which reaches the poor.[4]

Howard argues that tax expenditures have grown because they are easier to enact. For example, tax expenditures are harder to track and understand than traditional tax-and-spend appropriation programs.[5] In addition to ambiguity, tax expenditures enjoy procedural and institutional advantages over direct expenditures. Tax expenditures are components of revenue bills that must pass or the government shuts down. Howard claims that this requirement made it possible for the Targeted Jobs Tax Credit to pass as an amendment to the Revenue Act of 1978 rather than as part of President Carter's plagued urban aid package. In addition, tax expenditures go through the powerful committees that oversee all tax and revenue legislation, Ways and Means in the House and Finance in the Senate. Last, appropriations must be authorized by one congressional committee and funded by another in each House, whereas tax expenditures are authorized and funded by the same committees (Howard 1997).

Perhaps the most important advantage for tax expenditures, however, is that they are perceived differently. Instead of selling the merits of a particular program, tax expenditures can be portrayed as both aid to the needy and tax relief. Furthermore, tax credits offer new business for third-party service providers and are viewed as an alternative to "big government" programs. In 1978, for example, the Targeted Jobs Tax Credit was presented as a jobs program for disadvantaged workers and as a wage subsidy to small business. Moderate and conservative members of both parties also saw the program as an alternative to increases in funding for AFDC (the precursor to the current program, Temporary Assistance to Needy Families), unemployment insurance, and traditional job training programs (Howard 1997).

Increased use of tax expenditures was also possible because postwar growth in gross domestic product generated increasing tax revenue that did not require tax increases or cuts in spending. Even as the conditions of some middle- and lower-class wage earners were getting worse, economic growth through the post–World War II period provided increased revenue to the federal government. In addition to added revenue, military expenditures as a percentage of GDP dropped steadily from their post–World War II peak in 1953 of 14 percent to between 5 and 7 percent in the 1970s and 1980s.[6] More resources allowed the state to expand to "an unprecedented scale in American life," according to Julian Zelizer (1998, 3).[7]

Reliance on Nonprofits and on For-Profit Organizations

As Hacker, Howard, and Zelizer show, taxes were often used to provide incentives for welfare state services, but other incentives—grants, favorable regulation, loan guarantees—also encouraged for-profit and nonprofit corporations to work toward government goals. In the late 1960s and 1970s, nonprofits experienced a dramatic growth in federal funding and other financial incentives to provide a variety of social services, including neighborhood health centers, community drug and alcohol rehabilitation centers, battered-women shelters, rape crisis programs, and emergency shelters for runaway youth. In the 1980s, the federal government relied on nonprofits to combat the problems of mental health, AIDS, homelessness, and hunger (Smith 1999; Smith and Lipsky 1993).

The following is the story of how in one area, affordable housing, new policy actors outside the traditional welfare state (nonprofits and local government, among others) lobbied successfully for new tools and more resources. The details are particularly important, because what we see is that this coalition had allies across the political spectrum and was especially effective in securing increased funding. The story also speaks to the larger issue of how the welfare state continued to grow and evolve in unpredictable and often overlooked ways.

New Tools for Affordable Housing

Two programs stand out as important sources of new funds for affordable housing construction in the late 1980s: the Low Income Housing Tax Credit (LIHTC) and the HOME block grant that were created by the National Affordable Housing Act of 1990 (NAHA). The debates over tax credits started in 1985 but continued intermittently through the 1990s and into the early 2000s. I begin with the NAHA debates, because they have more defined beginning and end points. The policy debates demonstrate how a new political coalition that backed the decentralized housing network operated: who was involved and the arguments they made for their cause. In a reversal of circumstances from what prevailed in the 1970s, the new prohousing coalition brimmed with ideas and enjoyed substantial political momentum. These organizations had painstakingly built a new model for low-income housing production and now had a track record and the political clout to win new respect from Washington.

Findings and Recommendations of the National Housing Task Force

In 1987, the Senate Subcommittee on Housing and Urban Affairs of the Committee on Banking, Housing, and Urban Affairs assembled an all-star team to review the nation's housing situation. The team, known as the National Housing Task Force, was a group of 26 individuals drawn "from business, banking, community service, and state and local government" (National Housing Task Force 1988, ii). The committee tapped one of the leading members of the decentralized housing network, Enterprise Community Partners founder Jim Rouse, to head the blue-ribbon investigative commission. Rouse was cochair of this study with David Maxwell, chief executive officer of the Federal National Mortgage Association (Fannie Mae).[8] Maxwell was an important symbolic choice, too, since government-sponsored enterprises were also significant players in the decentralized approach as major purchasers of low-income housing tax credits.

The task force's report noted that state and local government, along with nonprofit and private corporations, had managed to develop innovative programs and build affordable housing in spite of federal cutbacks during the 1980s, which provided a potential foundation on which to build even more effective policy. The task force advocated a renewed federal government commitment to housing that could invigorate "new alliances among the public, private and community sectors" in what the report described as a "new wave" for housing policy (National Housing Task Force 1988, 10).

The report forcefully argued that although the new approach was promising it never would succeed without an infusion of federal money and leadership: "The 80 percent decline in HUD funds for new housing commitments over the past decade has hindered the growth of this new system to deliver affordable housing" (10). For the "new wave" approach to be comprehensive and effective, it would need new energy, leadership, and, most important, financial support from the federal government.

The HOME Program. A variety of financing tools was proposed to make the decentralized approach more effective. "We have learned, over the last quarter century, that housing problems are varied and complex," the report said. "To be effective, housing assistance must assume different forms" (National Housing Task Force 1988, 11). These different forms, according to the task force, included boosting the consuming power of low-income tenants with vouchers and providing a financial toolbox for housing construction finance that included low-interest loans, loan guarantees, tax incentives, and federal insurance for at-risk mortgage capital. One of the most important financing mechanisms proposed was a new block grant program, which eventually became the HOME Investment Partnerships (HOME) program. In many respects, this program was modeled on Community Development Block Grant program. While the new block grant program was meant to have few strings attached, it did have specific performance goals, a requirement for local government to contribute matching funds, and dedicated funds for nonprofit community development corporations (U.S. National Housing Task Force 1988; Urban Institute 1999).

HOME is the largest federal block grant program for state and local governments created to promote affordable housing. It provides $2 billion annually in block grants for low-income households.[9] The program specifically sets aside funds for nonprofits because they bring a new perspective on, and commitment to, low-income tenants and their communities. "[Nonprofit CDCs] offer more than just numbers," according to the Maxwell-Rouse Report:

> They know local housing needs and are committed to serving them. They are determined to serve low-income residents on a long-term basis. They are willing to take on projects that are considered too risky or too small by financial institutions and other developers. (National Housing Task Force 1988, 24)

The report suggested that nonprofits needed outside expertise and encouraged building on the model established by intermediaries such as the Local Initiatives Support Corporation (LISC) and the Enterprise Community Partners. Intermediaries, according to the task force, "play a critical capacity-building role, help structure project financing, identify ways to cut construction costs, and encourage alliances between local nonprofit developers and state and local governments" (National Housing Task Force 1988, 28). The report concluded that new government agencies, in combination with the decentralized housing network—including nonprofit and for-profit developers, capacity-building consultants, and other players—would develop into a creative and vigorous decentralized housing institution capable of innovating and combining new tools "in hundreds of different ways in hundreds of different places" (19).

Political Environment for Passing New Funding Programs

Those who supported the vision of a decentralized approach to housing needed to pass legislation to fund it. While the political environment of the late 1980s was somewhat resistant to passing major new funding for social welfare programs, several events and trends promoted the decentralized approach to housing policy, including

- ideological shifts toward centrist policies facilitated by "kinder and gentler" conservatism and a growing confidence—even among liberals—in market-based models for social policy
- newly energized political coalitions for subsidized housing that included state and local government and the real estate and finance industries
- the increasingly visible problem of homelessness and the rising cost of housing (even for the middle class)
- the general attractiveness of program flexibility and local control
- Democratic political control of both houses of Congress after 1986
- the high-profile HUD and savings and loan corruption scandals

Michael Stegman, a former HUD assistant secretary, wrote about the long history of HUD scandals, observing that public confidence plunged after "periodic ethical lapses at the highest levels of HUD—including the criminal indictment during the Reagan administration of a sitting HUD secretary who reportedly was so bored that he spent some afternoons watching soap operas" (Stegman 2002, 68).

President George H. W. Bush promised "a kinder and gentler nation" at the same time that he promised "no new taxes." The spirit was willing, but the budget was weak. As the reporter for the *Congressional Quarterly* wrote, no one "in Congress has figured out how Bush can reconcile the conflicting imperatives of increased social spending and the steady deficit reduction required by the Gramm-Rudman-Hollings law." Although some doubted Bush's ability to achieve this combination of both more and less spending, no one doubted its political effectiveness. By appealing to compassionate conservative themes, Bush hoped to bring more moderate voters (especially women) into the Republican Party (Rovner, Morehouse, and Kuntz 1988).

While the Senate Banking Committee was debating the bill that would ultimately become NAHA, Republican and Democratic leaders from the House, Senate, and White House were engaged in the so-called budget summit, a budget-cutting exercise. Despite budgetary concerns, efforts to pass new affordable housing legislation had been gaining momentum since 1988. Many different groups sent similar messages to Congress that echoed the message of the Maxwell-Rouse Report: new proposals in housing must build on the local efforts of the 1980s but be infused with federal resources and leadership.[10]

In February 1988, the U.S. Conference of Mayors sponsored a National Housing Forum in Austin, Texas. The conference brought housing scholars, builders, government, and the private sector together for several days to debate federal housing policy. The final report carried a message that was increasingly familiar: "local models of public, private, and community-based partnerships working with such organizations as the Enterprise Community Partners and the Local Initiatives Support Corporation (LISC) should be encouraged throughout the nation." The report went on to argue that this new approach to building affordable housing, what they also referred to as "new wave," needed resources and mentoring from the federal government.

Two months later, Senators Alan Cranston (D-Calif.) and Alfonse D'Amato (R-N.Y.) convened the first hearings on the findings of the National Housing Task Force. In his opening remarks, Cranston said, "A year ago, Senator Al D'Amato and I asked James Rouse and David Maxwell to suggest a fresh, new framework for national housing policy—

one that can meet the country's housing needs over the next decade" (U.S. Congress 1988a, 1–2).

Rouse had a new framework in mind; he told the senators that the task force recommended "the creation of a new institution." He added, "The centerpiece of our proposals is a recommendation that the federal government should create and invest in a new housing delivery system— that's very crucial—designed to foster and stimulate state and local initiatives to develop, renovate, and preserve low income housing." The task force found that the new institution did not have to be developed from scratch: "The components of this new delivery system that has developed in the country have been in the making over the last decade," said Rouse. The task force observed that a new network of housing providers "emerged from the community level in response to local needs" (U.S. Congress 1988a, 21).

As hopeful as the "new wave" was, it was too limited in resources and geographic reach to build the affordable housing that the country needed. From existing fragments, however, the federal government had the opportunity to weld together a new decentralized housing delivery system that would be flexible, responsive to local needs, and infused with the financial power of the federal government. Even with federal support, however, the new system would have to find new sources of funds. "We could not rely on federal funds alone," Rouse said (U.S. Congress 1988b, 23).

In addition to the National Housing Task Force, Cranston singled out the MIT Housing Policy Project for praise, citing its efforts to provide expert perspectives to his Senate committee. An MIT professor, Langley Keyes, was a leading voice in the NAHA debates and praised NAHA's approach of marrying federal efforts "synergistically with local institutions throughout the country" (U.S. Congress 1988b, 23). Keyes looked back on the prior affordable housing initiatives, so clearly represented by their respective presidential commissions—Kaiser (the 1968 Washington-based initiative) and McKenna (the 1982 market-oriented one)—and said:

> 1968 looks to have been the high water mark of federal commitment to resources to housing and reflective of another era. Yet, the minimal federal role articulated in 1982 seems equally dated in today's world of homelessness, expiring use restrictions [an end to affordability restrictions on HUD-financed apartments], and a declining percentage of young homebuyers. The recent report of the National Housing Task Force reflects the tenor of the times in that it paints a picture of serious federal leadership in the nation's housing policy while recognizing that bud-

getary and political realities as well as the changing nature of program sponsorship at the local level preclude a return to the model of the 1960s. (U.S. Congress 1988b, 145)

The subsequent debates over housing legislation in some ways were trying to find a compromise between the spirit of 1968 and that of 1982. In many ways, policymakers were successful in combining the bureaucracy model and the market model into a new synthesis.

* * *

Broad Support for the National Affordable Housing Act

The themes from the task force dominated the debates hammering out the details of what became NAHA. One was how local efforts had made a difference in the lives of communities. These successes were also winning friends in high places. For example, Senator D'Amato, Republican co-chair of the NAHA legislation, addressed Paul Grogan and praised his work with LISC: "I have had an opportunity to see firsthand the results of the work that you have loaned yourself to, and I would hate to think of how much more desperation there would be in the neighborhoods of New York and our city were it not for your undertaking [to help build new affordable housing]." He continued, "I have seen . . . how the local development corporations have readily brought about a spirit of pride and a fighting spirit to save a neighborhood and to involve people and to bring civility to the area. It makes a difference" (U.S. Congress 1988b, 340).

Support of Housing Advocates. In the NAHA debates, housing advocates always coupled their message of hope with a call for more federal resources. Grogan said, for example, that while local initiatives were "more effective, efficient, and responsive to local needs than previous federally driven efforts," these local initiatives would never achieve the needed results without federal subsidy. "Unfortunately," he pointed out, "for the most of this decade the federal government has been the missing partner and it is the only partner with the financial capacity to make substantial production of low-income housing possible" (U.S. Congress 1988b, 564).

John Simon, president of the National Housing Conference, a long-standing advocate for affordable housing, told senators that only the federal government had the power to complete the transition to the decentralized housing network.[11] "It is the federal government that collects most of our taxes," he said, "and the federal government has an obligation to provide housing" (U.S. Congress 1988b, 355).

Barry Zigas, president of the National Low Income Housing Coalition, a group that represented thousands of CDCs and grassroots housing advocates nationwide, told senators that housing was a "human right" that the federal government was obligated to provide: "The federal government must bear the responsibility for ensuring the opportunity to obtain decent, affordable housing" (U.S. Congress 1988c, 445).

Simon, along with other advocates, wanted the money with a minimum of federal bureaucratic involvement. They hoped that any new federal effort would learn from HUD's mistakes. "As I said once before, HUD stands for 'Help Us Delay,'" Simon testified, "but we hope that a future HUD will be more efficient and be able to do the things that they have not done in the past, rather than having to create another agency. . . . We don't have the time to develop a new program, a new bureaucracy." The vision articulated by Simon, Zigas, Grogan, and others was to build on an existing network, creating a decentralized institution that would be stronger, larger, and more effective, thanks to new federal resources. In other words, they wanted HUD money, but not HUD.

Support of State and Local Governments. State and local governments weighed in on increased federal housing subsidies. A phalanx of lobbying groups—including the National League of Cities, the National Governors Association, the National Association of Redevelopment and Housing Officials, the National Council of State Housing Agencies, the Council of State Community Affairs Agencies, and the U.S. Conference of Mayors—applied steady pressure at the Cranston and D'Amato hearings.[12]

According to the director of the Joint Center for Housing Studies at Harvard, William Apgar, state governments were ready to make a difference: "If the Feds get back into the business they [the states] will really be able to deliver the program." F. Lynn Luallen, president of the National Council of State Housing Agencies, told the committee, "One of my goals here today is to convince you that state housing finance agencies are prepared to play a leading role as a delivery system for rental and home ownership housing." He said that up to 1988 state housing agencies had issued $23 billion in multifamily development bonds, financing more than 639,000 units of multifamily housing (U.S. Congress 1988a, 300). State housing finance agencies now had sufficient experience with capital markets and local housing conditions, he believed, to move "well beyond the simple capital conduit role of the past to that of entrepreneur and innovator." Luallen portrayed state housing finance agencies as more than entrepreneurs, though; he saw them as bridge builders with "long-standing relationships with housing developers, builders, lenders, real estate professionals, municipal governments, and local housing interests" (U.S. Congress 1988a, 304).[13]

Support of the Private Sector. The private sector promoted its interests in the NAHA debates through a wide array of organizations: the Mortgage Bankers Association, the Savings and Loan League, the National Association of Realtors, the National Association of Homebuilders, LIHTC investors, and the International Downtown Association. Business lobbyists reinforced many of the same themes as housing advocates and government witnesses, particularly with regard to flexibility and the need for federal resources. Not surprisingly, however, this group emphasized the advantages that private enterprise would bring to housing policy. John Teutsch, president of the Mortgage Bankers Association, said, "As the [National Housing] Task Force report points out, financing rental multifamily housing requires a variety of approaches. Federal, state, and local governments must share the responsibility for providing suitable multifamily rental housing. The governmental role, however, should be enhanced by the participation of private nonprofit and for-profit entities" (U.S. Congress 1988a, 53). Even though they were adamant about private-sector involvement, business lobbyists were wildly enthusiastic about the proposals of the Maxwell-Rouse Report.[14]

Nestor Weigand, Jr., president of the National Association of Realtors, said, "The National Association of Realtors concurs with the task force's fundamental assertion that housing plays a vital role in human and community development." He continued, "We share the goal that the revitalized national housing policy should be established rapidly and carried forward vigorously" (U.S. Congress 1988a, 82–83).

Michael Fried, president of the Related Companies, brought the perspective of a large real estate development and finance firm to the hearings. He boasted that his company had "raised over $450 million to acquire in excess of 45,000 units of low- and moderate-income housing"

(U.S. Congress 1988a, 298). Fried cautioned that as scarce as affordable housing was, it would get worse because so few new apartment buildings were in the production pipeline. "In short," Fried observed, "1989 may greet the next president with a major housing crisis for America's middle and low income [citizens]." The Maxwell-Rouse Report addressed this crisis. Fried said, "One of the most important contributions of the National Housing Task Force Report is its underlying message that appropriate tax incentives are necessary to encourage the private sector to develop and operate affordable rental housing" (U.S. Congress 1988a, 299). The representative for the National Association of Homebuilders agreed: "I think it's been proven very, very often that tax credits are the best way of getting housing on the market and the most cost-effective to the government" (U.S. Congress 1988b, 155).[15]

Downtown real estate interests were also eager to see the federal government back in the business of creating viable neighborhoods where they were needed most, in the pockets of poverty that crisscrossed every downtown in the nation. Ann Lang, chairman of the International Downtown Association said, "There are new opportunities to create affordable housing together with development in downtowns and close-in neighborhoods. IDA's members are well positioned to pursue and expand these opportunities through their experience in forging public-private partnerships" (U.S. Congress 1988b, 648). Lang praised what she referred to as a "new system" that comprised "not only existing government agencies and quasi-public groups formed under their auspices, but also the many private-sector non-profit groups and profit-making corporations that have become involved in housing production, rehabilitation, and management in recent years."[16]

Lobbying for the National Affordable Housing Act

Lobbying by the decentralized housing network was a key to passing NAHA. But this was not a classic lobbying story where the side with the most allies won. Perhaps even more important than lobbying muscle was a widespread agreement among members of Congress (especially senators) on new directions for housing policy. This new direction was anti-bureaucratic, enthusiastic about using market mechanisms whenever possible, and interested in an expanded role for for-profit and nonprofit corporations in service delivery. This approach allowed for a significant overlap of diverse ideologies, which one senator called a "marriage" of philosophies (U.S. Congress 1990). It may not have been a happy marriage, but there was an unusual amount of accord.

Compromise is at the heart of the legislative process, but what made NAHA easy to pass was that every faction could see its view represented. Missouri's conservative Senator Bond, for example, said, "For my colleagues who have reservations about housing, who look at government from a more conservative point of view, I would say philosophically this is sound."[17] George H.W. Bush's HUD secretary, Jack Kemp, claimed that capitalism's triumph over communism in Eastern Europe must have a similar victory in high-poverty areas of American cities. "As Berliners tear down the wall that has kept them from freedom for 28 years, so too must we tear down the walls that are keeping America's poor from the blessings of freedom and democracy in our own country," Kemp said. Winning the cold war will not be complete if there is no win in the inner city, according to Kemp: "I can't help but feel that history has linked the cause of freedom abroad with the cause of freedom, dignity, and justice right here in America's ghettoes and barrios in one great cause for good" (U.S. Congress 1992, S15943–44).

Despite the fact that NAHA (as well as the Community Development Block Grant Program and LIHTC) represented massive federal funding of local initiatives, something about local groups' meeting their own housing needs seemed to fit the Republican affinity for individual initiative. Kemp observed, "As I go across our nation, I see non-profits, neighborhood groups, and community housing efforts taking the boards off vacant and foreclosed property, rehabilitating that property . . . and turning thousands of dilapidated houses into decent, quality housing for low-income people" (U.S. Congress 1992). Here was a multibillion-dollar, federally subsidized housing program that had a Horatio Alger feel to it.

Both conservatives and liberals embraced nonprofits because they were perceived as incorruptible, caring, and efficient. Senator Robert Kasten (R-Wis.) contrasted funding for nonprofits favorably with more funding for HUD, which he said would only "expand HUD programs and policies which are the same magnets for the waste, fraud, abuse, and influence peddling that we all claim to deplore" (U.S. Congress 1992, S15942).

Role of Nonprofit and For-Profit Organizations

Most senators agreed with the Maxwell-Rouse Report's description of community development corporations as advocates for their respective communities. Senator Connie Mack (R-Fla.) explained that "nonprofits are of, by, and for the people of the community," as opposed to "HUD's massive, distant bureaucracy." Nonprofits, he said, "consist largely of local people who care about their communities and who are sensitive to local needs" (U.S. Congress 1992, S8881). As locally based, bottom-up, politically connected institutions, they are nearly the opposite of HUD.

Most senators also agreed that because of their ability to respond to market signals, corporations—both for-profit and nonprofit—would be the saviors of the inner city. Senator Grassley (R-Iowa) said, "We have the opportunity to say no to excessive government bureaucracy. We have the opportunity to vote for a piece of legislation that will unleash the free market system toward providing affordable housing for areas of the country that are being restricted from this goal." Confidence in the anticipated efficiency and equity of this new decentralized approach to delivering housing ran high. Consider Senator Boschwitz's (R-Minn.) comment that the private sector would create housing more cheaply, but, even more amazingly, "without the potential for corruption or mismanagement" (U.S. Congress 1992, S8851–52).

All the pro-NAHA comments above came from Republicans; Democrats may have disagreed on emphasis, but they agreed on the policy. Connecticut's Democratic Senator Christopher Dodd was drawn to the new approach since it was "consolidating several rigid categorical programs into a more flexible block grant approach. [HOME] requires cities and states to identify their housing needs, and then channels federal money to them to be used in ways that they—not Washington—think best." Paul Sarbanes (D-Md.) also agreed with Dodd and acknowledged the important role of the Maxwell-Rouse Report in shaping the new HOME program. Sarbanes said that HOME "is really a partnership with state and local governments, nonprofit groups, and others who are best suited to develop housing solutions in each area of our country" (U.S. Congress 1992, S13253–54). Even an ardent housing advocate like Barry Zigas of the National Low Income Housing Coalition could call the measure "a good step forward," adding, "It's not enough, but it's a substantial step forward from the last decade."[18]

Opposition to the National Affordable Housing Act

As much praise as there was for a decentralized affordable housing network, there was an echo of Robert Kennedy's Economic Opportunity

Act debates and his concerns that local governments would be either incapable or unwilling to take a lead in affordable housing development. As Senator Alan Cranston noted, some local governments "are committed to providing affordable housing, and others are not so committed" (U.S. Congress 1988b, 205).

The House Banking Committee Chairman Henry Gonzales (D-Tex.) opposed the decentralized approach to housing. He said, "The patchwork system of tax credits and piecemeal funding from states, local governments, and the federal government, as innovative as it may be, often results in significant leakage of subsidy funds. This makes the system less efficient and more complicated to [administer than] the direct spending approach" (Kaltenheuser 1990, 29). Gonzales proposed a competing housing bill that put more emphasis on expanding funding to HUD and other traditional housing programs. House and Senate conferees worked on a compromise bill, and despite Gonzales's objections, the final bill that emerged from the conference committee was largely unchanged from the Senate version, with some minor changes to the block grant program.

Passage of the National Affordable Housing Act

The compromise bill passed in the Senate 93-6 and in the House by a voice vote. The National Affordable Housing Act of 1990 was signed into law by President George H.W. Bush on October 27 and authorized an annual direct expenditure increase of $3 billion. The centerpiece of the legislation was the new block grant program, HOME Investment Partnerships (Zuckman 1990).

Support for the law was nearly unanimous outside Congress, too. Both development-oriented and tenants' rights organizations were pleased with the legislation, according to a postpassage analysis by *Housing and Development Reporter* (1990, 454). Two years later, an Urban Institute study on HOME found that the legislation was having a dramatic effect on the funding available to local governments. In fact, the study found that local government had nearly double the housing subsidies that they had before NAHA (Urban Institute 1999).

Passage of NAHA (and other decentralized funding programs) was more significant than simply providing more dollars for subsidized housing: it facilitated the transition to a new kind of institution. Don Campbell, staff director of the Senate Housing Subcommittee, said that in the past too much attention had been given to particular programs—their rules and regulations, the target groups, outcome measures, and the like. Campbell said that focus was misplaced and that these individual programs were too rigid. What NAHA provided was a new network of more nimble institutions. "Institutions can survive because their program design is an ongoing adaptive process," he said. "That's what the Cranston-D'Amato bill [NAHA] proposes, the creation not of a new program but of a new institution . . . tailoring the best approaches to changing needs" (Kaltenheuser 1990, 29).

Low Income Housing Tax Credits

The Low Income Housing Tax Credit was a pilot project in the ambitious tax reform package that became the Tax Reform Act of 1986 (TRA 86). For many years, tax treatment of real estate had been an essential part of all aspects of the real estate market (affordable and market rate, residential and commercial, apartments and single-family homes).

Tax Treatment of Depreciation

One tax aspect that was particularly important for investing in apartment buildings was how depreciation was treated. In concept, depreciation tries to capture the part of something that is "used up" over time. Since this is a type of loss, the IRS allows tax payers to deduct part of this loss from their income, in effect providing an implicit subsidy. Karl Case, an economist at Wesleyan University, wrote that "under the rules in effect prior to 1981, owners could depreciate the full cost of a development over 40 years by using accelerated depreciation rules. As long as maintenance and repair expenditures were adequate, buildings did not actually lose value. In fact, in many instances projects appreciated in value" (Case 1991, 345).

Case conducted a series of estimates of the present value of tax benefits from a $10 million investment in an apartment building in three eras: before the Economic Recovery Tax Act of 1981 (ERTA), and the periods before and after the TRA 86. In his estimation in the pre-ERTA era, the developer could reap a $650,000 present value tax benefit. This amount shot up after ERTA to $1.5 million. "Little wonder tax shelter activity boomed from 1983 to 1985," he commented (Case 1991, 348). But TRA 86 "dramatically reduced the value of the implicit subsidies to real estate investment, including low-income housing." According to Case's calculation, the present value tax benefit after TRA 86 dropped to $183,000. Housing experts Denise DiPasquale and Jean L. Cummings (1992) had similar, if not as dramatic, findings.[19]

A simple review of the number of multifamily units provides at least a partial corroboration of this analysis. Table 3.1 shows the number of apartment units completed by year from 1980 to 1995 in buildings with five or more apartments.

The loss of such a significant subsidy for apartment construction after 1986 made the issue of tax subsidies, even those specifically targeted to low-income renters, a concern for the larger real estate industry. The Mortgage Bankers Association explained the original TRA 86 affordable housing provisions this way:

> MBA [the Mortgage Bankers Association] believes that the president's tax pro-posal would virtually preclude investment in low-income housing. Under current law, low-income housing is depreciated over 15 years, as opposed to 18 years for

Table 3.1. New Privately Owned Housing Units Completed, 1980–95

Year	Units built[a]
1980	426,300
1981	335,700
1982	293,100
1983	374,400
1984	514,800
1985	533,600
1986	550,100
1987	474,600
1988	388,600
1989	337,900
1990	297,300
1991	216,600
1992	158,000
1993	127,100
1994	154,900
1995	212,400

Source: U.S. Census Bureau, "New Privately Owned Housing Units Completed," http://www.census.gov/const/www/newresconstindex.html.

a. In buildings with five or more units.

other income property. Under the proposed CCRS [Capital Cost Recovery System], the recovery period for low-income housing would be 28 years—[a less] attractive incentive for investors.[20]

Members of the Senate committee had some sympathy with those who testified that tax incentives were the one remaining federal production program for low-income housing and that there might be a way to structure the incentive in a more efficient and effective way than the accelerated depreciation schemes outlined above. Paul McDaniel, a Boston College law professor, posed the following question to the senators:

> **Mr. McDaniel:** I think the question really is: could you design a program that is more efficient and doesn't cost the federal government so much money for the amount of housing to do that?
> **Senator Heinz:** I assume we are smart enough to do that.
> **Mr. McDaniel:** Yes, I think you are.
> **Senator Heinz:** I don't want to put that to a vote [Laughter].[21]

In the hearings, many echoed the sentiments of the National Advisory Council of HUD Management Agents, who argued that while the tax code might not be the best tool for promoting affordable housing, "it is, for better or worse, the only remaining tool."[22]

Barry Zigas told the senators that if the original proposals for TRA 86 were enacted without the tax incentives, the private sector would withdraw its support from nonprofit development of low-income housing. Zigas did concede that the current system was not perfect and that "it could and should be better targeted."[23]

Zigas introduced the idea of housing tax credits to Senator Bob Packwood's (R-Ore.) staff. Zigas said progressive housing activists and the senator's staff preferred tax credits as a more targeted subsidy over the unwieldy subsidies in ERTA. More important, the tax credits also had a champion in George Mitchell (D-Maine). In time, and with some adjustments, the real estate industry saw the tax credit as a worthwhile compromise.[24] In the end, Congress included the Senate version of the LIHTC program in TRA 86 as a temporary demonstration project. The three-year program allowed state agencies (usually housing finance agencies) to allocate roughly $3 billion in credits per year. Each state received an amount of tax credit weighted to its population ($1.25 per person in 1986).[25] Tax credits are tax expenditures, as opposed to direct expenditures from the budget; they create an incentive for a particular activity (e.g., research and development, home ownership) that is rewarded through the tax code.

How the Low Income Housing Tax Credit Works

The LIHTC is something like a tax coupon that is awarded to affordable housing developers. The developers sell the coupon to investors (usually corporations) in exchange for providing equity capital to build apartment buildings that are rented to low-income tenants.[26] Investors use this coupon to pay their tax obligations to the IRS in lieu of cash. To claim the coupon, however, the investors must become partners in a limited partnership legal structure. In essence, they become a legal partner in every deal in which they invest. This has other tax benefits, including the ability to take losses from the project to offset investor income. To be considered "low income," a renter must earn less than 50 or 60 percent of the local area median income as measured by an annual county-by-county HUD survey.

The amount of tax credit equity from an investor that goes into a typical project can vary but is rarely more than 40–50 percent of the necessary funds for construction. Additional funds usually come from federal block grants—HOME and CDBG—and state and local funds. The final piece of financing is typically a mortgage from a private-sector credit provider (usually a bank) that is sized to the limited cash flow coming from tenants' statute-restricted rents.[27] The project is able to keep rents low, thanks to the infusion of low-cost tax credit equity, other low-cost debt, and grants from programs such as block grants. Tenants' rents can also be subsidized slightly by a below-market mortgage from a bank motivated by the Community Reinvestment Act (CRA). In this finance structure, there is no ongoing subsidy to the project, although as we will see in the case studies in the next chapter, many tenants also receive Section 8 or other rent support as individuals, which ultimately flows to the project's bottom line.

States (and a few cities) are awarded tax credits, which they then allocate based on what is known as the Qualified Allocation Plan. State and local governments must meet certain guidelines, such as a minimum 10 percent allocation to nonprofits. Otherwise, however, they can set goals to achieve local objectives, such as building more large apartments for families or encouraging "green" building techniques.

Many housing activists were wary of tax credits, according to Zigas, but after the Reagan cutbacks, there was a sense that "if we lose this [tax credits], there will be nothing."[28] And support for these credits grew. "At the time, I don't think many people thought this program was going to amount to much because it had been done on the quick with little research," William Apgar remarked. "But the states and the nonprofits and others have learned how to take this credit and make it into housing."[29] By 1989, the *New York Times* could editorialize that while "the housing industry originally doubted the effectiveness of the tax credit plan, results have surpassed even optimistic predictions."[30]

Making the Tax Credits Permanent

Although popular, the LIHTC program was vulnerable since it was a demonstration program. It was modified in 1988, in 1989, and again in 1990, mostly to correct errors and strengthen oversight.[31] But the program was still not permanent.

As with NAHA, conservatives joined liberals in support of the tax credit. A 1989 column in the *Wall Street Journal* by a for-profit real estate investor called on HUD Secretary Jack Kemp to support the credits:

> If experience has taught us anything, it is that government-built and controlled housing is fraught with fundamental weaknesses, not the least of which is the basic inefficiency of the bureaucracy in maintaining properties and the frequent failure of such housing to provide safe, or even humane places to live. Mr. Kemp shares that view. The looming question, then, is whether in spite of his aversion to tampering further with the tax code, he will swallow a broad program of tax incentives in order to inspire an alternative.[32]

Kemp did indeed swallow the tax credit program; he proposed making it permanent. In the hearings of the tax law–writing Housing Ways and Means Committee, Kemp urged Committee Chairman Charles Rangel to "rise above the left-right debate and find consensus as to what our nation can do to fight poverty." Kemp went on to praise both liberals and conservatives on the committee for their "willingness to walk away from ideology" (U.S. Congress 1989, 6).

Liberals on the committee, like Rangel, could voice their opposition and still embrace Kemp's proposals. Rangel said, "I am outraged at some of the things that have happened to my country in the last eight years, but you have to play the hand that is dealt you." True to his statement, Rangel spent a great deal of time during the hearing seeing how to make the credit more attractive to corporate investors. "We are just here to make certain that we can provide the incentives that are necessary to the investors," he said (U.S. Congress 1989, 177, 235).

In their effort to make the tax credits permanent, Rangel and Kemp received ample feedback from the business community. Several of the country's largest financial and real estate industry firms also testified in the LIHTC hearings, including Lehman Brothers, Boston Capital, and a representative of the National Association of Home Builders.[33] The for-profit business community lobbied that housing tax credits were good for business.[34] According to the *National Real Estate Investor* magazine, out of 250,000 apartment buildings that began construction in 1994, 100,000 were financed with the help of LIHTC (McQuiston 1996). A *Wall Street Journal* article in 1992 explained that LIHTC provided much-needed help during the recession of the early 1990s. The tax credit program "staved off a lot of bankruptcies in the industry that would have occurred without the program," said Martin Flounoy, chairman of the builders committee at the National Apartment Association. The article concluded that a number "of real estate industry and not-for-profit groups are lobbying the president to sign the bill" to extend the tax credit program permanently.[35]

Another *Wall Street Journal* article explained that many Fortune 500 companies were eager to purchase housing credits. James Ross, president of BP America (a subsidiary of British Petroleum), said that the return on investment for tax credits was "reasonably competitive" with other corporate investments. During this time, the financial returns on money invested in LIHTC averaged 20 percent—a return higher than most junk-rated bonds (Cummings and DiPasquale 1999).

Affordable housing advocates also made their voices heard. In a 1991 pro-LIHTC press conference with U.S. mayors, Paul Grogan said, "This credit is directly responsible for the creation of 120,000 homes for the poor annually in this country. This program has only been in existence since 1987, but we believe it to be the most successful federal housing program in history."[36]

In a *Washington Post* opinion piece, Grogan compared the advantages of tax credit programs with those of the Great Society housing programs. "While the Great Society programs of the 1960s had many positive results," he wrote, "they also showed the limitations of the top-down approach. But the federal government does have a role, mostly through flexible programs that support and encourage community initiative."[37]

Critics of Low-Income Housing Tax Credits

Although housing advocates testified in favor of LIHTC, there were divisions within the ranks on whether to push for an extension of the tax credit program. Some activists wanted the federal government to stop a program they perceived to be a shell game and that, in the end, was more beneficial to wealthy taxpayers than to low-income tenants. Others, however, saw it both as politically popular and as good public policy. The housing activist magazine *Shelterforce,* which started as a pro-affordable housing collective in the 1970s, aired both sides of the debate in 1992. On one side was Chester Hartman, and on the other were Paul Grogan and Benson Roberts of LISC (Hartman, Grogan, and Roberts 1992).

Hartman, executive director of the Poverty and Race Research Council, questioned the logic of tax expenditure support for affordable housing. Much of his criticism stemmed from his central question: "Why do something indirectly rather than directly?" In addition, he said tax credits were so complex that they were almost by design an effort to shift power from activists at the community level to technocrats and "middlemen" (Hartman 1992, 12). His strongest criticism, however, was over the method of subsidy delivery: "It is unseemly and redistributively unjust to help the poor by helping the rich—those upper-income investors and big corporations that avoid paying parts of their income taxes by offsetting these obligations via investment in low income housing." This program seemed to reward "rich investors" by providing photo opportunities with mayors, low-income tenants, and housing advocates— all a charade for participating in a lucrative tax scheme.

Paul Grogan, as head of LISC, was involved in selling tens of millions of dollars of those tax credits, and he disagreed with Hartman. In the same issue of *Shelterforce,* in an article titled "Good Policy, Good Politics," Grogan and Benson Roberts (1992), also at LISC, praised the multilayer approach to financing. They wrote that in 1985, when the idea of the tax credit was introduced, they were skeptical. But since it was the only option politically, they endorsed it. Since then, however, they had become converts. They addressed Hartman's points about the fairness of the credit, explaining that while it was true that rich investors were the ones who could make use of the credit, they paid a fair price to participate in the program. "If it lets them do well while doing good, if it broadens political support for good social policy, that's a plus, not a minus," they argued (Grogan and Roberts 1992, 13).

More than politics, the participation of private-sector investors helped create better housing, according to Grogan and Roberts. It was also true that these investors insisted on higher underwriting standards and safeguards, such as reserves.[38] Under the old programs, private owners with little or no investment stake in the project were likely to "walk away" at the first sign of trouble. But the tax credit program meted out significant penalties to investors if the project had problems during at least its first 15 years of operation.[39] "That kind of performance incentive means that housing will be planned, built and managed to last. No wonder Congress likes it," they wrote (Grogan and Roberts 1992, 13).

Tax credits also offered flexibility, according to Grogan and Roberts. They could be used for many different housing types, and communities, "not some federal bureaucracy," determined its uses. And while the tax credit program was complicated, it was not wasteful, according to the authors. Comparing this program with previous Washington-based ones, they wrote:

> Just ask any CDC that has had to spend 15 months of staff time getting a federal agency to sign off on a project the city and state have already approved. A thinly capitalized CDC could die before the project goes through federal approvals. Not to mention the costs of having to re-bid construction contracts that have expired in the meantime or the cost of federal agency staff and the consultants retained to satisfy them. (Grogan and Roberts 1992, 15)

Increasingly, housing advocates agreed with Grogan and Roberts. Patrick Clancy, then executive director of Greater Boston Community Development, Inc. (and later head of The Community Builders), defended the efficiency of LIHTC. Clancy (1988, 9) wrote, "Those producing affordable housing can achieve more direct access to assistance with less bureaucratic inefficiency through investment incentives than if the same assistance is provided through direct expenditures."

Passing the Extension of LIHTC

As early as 1991, housing advocates in the network understood their connection to one another and lobbied effectively as a group for the LIHTC extension. To bolster the case for extending LIHTC, Rangel included a letter in the *Congressional Record* that was signed by over 500 community-based housing nonprofits from across the nation. The letter both urged Congress to extend the tax credit and praised the role of for-profit corporations as part of the network of affordable housing providers: affordable housing "requires the kinds of creative solutions and especially the private sector involvement that the credit has stimulated"

(U.S. Congress 1991, E3640). Left in the wild, these groups were natural enemies, but by 1991, they recognized that their political and economic futures were linked.

It was clear that the tax credit program had broad support, but it still had to fight for resources during a period of belt-tightening. In 1991, when Charles Rangel introduced legislation to extend tax credits permanently, he went to great lengths to explain how the program had been improved with new oversight to guard against graft and corruption in the program. Looking back on five years of the program, Rangel argued:

> The credit has also fulfilled one of the original goals of its framers: to encourage additional government and private-sector support for housing. It has successfully created a partnership with state and local governments and nonprofit groups who have supplemented the credit with additional assistance. States and local governments are providing subsidies, low-interest loans, land, tax abatements among other forms of assistance. Nonprofits are organizing tenant and community groups to empower people on their way to providing housing for themselves and their neighbors. (U.S. Congress 1991, E3640)

Again, the familiar cadre of subnational government and private sector firms joined housing advocates to push for a permanent extension of LIHTC. A *New York Times* article, "Tax-Credit Program on Borrowed Time," showcased this diverse coalition. Republic National Bank Executive Vice President John Tamberlane was quoted urging support for the program because it, "benefits the bank with significant tax credits" and "it benefits the community by providing affordable, rehabilitated apartments for individuals with low and very low incomes."[40] Also quoted in the article was John McEvoy, executive director of the National Council of State Housing Agencies, who claimed that the few who opposed the program did so out of concern over its cost, not its effectiveness.[41] New York City Mayor David Dinkins claimed that cities needed LIHTC to be made permanent for it to be effective: "The annual lobbying to extend the credit has a detrimental effect on the production of affordable housing," he said. Grogan added, "No one could rely on assurances or raise any capital if the program isn't there at the end of the year." Such an array of advocates—mayors, bankers, state government bureaucrats, and housing activists—demonstrated that broad interests were working in concert to save LIHTC.

The Los Angeles riots in the spring of 1992 also gave weight to efforts for new urban relief initiatives, including the permanent extension of the tax credit. In an editorial, the *Los Angeles Times* argued that the "riots changed the political climate and put the problems of cities back on the national agenda." The LIHTC permanent extension did pass in the House, and going into the debate in the Senate, over 80 senators were on record in support of permanent LIHTC extension.[42] Echoing sentiments in editorials in the *New York Times,* the *Washington Post,* and the *Wall Street Journal,* the *Los Angeles Times* wrote: "The tax break deserves renewal because it remains the primary federal resource for financing additional new and affordable housing. It also forms the cornerstone of the numerous public/private partnerships that are increasingly the salvation of cash-short cities and states."[43]

Threat to LIHTC from Congress

The permanent extension passed in 1993, but that was not the end of the story.[44] The new Republican congressional majority in 1994 was on a crusade to cut the federal budget and simplify the tax code. The new chair of the House Ways and Means Committee, Bill Archer (R-Tex.), vowed to cut the housing tax credit (Shashaty 1997). To strengthen his case, Archer claimed the credits were an inefficient use of federal money. He cited a critical report by the IRS as justification for doing away with the program. The IRS estimated that "fraud in the amount of approximately $6.0 billion could be associated with alleged abuses of the program" (McQuiston 1996, 14–19). Archer demanded that the Government Accountability Office do a follow-up study of the LIHTC program. Although it found some inconsistencies and complexities to the program, it found no fraud. In fact, the report was generally positive on the role LIHTC played in housing economically vulnerable people (GAO 1997).

As Archer's evidence evaporated, so did his political allies in Congress. Moderate Republicans flocked to LIHTC. Jack Metcalf (R-Wash.) founded a Republican affordable housing caucus and was joined by other members, including Nancy Johnson (R-Conn.), Rick Lazio (R-N.Y.), Jerry Weller (R-Ill.), and Phil English (R-Pa.). The goals of the caucus were "to encourage the development of innovative, cost-effective and efficient approaches to providing affordable housing." Its charge was to "blend the energy and capital of industry with the public spirit of government and the incentives we can offer through law," Metcalf said ("New Republican Caucus" 1996, 74). Among those who made up the advisory committee of the caucus were Paul Grogan of LISC, John McEvoy of the National Council of State Housing Authorities, and F. Barton Harvey III, CEO of the Enterprise Community Partners. The advisory committee also included representatives from Boston Capital, the National Association of Home Builders, and the National Association of Realtors. Lazio, who was chair of the House Banking Committee's housing subcommittee, said, "The tax credit does everything that we Republicans say we want to do with housing. It puts private capital at risk. It leverages public dollars. It ensures income mix" (Seiberg 1995, 1).

As we have seen before, when the interests of the decentralized housing network were challenged, the coalition to save its funding programs proved to be a formidable opponent. In the fall of 1995, LISC and the Enterprise Community Partners rallied supporters of tax credits—mayors and governors, Wall Street investors, consultants, CDCs, banks, and corporations—to oppose the efforts of the House Ways and Means Committee chair. Antipoverty activists also joined the battle against Archer. John Taylor, president of the National Community Reinvestment Coalition, said that Archer's attack "just reveals the absolute lack of commitment by this Congress to housing the poor" (Seiberg 1995, 1).

In the fight against Archer, banks were important allies. "Dozens of banks" rallied to protect LIHTC, "including First Chicago Corp., Chemical Bank, and Wachovia Corp.," according to an article in *Mortgage Banking* magazine (Seiberg 1995, 1). "We believe people should have safe, clean, and affordable housing," said Donald Mullane, executive vice president at Bank of America. "As a matter of social policy, it is a good thing. This program [LIHTC] is a win for the community, a win for us, and it is a win for our shareholders" (Seiberg 1995, 2). Banks also had extra incentive to invest in credits because they were able to make a good tax-saving investment and get credit for complying with the Community Reinvestment Act. The *Journal of Housing and Community Development* wrote, "The combination of CRA compliance credit, attractive effective yields and goodwill created from investing in the local community makes the investment in tax credit projects increasingly popular for many banking institutions" (McQuiston 1996, 14–19).

The coalition to save the tax credit was broad and diverse, but it was also sophisticated. As an example of how proponents of poverty programs could play the lobbying game as effectively as any other special interest group, the *Wall Street Journal* reported that tax credit advocates were making donations to political allies of Archer's in an effort to sway him on LIHTC. The *Wall Street Journal* reported that Herb Collins, a top executive at Boston Capital, was leading the lobbying efforts to save the credit. He arranged meetings with tax-credit investors and Archer, and, according to one investor, instructed those with a stake in the program to make contributions to the congressional campaign of Archer's son-in-law.[45] For the first time, a federal poverty program was in the knife fight of budget politics, armed with a knife.

Archer's sunset proposal to kill LIHTC was part of the House version of the Revenue Reconciliation Act of 1995 that was famously vetoed by President Clinton.[46] Bipartisan lobbying removed the sunset provision from the compromise budget legislation. Archer had tried to reintroduce the sunset proposal to kill LIHTC in the compromise legislation, but according to the *National Real Estate Investor*, "he backed off after the credit received a strong endorsement from both Republican and Democratic members of his committee" (Jacobs 1997, 30). After the budget was passed, the *Journal of Housing and Community Development* wrote, "There appears to be no imminent threat to the tax credit program, and it would not be surprising to see additional growth in affordable housing through investment spurred by the program" (McQuiston 1996, 19).

Archer backed down from any further attacks on the LIHTC program after 1996. In April of 1997, the General Accounting Office (later renamed the Government Accountability Office) published a highly positive report on LIHTC. Many saw this as a vindication of the program that had come so close to termination. "After reviewing the GAO report," Archer conceded, "it appears that the housing projects using the credit are benefiting the right people—households with very low incomes" (Mishra 1997, 64).

Congress increased funding to the program in 2000 by increasing the allocation formula based on population in each state. The original amount based on $1.25 per person was increased to $1.50 in 2001 and then again to $1.75 in 2002. In 2003, future adjustments would be made to keep pace with inflation (OMB 2006). The Office of Management and Budget estimated the cost of the 2005 housing tax credit subsidy to affordable housing to be $3.88 billion.

Threat to LIHTC from the George W. Bush Administration

The LIHTC program faced one more significant threat. In 2003, the Bush administration proposed to exclude corporate dividends from taxation as part of a package to stimulate the moribund economy, a change that cut the value of LIHTC significantly. An analysis performed by Ernst and Young (2003) for the National Council of State Housing Agencies estimated that this change in tax law would result in significantly less tax credit equity going to housing; the likely result was 40,000 fewer LIHTC apartments per year, according to the report.

As in years past, an impressive coalition of advocates, state and local government, and some private-sector firms came together to protect the credit.[47] Within days of the proposal, Charles Rangel, a long-time supporter, sent a letter to HUD Secretary Mel Martinez in which he attacked the proposed change as "unfair and reckless." He wrote, "Corporations who had purchased low-income housing credits in the past will find they paid full value for something that is now worthless."[48] After intense lobbying through the spring, the final version of the bill that was approved by the House and narrowly in the Senate (Vice President Dick Cheney had to break the tie) had a modified dividend tax cut that did not severely affect LIHTC. The president fared poorly in the scrape: "The White House aggravated GOP senators by pushing them to support the full dividend tax cut and then retreating," according to an article in the *Washington Post*.[49]

Over its life, the LIHTC program has been attacked from the right as distorting the marketplace (Husock 2003) and from the left as "backroom politics" and a corporate-engineered tax giveaway (Guthrie and McQuarrie 2005).[50] But these attacks do not detract from the enormous popularity the program enjoys in the mainstream. In 2000, Congress assembled a bipartisan Millennial Housing Commission to take a comprehensive look at U.S. housing policy. Its members came from all across the political spectrum. Their widely cited 2002 report praised the decentralized housing network: "The LIHTC and HOME programs represent a true and strong paradigm shift away from some of the less effective federal policies and programs of the past." The program provided for local needs: "States and cities—not the federal government—now determine how to use most housing resources," it said. And the program managed to harness the energy of the private sector in a positive way by building "on lessons learned about providing incentives for private-sector involvement in housing. LIHTC's program design eliminates many of the perverse incentives that resulted in costly long-term problems with the privately owned, subsidized stock" (Bipartisan Millennial Housing Commission 2002, 64).

Other Financial Developments in the 1990s and 2000s

By the mid-1990s, the financial backbone of the decentralized housing network was in place with CDBG, LIHTC, and HOME. Two other financial developments of note in the 1990s were the expansion and strengthening of the Community Reinvestment Act in 1995 and the Community Development Banking and Financial Institutions Act of 1994.

The Community Reinvestment Act

The commercial lending world was of two minds on CRA. Bankers would admit that they often received a decent return on the loans they made to low-income areas and that they enjoyed the good public relations that these loans engendered. An article from American Bankers Association, the trade group representing banks, suggests that CRA helped banks to develop a "deeper understanding of the perspectives of all parties" in the communities in which they operate. "The American Bankers Association believes that bank compliance with the spirit and the letter of the Community Reinvestment Act is healthy, reflecting the fact that bankers, regulators, and community groups have all learned from one another over the past 30 years" (American Bankers Association 2009).

Representatives for banks and savings and loans also make the point that some of their competitors in the financial services industry—mortgage lenders such as Countrywide and credit unions, for example—have had an unfair advantage because they were not subject to CRA regulation. The evidence was clear that CRA motivated banks and savings and loans to lend more to low-income individuals and communities. A study by the Joint Center for Housing Studies at Harvard University for the Ford Foundation concluded that CRA-regulated institutions lent significantly more capital to underserved groups than institutions that were not regulated by the CRA (Fishbein 2003, 18).

Housing advocates, too, were critical of CRA. According to them, almost all banking institutions got a passing grade from CRA regulators (more than 90 percent), implying that the standards applied to the banks were too low. After an overhaul in 1995, new rules "shifted the emphasis for rating banks to more statistical performance measures and away from the procedure-oriented measures that were used before," noted CRA expert Allen Fishbein. Most banks continued to receive passing grades from regulators after 1995, but, according to Fishbein

(2003, 18), the "1995 revisions require banks to work harder to achieve their grades."

The Community Development Banking and Financial Institutions Act of 1994

The Community Development Banking and Financial Institutions Act of 1994 was a central part of the Clinton administration's new urban policy. It was modeled on successful efforts by community-oriented banks such as ShoreBank in Chicago and its Arkansas affiliate, Southern Development Bancorporation. The act intended to create 100 similar institutions nationwide to provide "small real estate and business loans, and provide technical assistance to borrowers in economically disadvantaged urban and rural areas," according to an article in the *Journal of Housing* (Metzger 1993, 83). It also created another pilot tax credit program (the prototype for what would become the New Markets Tax Credit program), to promote investment in small businesses in low-income neighborhoods.[51] NMTC was established as part of the Community Renewal Tax Relief Act that Bill Clinton signed weeks before leaving office. The tax credits are awarded by a new department of the U.S. Treasury, the Community Development Finance Institution Fund (Rubin and Stankiewicz 2005). In many instances, NMTC helped finance the commercial portion of mixed-use apartment buildings (i.e., those with commercial space in addition to apartments).

The government-sponsored entities also played a part in promoting the development of the decentralized housing network. The Federal Housing Enterprises Financial Safety and Soundness Act of 1992 had new regulatory provisions for the HUD secretary and the newly created Office of Federal Housing Enterprise Oversight. The 1992 act mandated yearly goals for Fannie Mae and Freddie Mac in the following categories:

- low- and moderate-income housing, targeting families with incomes below the area median
- special affordable housing, targeting very low income families
- underserved areas housing, targeting families living in low-income census tracts or in low- or middle-income census tracts with high minority populations

According to HUD, "The housing goals are expressed in percentage terms, as the minimum share of housing units financed by a GSE's [government-sponsored entity's] mortgage purchases in a particular year, and include units financed by the GSE's purchase of both single-family and multi-family mortgages" (Federal Home Loan Mortgage Corporation 2008).

As was shown in chapter 2, the percentage of affordable multifamily mortgages that Fannie and Freddie purchased doubled in the 1990s. And the government-sponsored entities became a significant participant in the LIHTC market. To provide a sense of how important Fannie Mae was to this market before the government takeover in 2008, consider the following comparison: in the first six months of 2007, Fannie Mae purchased $620.5 million in tax credits; in the first six months of 2008, that number had dropped to $10 million (Kimura 2008).[52]

A New Direction for HUD in the 1990s

Perhaps the most dramatic example of the new HUD was the appointment of Henry Cisneros, a young, dynamic mayor, to head the department. The former mayor of San Antonio said he had never considered working for HUD before. "HUD was largely irrelevant to the kind of entrepreneurial government we were trying to build in San Antonio," he said. "It was more of a problem than a help. I feel strongly we must change that perception and reputation" (Fulton 1993, 18).[53]

One of the most important new HUD programs in the 1990s was HOPE VI.[54] Initially known as the Urban Revitalization Demonstration Program, this program has been used to demolish poor-quality public housing stock and replace it with lower-density housing, often mixing in middle-income properties. It can also be used to rehabilitate properties and has social services as part of the effort as well. For example, there are funds for relocating existing tenants, including providing vouchers for those who do not return to the rebuilt housing.[55] From its beginning through fiscal year 2006, HOPE VI spent nearly $6.3 billion in demolishing and rebuilding public housing sites (HUD 2007). Nearly 165,000 of the worst public housing units had been approved for demolition by 2004 (Solomon 2005).

The program has also been successful in building capacity in local public housing authorities. To rebuild the public housing sites, the local public housing authorities often partnered with familiar members of the decentralized housing network—community development corporations and local and state government—and used familiar additional financing tools—LIHTC, CDBG, and HOME (Popkin et al. 2004).

The program was not without controversy, however. The physical improvements were impressive, but it is still not entirely clear how the tenants, many of whom were hard to house, fared in this program (Popkin 2002).

Funding for the HOPE VI program was significantly cut back by the George W. Bush administration. Funds in fiscal year 2004, for example, dropped to $150 million from $574 million in the previous year (Solomon 2005, 23). According to Rachel Bratt, in the fiscal year 2006 bill, the program was cut again to $100 million, or about 18 percent of its appropriations five years before (Bratt 2007).

Conclusion

This chapter charts the growing power and legislative victories of the decentralized housing network in the 1980s, 1990s, and early 2000s. These successes continue down to the present with the successful lobbying, over the Bush administration's objections, for a $4 billion community stabilization fund in the Housing and Economic Recovery Act of 2008. The new law attempted to correct the problems associated with subprime lending and foreclosures but had numerous provisions to boost the LIHTC program (Roberts 2008).

Looking back on the changes within the affordable housing community during the 1980s and 1990s, Avis Vidal wrote in the *Journal of the American Planning Association,* "Despite dramatic and unfortunate changes in the nation's urban neighborhoods and its political and fiscal climate since the community development movement began 30 years ago, the movement has matured into an industry" (Vidal 1997, 429). This new industry was built by people like Dorothy Mae Richardson, Paul Grogan, Patrick Clancy, and Jim Rouse. It was built by institutions like the National Council of State Housing Agencies, Boston Capital, Bank of America, and the National Association of Home Builders. The industry lobbied for, and secured, new funding—a job made easier by the popularity of this new approach to social policy among politicians across the political spectrum. Thanks to renewed federal resources, the decentralized network grew dense during the 1990s and 2000s. The next chapter looks at how the pieces fit and worked together to build housing "in hundreds of different ways and hundreds of different places," as the Maxwell-Rouse Report predicted.

4

Lessons Learned from What Was Built

I n the 1980s and early 1990s, production of new apartments by non-profit and for-profit real estate developers took off. But what did this evolving network build? How were the transactions structured? Who lived in these homes? And how did these projects perform over time? This chapter offers answers to these questions through a detailed look at actual projects. Two groups of case studies, one from the Fannie Mae Foundation and the other from the Urban Land Institute (ULI), feature projects from both the early period of the program (late 1980s to the early 1990s) and from the most recent period (2003 to 2007). The Fannie Mae Foundation projects won the prestigious Maxwell Award (named for David Maxwell from the Maxwell-Rouse Report), and the Urban Land Institute case studies were selected as exemplary affordable housing developments. In this chapter, I also draw from a large sample of projects from the National Equity Fund (a division of the Local Initiatives Support Council) from a middle period (1994–96).

The Maxwell Award Winners, 1988–92

The five projects discussed in this section received the Fannie Mae Foundation's Maxwell Award for the Production of Low-Income Housing. The award was designed to "identify, recognize and showcase the outstanding work of nonprofit organizations developing and maintaining housing for low-income Americans" (Rohe et al. 1998, ix). The Maxwell Award was a nationwide competition that evaluated projects on their "creativity in addressing housing needs, quality of the designs, originality of financing, affordability, and success in implementing the developments" (Rohe et al. 1998, ix).

In 1998, the Fannie Mae Foundation funded a study of Maxwell Award winners, enlisting the Center for Urban and Regional Studies at the University of North Carolina at Chapel Hill to assess the operational history of those projects and to see what factors contributed to their success or failure. The following is a review of five award winners from 1988 to 1992.

Case Study 1: Guyon Towers

Guyon Towers was once the pride of Chicago, an elegant downtown hotel now on the National Register of Historic Places; in its glory days, it hosted big bands in its Paradise Ballroom. By the 1980s, however, it was a symbol of inner-city blight. The hotel, like its neighborhood of West Garfield Park, had experienced terrible decay since the 1940s. In fact, former president Jimmy Carter chose Guyon Towers as a place to spend the night on his nationwide tour to raise awareness of intolerable housing conditions (Reed 1988, 31).

The renaissance of the old icon came about partly through a partnership between Chicago banks and housing activists. The Chicago Rehab Network, a coalition of community groups, pressured three big downtown banks—First National Bank, Harris Bank, and Northern Trust Co.—to get them "back into the business of lending to the neighborhoods," according to Gale Cincotta, a long-time community activist (Reed 1988).[1]

One of the groups pressuring the banks was Bethel New Life, a faith-based community development corporation founded in 1979 by the Bethel Lutheran Church. Bethel teamed up with Harris Bank to rehabilitate Guyon Towers. "We started out as confrontational, but became partners," according to Bethel New Life's president, Mary Nelson. Learning how to orchestrate a complicated transaction like Guyon Towers (requiring six separate sources of funds, see table 4.1) was difficult for all the parties involved: "These are complicated deals that require decisions you don't learn in textbooks," said Cincotta (Reed 1988).

The building was seriously delinquent on its property taxes, allowing Bethel New Life to acquire the building for $2,000 through a Cook County program to facilitate the sale of delinquent projects to nonprofits (Rohe et al. 1998).[2] Bethel converted the old hotel into a 114-unit apartment building with eight storefronts on the street level. Although the project received recognition as a model project with a Maxwell Award in 1989, it had many problems over the years.

The Sponsor

Bethel New Life got its start in housing with Guyon Towers, and its area of concentration has been Chicago's West Side. At the time Bethel received the Maxwell Award in 1989, it had an operating budget of $2.5 million and a staff of 142 full-time employees. Up to that point, it had developed 387 units of housing and had another 452 in development. Ten years later, Bethel had enlarged the number of housing units developed, its staff, and its services offered. It had developed a thousand units of housing, its staff had grown to 400, and its annual budget was approximately $10 million. Its services now included programs in employment, economic and small business development, health, and family support services. All this growth happened under the leadership of Mary Nelson, the original president. By 2008, Bethel New Life had built more than a thousand homes and branched out into developing community facilities for small businesses and social services.[3]

Who Was Served?

Rents were restricted to tenants who earned 60 percent or less of the Cook County median income, to conform with the requirements of low-income housing tax credits. The units were relatively small since they were converted hotel rooms, which made this project more attractive to seniors, singles, and small families. All the tenants were African American.

Financing

During the construction phase of the project, financing came from two subsidized loans: one from the city of Chicago, which used its Community Development Block Grant money, and the other from the Enterprise

Foundation. A nonprofit consultant, the Chicago Equity Assistance Center, assisted in arranging the permanent financing, which is summarized in table 4.1.

According to the sponsors, the financing of this project had problems from the beginning, with a smaller than expected first mortgage and confusion over its construction loan. Harris Bank reduced the first mortgage because the appraisal of the building's value was lower than expected.[4] The low appraisal stemmed from two issues: first, it was in an undesirable neighborhood and, second, the rents were restricted by LIHTC. Since the bank lends money based on the building's value and its income potential, it was forced to underwrite a loan that covered only 26 percent of the development cost. With a smaller first mortgage, the project required an additional subsidy from the Illinois Department of Housing. To make matters worse, the city caused delays because it had limited experience with using CDBG as a construction loan.

In the end, the financing of Guyon Towers worked because the building was cheap—thanks to Cook County—and it had significant subsidies, nearly 75 percent of the total development cost. The financing was a cocktail of different federal, state, and local subsidized lending programs.

Table 4.1. Funding for Guyon Towers

Source	Amount ($)	Percentage of costs	Terms
Harris Bank	1,549,588	26	8% fixed; 30-year term
Chicago Department of Housing (CDBG)	1,960,626	33	0% fixed; 30-year term
Illinois Department of Housing	1,000,000	17	3% deferred; 30-year term
Chicago's Department of Economic Development	41,000	1	Grant
Illinois Solar Bank	50,000	1	Grant
Chicago Equity Fund (an affiliate of the National Equity Fund and LISC)	1,262,720	22	Tax credit equity investment
Total	5,863,934	100	
Total per unit	51,438		

Source: Rohe et al. (1998, ix).

The largest portion, 33 percent, came from the Chicago Department of Housing's CDBG funds. The second-leading contribution, 22 percent, came from the equity that the Chicago Equity Fund was able to raise by selling the project's LIHTC to corporate investors.[5] The last major piece came from the Department of Housing and Urban Development, with funds that were under the discretion of the Illinois Department of Housing. Bethel secured small grants to improve to the building's historic façade and to make energy-saving changes.

How the Project Fared

Guyon Towers had problems in its first year. When the drug and crime problem in the neighborhood intensified, the sponsor responded by hiring security guards, adding nearly $60,000 per year in operating costs. In addition, maintenance problems—particularly problems with the elevators and plumbing—caused higher than expected operating costs and fueled tenant dissatisfaction. As a result, tenant recruitment and retention suffered. Poor on-site management contributed to an already bad situation. Bethel had difficulty renting all the apartments; as costs went up, revenue dropped.

Nelson admitted making a damaging mistake by taking too long to solve the property management problem on her own. "We wasted six months," she said. "One of the lessons I would [offer] others in my position, is 'don't go it alone'" (Hornung 1991). But new property management was not enough to stop the flow of red ink. By 1993, the project was unable to pay its mortgage, triggering a loan restructuring with Harris Bank. The bank lowered the interest rate from 8 to 3 percent (a generous move that was facilitated by much lower interest rates available in the capital markets at that time).

As part of the restructuring, the bank insisted that the Chicago Equity Fund (a division of LISC) assume responsibility for the management of the building. The fund hired a new private property management company to handle the day-to-day operations and contributed money to get the project back on its feet. It was strongly motivated to restore the project to financial viability because it would be forced to return the tax credits to the IRS and pay a substantial penalty if the building failed. Subsidies from Harris Bank and CEF, along with better management such as more effective tenant screening and prompt repairs and an improving neighborhood, contributed to the ultimate success of this project. With new resources and new management, the project achieved occupancy rates above 90 percent after years of hovering closer to 70 percent. This improvement boosted revenue at a time when mortgage and operational expenses dropped.

Case Study 2: West Side Development

The West Side Development was a substantial redevelopment of Belcher's Quarters, an area in the west side of town that was one of the worst slums in Tuscaloosa, Alabama. "It doesn't take a Rhodes Scholar to know that a lot of the things that the City of Tuscaloosa offers, the west side does not have access to," according to Ronnie Miller, a local housing activist (*Speakin' Out News* 2000, 3).[6] The project sponsor, the Community Service Programs of West Alabama (CSP), used equity from the sale of LIHTC to buy 60 shacks in a dilapidated western neighborhood. It demolished the old homes and built new ones in their place, completing the project in 1990. West Side Development received the Maxwell Award in 1992 (Rohe et al. 1998).

The project was the first new low-income rental housing built in Tuscaloosa in 10 years. It also was the city's first project to use LIHTC. While most of the original buildings were abandoned, CSP was able find temporary housing for the tenants of Belcher's Quarters during construction. Most of the displaced tenants moved back to the newly built apartments.

The development, which occupies a city block, comprises 16 duplex units and one six-unit building. The duplexes are single-story ranch-style units arranged around a central courtyard. The courtyard has play and picnic areas and a basketball court. The six-unit building is across the street. In all, the project has 11 one-bedroom, 5 two-bedroom, 12 three-bedroom, and 10 four-bedroom apartments.

The Sponsor

Community Service Programs and its executive director Bill Edwards exemplify important aspects of the decentralized housing network. They both had their roots in the Great Society; CSP was originally a War on Poverty community action agency, and Edwards was a Californian who came to Alabama in 1969 as a VISTA volunteer. "My chief purpose for coming to the South was to help bring positive social change and try to do something about poverty," he said. Noting that he arrived with long hair, a long beard, and holes in his jeans, he acknowledged that he "was probably viewed as an outside agitator by some people."[7]

Edwards became director of CSP in 1982, and over time, he and the organization changed tactics. "I want to create real, long-lasting substantial social change," he said. "And that is more difficult than trying to organize a voter registration rally. It might be kind of cliché to say, but I just felt I could get more done by working within the system."[8]

CSP operated in communities across western Alabama, providing economic development, social services, Head Start, child-care management, youth development, education, and affordable housing consulting and development. In 1992, CSP had 168 employees. By the time of the Fannie Mae study in 1998, it had grown to 284 employees, with an annual operating budget of $808,000. CSP started its affordable housing development with Belcher's Quarters, and by 1998, it had developed 620 such units. It had developed 15 apartment complexes by 2008.[9]

The reporter profiling Edwards for the *Birmingham News* wrote, "The effort at better housing, [Edwards] said, is a result of a new attitude in the state, which has brought together the business community, local governments, as well as state and federal agencies, and black and white churches."[10]

Who Was Served?

The LIHTC program restricted rents at West Side Development, requiring eligible tenants to earn 60 percent or less of the area median income. The project's first tenants were the former residents of the demolished shacks of Belcher's Quarters. They tended to be elderly; subsequent renters tended to be younger, single-parent families. All the tenants at the time of the 1998 Fannie Mae study were African American.

Financing

The bulk of the financing came from LIHTC equity, with smaller grants coming from city and state governments (table 4.2).

There was no conventional mortgage on the property, but in an unusual development, the project made a monthly payment to its two LIHTC equity investors, First Alabama Bank and the Bank of Tuscaloosa. Excess revenue generated by tenants' rents went to project maintenance and financial reserves. CSP did not obtain a separate loan to fund its construction phase.

Table 4.2. Funding for West Side Development

Source	Amount ($)	Percentage of costs	Terms
First Alabama Bank	1,358,425	78	Tax credit equity investment
Bank of Tuscaloosa	166,608	10	Tax credit equity investment
City of Tuscaloosa (CDBG funds)	175,000	10	Grant
State of Alabama-Community Services Block Grant	40,000	2	Grant
Total	1,740,033	100	
Total per unit	79,092		

Source: Rohe et al. (1998).

How the Project Fared

The strong organization of CSP, combined with conscientious property management and good-quality construction, made this project a success in its first eight years of operation. CSP relied on substantial tenant screening, including credit and police checks and in-home interviews as a way to ensure responsible tenants. In addition, CSP was able to enrich the living environment for its residents because it was also a service provider.

Initially, city hall offered some resistance to this project. For one thing, the city did not want the expense of demolition and relocation of the existing tenants of Belcher's Quarters. In response, CSP coordinated a political campaign to convince the city and other local institutions that a large-scale renovation was not only possible but also necessary. CSP organized a march in support of the project. The march had a persuasive effect, as one city council member noted:

> There were those on the [city] council who claimed they did not know that such a place existed and this march opened their eyes. There was a lot of debate about whether the city was rewarding a slumlord by assisting with the purchase of the property—but finally CSP purchased the land. CSP's strong reputation in the community as a service provider was instrumental in convincing local leaders to support the project. (Rohe et al. 1998)

This successful project changed negative community attitudes toward low-income housing and launched CSP's career in affordable housing development. In the Fannie Mae report, one resident of West Side Development said, "I never believed that they could really change this place and get rid of those falling down houses but they did and I got a new home . . . it was nice and has brick walls and big rooms."

Case Study 3: Frank G. Mar Community Housing

The organization that built the tremendously complicated Frank G. Mar Community Housing development in Oakland got its start in an old abandoned warehouse in Oakland's Chinatown in 1975. "We were just a bunch of kids, really," said Ted Dang, a founding board member of the East Bay Asian Local Development Corporation (EBALDC) (Gan 1988, 19). Dang was not simply being self-deprecating about his age; many who founded EBALDC really *were* kids (or at least college students). Seventeen years later, however, Fannie Mae presented a Maxwell Award to this nonprofit community development corporation for an ambitious project that combined 119 residential apartments with 12,000 square feet of commercial development in Oakland's Chinatown (Rohe et al. 1998). The project won many architectural design awards and signaled a new era for EBALDC.

The Sponsor

EBALDC was incorporated as "a community development organization dedicated to the betterment of the East Bay Community, particularly the low-income and Asian and Pacific Islander population, through development of physical, human, and economic assets for individuals and community organizations." At the time of the Maxwell Award, EBALDC had 11 full-time staff and an annual budget of $600,000. By 1998, it had 40 full-time employees, had an annual budget of $1.3 million, and had built 573 homes for low-income tenants.

A project on the scale of Frank G. Mar, however, required more development expertise than EBALDC could muster, which prompted the collaboration with BRIDGE, a developer that I. Don Terner founded in 1982.[11] BRIDGE was not a local CDC in the tradition of EBALDC. Rather, Terner saw BRIDGE as a nonprofit competitor to its for-profit real estate developer rivals. BRIDGE's aggressive practices helped make it one of the nation's largest nonprofit housing developers.

Both EBALDC and BRIDGE continue to be major players in affordable housing development. By 2008, EBALDC had developed over a thousand affordable apartments and single-family homes, and BRIDGE had build more than 13,000 homes.[12]

Who Was Served?

Frank G. Mar project was overwhelmingly occupied by low-income Asian households (91 percent). At the time of the Maxwell Award in 1992, 108 of the 119 families had incomes below 50 percent of the area median income. As intended, a mix of elderly and younger families lived in the project. In 1998, the project had a 97 percent occupancy rate, and there was virtually no change from its original tenant demographics (race, family size, or income).

Financing

A remarkable feature of the financing for the project was that only 19 percent of the more than $17 million in development costs was in the form of a conventional first mortgage. The other two loans were low interest (relative to the rates at the time) and deferred, which meant they did not require a scheduled payment. The deferred loans were paid with excess cash flow above the costs of the fixed first mortgage, maintenance costs, and funding reserve accounts. In practice, however, sponsors often found ways to spend revenue, partly by funding all conceivable maintenance costs and keeping generous reserves fully funded. On the revenue side, sponsors also preferred to keep rents low for their tenants rather than paying down the deferred mortgages.

Another unusual aspect was the large HUD Housing Development Action Grant and the grant from the U.S. Department of Health and Human Services. These two grants accounted for 35 percent of the development costs. The sponsor, EBALDC, had to plug development cost overruns with part of its developer fee. Otherwise, the other sources of funds were familiar: CDBG funds from the city of Oakland and LIHTC equity from a corporate investor, Mission First Financial (an affiliate of the utility Southern California Edison). These last two sources amounted to 23 percent of total development costs (table 4.3).

The HUD grant and a loan from Wells Fargo Community Lending Bank for $3,350,000 paid for the construction phase of the project. Additional construction-phase financing came from the Oakland Redevelopment Agency ($4 million loan) and the Oakland Parking Authority ($2.5 million loan).

Table 4.3. Funding for Frank G. Mar Community Housing

Source	Amount ($)	Percentage of costs	Terms
Citibank	3,350,000	19	10.47%; 30 years fixed
HUD Housing Development Action Grant	5,523,579	32	3%; 30 years deferred
Oakland Redevelopment Agency	1,250,000	7	3%; 50 years deferred
U.S. Department of Health and Human Services	500,000	3	Grant
City of Oakland Parking Authority	3,400,000	20	Equity investment
Mission First Financial	2,750,000	16	LIHTC equity investment
EBALDC	507,636	3	Sponsor's equity
Total	17,281,215	100	
Total per unit	145,220		

Source: Rohe et al. (1998).

How the Project Fared

Frank G. Mar Community Housing was an important achievement for Chinatown, an area of the city that had lost hundreds of apartments and homes in the previous 10 years. Appropriately, it was named after one of the leading lights of the East Bay Asian community. The Reverend Frank G. Mar was an immigrant to the East Bay in 1934, a graduate of the University of California at Berkeley, and a minister for Oakland's Chinese Presbyterian Church. As a community activist since the 1960s, Mar was frustrated with the halting progress of the housing the "community [had] fought for many years." The minister saw a mission in EBALDC's work; if successful, it would have an impact on "all of Oakland and other cities like Seattle and Los Angeles. The success will tell others, 'Hey, we can do it!'" (Pomar 1986, 15).

EBALDC needed that kind of optimism, because the project was complicated. It was physically large, covering a city block, and involved a number of building types—a mid-rise apartment tower, underground parking garage, commercial spaces, and townhomes. It was in a downtown location in an older city and had problems with toxic soil contamination. There were many participants—two nonprofit sponsors; two banks; federal, state, and local government; the Oakland Parking Authority; and an LIHTC equity investor. Because of the strong demand for affordable rental property, the housing aspect of this project was low risk from the perspectives of the lender and equity investor. The commercial aspects of the project, however, made it a riskier investment. Unlike housing, commercial vacancies can vary wildly. It was unusual at the time for a bank to lend to a combined housing and commercial project. The environmental remediation, commercial vacancy risk, and general complexity of the project contributed to a start-to-finish development period of six years.

The project was physically attractive and located in a good neighborhood with access to shops, services, and transportation; rents were low, and the property was well maintained. Unhappy with the original property management company, EBALDC fired the firm and took over the management itself. EBALDC developed a good reputation for managing the building by including residents in decisions, carefully screening tenants (conducting home interviews, for example), and regularly inspecting units for maintenance problems. Security guards were present in the evening, paid for by the commercial tenants, which included a day-care center, a parent-child resource center, and a variety of retail shops.

Case Study 4: Quality Heights

The key to successful community development, according to Colleen Hernandez, director of the Kansas City Neighborhood Alliance (KCNA), is getting results that allow people to feel "a flicker of hope." "Then," she says, "their brain clicks in to other things they can do, ways they can get other people involved. It's about power, and it is really potent" (Leifer 1993, 44). That kind of drive was necessary for KCNA, formerly a service delivery nonprofit, to jump into the world of real estate development. KCNA successfully completed its first housing project, Quality Heights, in 1988; the project won the Maxwell Award in 1989.

Quality Heights was a two-phased project consisting of 40 single-family homes and 68 duplex apartments built over several city blocks in the Wendell Philips neighborhood in Kansas City. The homes in Quality Heights had three bedrooms, one and a half baths, central heating and air conditioning, small porches, and driveways. It was the first new construction in that neighborhood in 40 years (Rohe et al. 1998, 163–70).

The Sponsor

KCNA got its start in 1979 as a nonprofit dedicated to serving neglected Kansas City neighborhoods. Before building Quality Heights, KCNA was primarily a training organization, providing technical housing assistance (home purchase and development) to individuals, other community development corporations, and neighborhood advocacy groups. For example, KCNA supported programs that encouraged small contractors to refurbish inner-city homes and counseled low-income tenants about negotiating mortgages and home ownership. KCNA launched its affordable housing development career with Quality Heights, but the organization was destined for much more. The CDC used its contacts from the Quality Heights transaction to produce more housing and by 1998 had developed 173 more homes for low-income tenants. The organization had eight staff members at the time of its Maxwell Award in 1989 and grew to 15 by 1998. KCNA had an annual budget over $1 million in 1998. In later years, KCNA hit on hard times and transferred many of its programs to other entities. It finally closed down.[13]

The sponsor was an earlier pioneer in the use of low-income housing tax credits. In the course of building Quality Heights, KCNA made important connections with the National Equity Fund, LISC, and the Missouri Housing Development Commission. It used those partners again in subsequent low-income housing transactions.

In another high-profile effort, KCNA partnered with a fledgling community nonprofit to rehabilitate an entire neighborhood. The story is told in a Kansas City alternative weekly paper, the *Kansas City Pitch*. The headline read, "Here's How One Neighborhood Conquered White Flight, A Slumlord, Crack Wars and City Neglect." With federal funds and what it raised from the Pew Charitable Trusts, the Kaufman Foundation, the Hall Family Foundation, and the Community Foundation, KCNA and its nonprofit neighborhood partner bought dilapidated homes, helped home owners make improvements, and cleaned up neighborhoods streets. In what the article described as a "slowly evolving shift in government policy," nonprofits now "rule urban redevelopment" because "federal officials have moved away from sweeping top-down solutions for problems."[14]

Who Was Served

As a project funded by low-income housing tax credits, the homes are restricted to tenants who earn 60 percent or less of the median income in the Kansas City area. A majority of the tenants were single-parent families and African American.

Financing

Compared with Frank G. Mar, Quality Heights had a relatively simple financing structure. It had a first mortgage from the state of Missouri's Housing Development Commission (the state housing finance agency and LIHTC allocator) and a deferred second mortgage from HUD. Equity from the sale of low-income housing tax credits and a small grant from LISC provided the balance of the development costs.

Because this project used factory-built housing components, which were assembled on site, there was no lengthy construction period requiring separate construction financing.

How the Project Fared

Clergy from the Wendell Philips neighborhood initially proposed the project. Having local churches on board, however, was not enough to quell the concerns of the existing neighborhood association. Even low-income neighborhoods can engage in not-in-my-backyard politics, and KCNA spent a great deal of time meeting with neighborhood representatives in an effort to get their support for the project. According to

Table 4.4. Funding for Quality Heights

Source	Amount ($)	Percentage of cost	Terms
Missouri Housing Development Commission	800,000	36	First mortgage
HUD Housing Opportunity Development Action Grant	750,000	34	Second mortgage
National Equity Fund (LISC affiliate)	612,000	28	LIHTC equity
LISC	49,000	2	Grant
Total	$2,211,000	100	
Total per unit	$20,472		

Source: Rohe et al. (1998).

Hernandez, neighbors "were convinced it was a Wayne Minor [a local crime-ridden federal housing project built in 1962] in their front yard." In a bold strategic move, Hernandez made the neighborhood association a co-owner in the limited partnership that developed Quality Heights. The neighborhood association then embraced the project once it had more say in its development. Success in phase one provided a track record, ensuring local support for phase two.

The use of prefabricated components seemed to work well for this project, in part because the construction quality was high. A problem came later when hard-to-find nonstandard components like closet doors had to be replaced.

Two other problems plagued the project. First, inadequate financial reserves prevented the sponsor from some routine maintenance and would have been a significant problem if a major fix had been necessary— roofs, plumbing, and the like. Reserves for cash shortfalls were also inadequate, which was a potential problem during times of slumping project income or rising expenses. This problem was flagged by a follow-up performance review by LISC. Armed with the LISC study, the sponsor negotiated with its financial partners in the early 1990s and won some concessions for more debt and equity to fund its reserves adequately. This adjustment solved the problem: the project had sufficient cash reserves from the early 1990s until the Fannie Mae study in 1998.

Second, the project had difficulty with property management and occasional high vacancy, which triggered revenue shortfalls. Originally, the sponsor was also the manager, but it did not have the expertise for the job, and conflicts emerged when it had to act as a tough rent-collector on the one hand and as an encouraging service provider on the other. KCNA hired a local property management firm, but the new firm had problems as well. The third outside manager who took over at the time of the Fannie Mae study appeared to be an improvement. According to one resident, "In the two years I have been here, having three management agents has been pretty tough." Another tenant commented, "Only recently have they [the management] begun to live up to my expectations."

Despite management and financial problems, innovative staff and an involved board of directors made this project a success. Both provided important help in problem solving, such as making the neighborhood group a colimited partner and renegotiating reserves with the lenders. They also responded aggressively when a trusted outside source (LISC) warned them about their reserves.

Overall, the prospect of a single-family home or duplex was very attractive to tenants. One resident commented during an 1998 interview, "My neighbors have been great . . . it's good living in a house . . . at least this place is not stigmatized as public housing—it's great to order a pizza and they agree to deliver once they hear your address" (Rohe et al. 1998).

Case Study 5: Peter Claver Community

Considering that President Reagan did not use the term AIDS publicly until 1987, it is surprising that in 1988 local leaders in San Francisco were able to use federal funds to open one of the nation's first subsidized housing projects for AIDS sufferers. The new facility, the Peter Claver Community, was a single-room occupancy (SRO) development for formerly homeless people diagnosed with AIDS (Rohe et al. 1998, 171–80). It had 32 furnished private rooms, with shared kitchens, bathrooms, common rooms, and an outside patio deck. In addition to housing, residents received support services, including meals, counseling, 24-hour nursing care, and financial planning. Offices for counselors and nurses were on site. The renovated building, formerly a church, was located in the Fillmore District, near shopping, cafes, services, and transportation. The project received the Maxwell Award in 1990.

The Sponsor

Primarily a charitable social service organization, Catholic Charities of the Archdiocese of San Francisco was founded in 1907 to help San Francisco residents recover from the 1906 earthquake. It became an early leader in housing people with AIDS (*Sun Reporter* 1995, S5). Early developments like Peter Claver allowed it to leverage development relationships with lenders, foundations, and the city of San Francisco to continue to build some affordable housing. Another Catholic Church affiliate, Mercy Charities (a more experienced housing developer), was also instrumental in creating the Peter Claver Community.

Who Was Served?

After the AIDS crisis exploded in the mid-1980s, this new type of service-enriched housing was much in demand. The city of San Francisco maintained a waiting list of several thousand eligible tenants who needed a home like the Peter Claver Community. At the time of the Maxwell Award in 1990, the residents were exclusively gay white men. By 1998, however, the tenants had diversified with more women and transgender residents. A majority of residents were white, but one-third were African American and 12 percent Hispanic. Most tenants were formerly homeless, had no jobs, and paid rent from their monthly allowance from SSI, the Social Security program for the indigent.

Financing

Two-thirds of the total financing came from two nearly equal sources— LIHTCs and a private donation. Grants from two foundations and the Macy's Corporation accounted for 4 percent of the total construction cost. The remainder was a first mortgage (14 percent) from the Savings Association Mortgage Company, a consortium of savings and loans of northern California that specialized in affordable housing lending. San Francisco's redevelopment agency provided a deferred loan from its CDBG funds (16 percent of the total). Table 4.5 breaks down the sources and uses of the funding.

Catholic Charities, and its affiliate Mercy Charities, used the donated property along with CDBG funds and grants to start construction of this project. Additional construction-phase financing came from a nonprofit

Table 4.5. Funding for the Peter Claver Community

Source	Amount ($)	Percentage of costs	Terms
Savings Association Mortgage Company	355,000	14	Conventional mortgage
City of San Francisco Redevelopment Agency (CDBG)	400,000	16	Conventional loan
Irvine Foundation	50,000	2	Grant
Koret Foundation	20,000	1	Grant
Macy's	18,000	1	Grant
Private donor	875,000	34	Donation
LIHTC	830,460	33	Tax credit equity
Total	2,548,460	100	
Total per unit	79,639		

Source: Rohe et al. (1998).

affordable housing lender, the Low Income Housing Fund, based in San Francisco, and the McAuley Housing Fund, a charity related to the Catholic Church.[15]

Operational funding for services at Peter Claver Community came from four government grants: one from HUD's Housing Opportunities for People Living with AIDS, by far the largest source; two grants from the San Francisco Department of Public Health for mental health and homeless assistance; and one from the federal government's Ryan White CARE program for AIDS services. In addition to the small rents that tenants paid (30 percent of their monthly income), the project was supported by project-based HUD Section 8 funding.

How the Project Fared

The San Francisco Department of Public Health first approached Catholic Charities in 1987 to build service-enriched housing for people with AIDS. Working together, the city and Catholic Charities were able to finish the project in record time: it opened its doors in August 1988.

Early on, the turnover of residents was high, nearly 63 percent in 1988. While the primary cause of the frequent turnover was death, occasional evictions came about because of behavioral problems. Given the long waiting list, though, the project lost very little income through vacancies. By 1998, the death rate had declined dramatically, thanks to medical advances in treating AIDS. In response, Catholic Charities adjusted its tenant services, offering more job and independent living training for residents who were living longer.

The Peter Claver Community was heavily dependent on continuing federal grants, resources that had been on and off the budget chopping block. In response, the city of San Francisco and Catholic Charities were exploring how they could cut back on costs and continue operating the facility with most of its services if funding were cut. In 1998, the chief operating officer of Catholic Charities said, "I don't think Catholic Charities would be in a position to fund the operation of Claver . . . without substantial public funding" (Rohe et al. 1998).

Themes from the Early Maxwell Winners

The variety in this small sample of early Maxwell Award winners illustrates a number of features of the new approach to delivering affordable housing. Each project required the coordinated effort of diverse development teams: local community-based groups, local banks, and local government. They were also infused with money and expertise from state and federal government and nonprofits with national reach (e.g. Local Initiatives Support Council, National Equity Fund, and Enterprise Foundation).

The teams were also eclectic in the type of housing they built: single-family homes, townhomes, apartments, and rehabilitated historic buildings. Each participant brought an expertise in government programs, finance, construction, social services, or the needs of tenants. The teams navigated skillfully around obstacles, whether they were political, construction related, or market derived. In this sense, they exhibited the kind of institutional adaptability that was predicted in the Senate debates over the HOME program in chapter 3.

What the Case Studies Show.   In spite of their differences, the projects had similar financing structures. Each had a small first mortgage (a conventional real estate loan) that covered between 14 and 36 percent of its development costs. Equity in the project primarily came from LIHTC investors, which ranged from 16 to 88 percent of total development costs. Sometimes, the sponsor would lend part of its own capital (sometimes in the form of its developer fee) to a project, as EBALDC did in the Frank G. Mar project. The balance of financing in every case consisted of subsidized loans from state and local governments, the bulk of this money coming from the federal CDBG and HOME programs.

The case studies also show how projects from the late 1980s laid the organizational groundwork for collaboration and subsequent affordable housing projects. The team of organizations assembled for one project often worked together on later ones. The next development was easier because all the participants knew how to use new tools (e.g., LIHTC) and how to work together. In other words, successful collaboration built trust and predictability, which lowered transaction costs. In addition to making transactions more efficient, repeated collaboration built up social capital in the community and strengthened the network capability of these loosely coordinated institutions.

Collaboration was woven into every transaction. At first glance, the financing plans of the projects in the case studies appear too complicated, involving from four to seven layers of financing.[16] But with multiple participants vetting critical decisions, mistakes were less likely. In addition, if something did go wrong, all had a financial stake in finding a solution because they all suffered if the project failed.

Guyon Towers was a vivid example of how a financing team came to the aid of a failing project. A deteriorating neighborhood, security problems, and maintenance difficulties were overwhelming, and turning things around required more than the dedication and pluck of the staff of Bethel New Life. The nonprofit asked its financiers for help. Because its syndicator of low-income housing tax credits, LISC, had a significant financial stake in the project's success (along with a mission-driven commitment to help), the project was able to find new resources and new solutions—better security and a well-respected property management firm that cut maintenance problems and boosted occupancy. LISC and Harris Bank also subsidized the project to get it back on its feet.

Earlier chapters of this study focused on the machinations of federal policymaking in Washington, D.C., but the decentralized housing network shifted political action to the local level. When the West Side Development CDC needed the support of the Tuscaloosa City Council, it organized a march on city hall to highlight the blight of the Belcher's Quarters neighborhood. And when the Kansas City Neighborhood Alliance experienced stiff local resistance by a neighborhood association, it acted strategically, making that association a partner in the future development. EBALDC and BRIDGE were able to partner with the parking authority in downtown Oakland, both as a way to secure a project site without a bidding war (the project was built on a parking authority lot) and as a way to accomplish the politically popular objective of providing more parking in downtown Oakland, a move that helped expedite the project's zoning approval. In each of these cases, the sponsors displayed a sophistication that disarmed community opposition.

Finally, these diverse teams showed they were adaptable. The Peter Claver Community, for example, evolved from hospice to transitional living facility. By 1998, the Archdiocese of San Francisco was offering less grief counseling and hospice care and more job training and education classes. The Kansas City Neighborhood Alliance fired itself as a property manager, then fired a second property management firm, and finally settled on a third company that was able to bring more effective management to the Quality Heights project. This adaptability shows how the elements of the decentralized housing network were capable of solving problems on their own. They had the flexibility, the partners, and the resources to attack problems without the need to apply for the federal bailout common to struggling large public housing projects (see, by way of comparison, HOPE VI) (Biles 2000, 265).[17]

Along the same lines, the case studies demonstrate how each development team in each project was able to incorporate the remnants of old housing programs and parts of existing social service programs into its own new programs. Bethel New Life, for example, combined many different subsidized lending programs with a Cook County program that sold tax delinquent properties to nonprofit sponsors. Another example was the West Alabama CDC, which got its start as a community action agency in the War on Poverty. The War on Poverty bequeathed an important legacy to the decentralized housing network of hundreds of organizations that became housing developers in the 1980s. Even more important, however, were the many thousands of trained and committed people like Bill Edwards, who got their start in the antipoverty programs of the 1960s, and, in a later era, became the human capital of the decentralized housing network.

The National Equity Fund Sample, 1994–96

A nationwide sample of 172 projects built between 1994 and 1996 confirmed many of the themes from the Maxwell Award winners. All these projects were funded in part by tax equity investments that were coordinated by the National Equity Fund (NEF), an affiliate of LISC. NEF was an early participant in the low-income housing tax credit program as a tax credit syndicator. In this role, the fund pooled tax credits from multiple projects and sold a share of the pool to corporate investors. Investors then received a portion of the tax credits and other tax benefits for buying a share.

NEF staff prepared a report for each project in the pool so that investors could assess the risk of participation. Each report contained detailed information about the housing project, its development team, and its financing. This sample is a good geographical cross-section, but its usefulness is somewhat limited because it includes few for-profit developers. In many cases, however, nonprofits teamed up with for-profit developers and finance consultants. And in all cases, the other parts of the network—state and local government, banks, and consultants—were the same for both nonprofit and for-profit sponsors.

The projects in the NEF sample resemble the Maxwell Award winners in their remarkable variety: how they were built, who built them, and whom they served. There are large projects (a few over 300 apartments) and small ones (fewer than 15 apartments). Projects are located in inner cities, suburbs, and rural areas. Some projects rehabilitated older historic structures, while others were new, with strikingly modern architectural elements. The sponsors and management teams also differ widely from project to project in the sample, and the projects themselves demonstrate notable differences in their financing and ability to mix and match existing housing subsidy programs and incorporate extant fragments from prior programs, including housing authorities from the 1940s and community action agencies from the 1960s. In the quasi market created by tax credits and block grants, no two projects are alike.

Variety in the Types of Programs in the NEF Sample

Many of the nonprofit developers were former community action agencies from the mid-1960s. The NEF sample includes the South East Alabama Self Help Association (founded in 1967), Self-Help Enterprises in San Joaquin Valley, California (1965), Southern Maryland Tri-County Community Action Committee (1965), and the Anoka County Community Action Program in Minnesota (1965). Veterans of the civil rights movement and the War on Poverty formed Mississippi Action for Community Education, Inc., a group "active in the Delta for more than 25 years," according to the NEF investor profile.

At times, sponsors were literally remaking old housing programs by rehabilitating existing HUD-built projects from the 1960s and 1970s. The massive 80-acre development in Louisville, Kentucky, for example, replaced over a thousand HUD-built units. In St. Paul, Minnesota, the Neighborhood Development Alliance (a nonprofit founded with city encouragement in 1989) teamed up with two for-profit real estate developers to help reconfigure and rehabilitate two existing HUD buildings, in addition to building some new townhomes and a park. The $8.4 million 73-unit project added new laundry, storage, and community rooms to the existing HUD project. The sponsor also "upgraded electrical systems, thoroughly renovated bathrooms, and added new windows, doors, decks, and balconies throughout" (Bluff Park Homes NEF96).[18]

In addition to the blending of past programs, the decentralized approach incorporated concurrent housing and service programs. For example, one of the new HUD programs of the 1990s was the McKinney Shelter Plus Care Program that provided operational assistance to projects that housed formerly homeless residents. In the Ludlow Street apartments, the Connecticut Department of Mental Health and Addiction Services supplemented federal McKinney aid to help the project's sponsor provide substance abuse counseling and other services to its formerly homeless residents in Stamford (Ludow Street, a.k.a. Colony Apartments NEF95). And like the Peter Claver Community in San Francisco, all the projects that housed tenants with HIV/AIDS also drew on HUD operational subsidy programs, such as Housing Opportunities for People with AIDS.

In addition to blending federal programs, projects in the sample combined federal with state housing programs. Layering funding program on top of program was quite common among projects in the sample. Most projects had a minimum of four to six sources of financing, but consider the 124-unit Alliance Apartments in Minneapolis, Minnesota. The Central Community Housing Trust (a nonprofit founded in 1982) developed it and targeted it to individuals (and especially veterans) who suffered from substance abuse. Alliance Apartments had 13 separate sources of funds—a low-interest first mortgage from the Federal Home Loan Bank, HOME and CDBG funds from the city, three zero-interest loans from the Minnesota Housing Finance Agency, two subsidized loans from the Veterans Administration, two subsidized loans from a local foundation, one loan from HUD, and LIHTC equity.

But sponsors were doing more than simply assembling financing sources in new combinations; they also *created* new programs with their government and private-sector partners. In one case, a local public housing authority acted as its own bank, issuing tax-exempt bonds (Maple Knoll Apartments, Vancouver, Wash., NEF96). In another, the Rhode Island housing finance agency had a special program for lending to projects that required lead-based paint abatement. One of the most elaborate new programs involved the New York Equity Fund, LISC, the Enterprise Foundation, and the New York City Department of Housing Preservation and Development that provided a special fund for rehabilitating partially occupied buildings throughout the city.

The decentralized housing network in different communities tailored national programs—such as LIHTC and HOME—to meet local needs. Consider the following examples:

- *Rebuilding after the Los Angeles riots of 1992.* As early as two years after the riots in Los Angeles (and after the new federal funding programs for inner cities—enterprise zones—failed to provide funds for Los Angeles), there were new low-income projects in the heavily damaged Koreatown and Mid-Wilshire neighborhoods. One example of an NEF project contributing to the rebuilding of this area was the 69-unit Los Altos Apartments, a $10 million historic renovation and mixed-income project (CEF96).

- *Attracting manufacturing jobs by improving housing stock.* Less-expensive and high-quality housing was used as a strategy to make a community more attractive and draw new businesses back to town. This was the motivation for the $2.4 million, 24-unit Luverne Family Housing project in Luverne, Minnesota. "Developing affordable rental housing in Luverne is essential if the town is going to maintain, or even retain, its economic growth," according to NEF (a.k.a. Rock Creek Town Homes NEF96).

- *Revitalizing decayed downtowns.* Amid the diversity of projects aimed at rehabilitating downtown neighborhoods, two that stand out built living space for artists. In anticipation of Richard Florida's theory that economic growth requires a city to have a mixture of creative people (the idea of "creative capital"), the Downtown Little Rock Community Development Corporation (created in 1993 with assistance from LISC) sought to bring artists back to downtown Little Rock (Florida 2004). The 22-unit Kramer School Artists' Lofts was a $3.3 million renovation of an old elementary school (NEF95). Another nonprofit specialized in developments for low-income artists. The Minneapolis Arts Commission created Artspace Projects, Inc., in 1979 "to serve as an advocate for affordable living and studio space for artists in the wake of gentrification in Minneapolis' Warehouse District," according to NEF. This group built housing for artists across the country. Its affiliate, Artists and Cities of Pittsburgh, which was created in 1995 with financial support from the Pittsburgh Foundation and the Howard Heinz Endowment, built the Constantin Project for low-income artists in Pittsburgh in 1995 (NEF96).

- *Achieving mixed-income development.* A project for senior citizens in Tiburon, California, attempted to keep low-income seniors in a community, "where per capita income is the highest in the state and, and the ninth highest in the nation," according to the California Equity Fund, the NEF affiliate in California (Cecilia Place CEF95). And in a master-planned community near Seattle, a nonprofit sponsor built a 51-unit, $6.7 million project that was indistinguishable from the larger luxury development that enveloped it (Highland Gardens, Issaquah, Wash. NEF96).

The flexibility of the decentralized housing programs allowed for a hundred schools of thought to contend. The program helped rebuild inner cities, reduced concentration of poverty by mixing low-income tenants with middle- and upper-income tenants, breathed new life into old HUD projects, and allowed communities to try to make their downtowns more "cool."[19] The decentralized program showed how it could be all things to all people, which helps explain why so many members of Congress—across the political spectrum, from large and small cities—found it an easy program to defend and promote.

Variety of Home Types

The variety of product type (that is, the types of buildings constructed) is also remarkable when compared with previous programs. For example, in any downtown in the country, the trained observer will be able to spot many apartment buildings constructed under the HUD 202 program for senior citizen apartments—a design that looked like something Stalin's architect had dreamed up. Under the decentralized program, no two projects look alike. In the NEF sample, they range in size from 12 to 350 units. Some were new construction, and others were rehabilitated existing structures. Some of the rehabilitated structures were historic properties that brought back architectural gems like old factories, schools, Victorian mansions, and abandoned car dealerships to a neighborhood. At times the program was used to build small, scattered-site, and infill projects. And sometimes the program gutted, cleared, and rebuilt areas the size of small cities.

The $5.3 million, 40-unit Sarah Allen Phase IV project was an example of an infill project in west Philadelphia. The sponsor built new duplexes in addition to rehabilitating several row houses and an old mansion on four separate sites (NEF95). At the other extreme were large projects coordinated by multiple sponsors or, as in the case with the Thompson-Walnut Housing Initiative project in Philadelphia, a single project that was part of a larger, coordinated effort to revitalize an entire neighborhood. The long-neglected Thompson and Walnut neighborhoods underwent considerable renovation and were the site of several NEF-financed developments, according to NEF (NEF95).

Many of these projects were expensive on a per unit basis. In high-cost areas such as California, New York, and Massachusetts, a project could have a total development cost as high as $207,000 per unit (Brooklyn). In other areas, the cost could be as little at $42,000 per unit (Gary, Indiana). In all cases, however, projects had to have many amenities to avoid being stigmatized as a "project." The $4.6 million Rumrill Place in San Pablo, California, was typical:

> The project's four two- and three-story buildings surround an interior courtyard with a lawn, benches, a community garden, and a play area with swings and a jungle gym for residents' children. Tenants have access to off-street parking, a community room with a kitchen and laundry facilities, and a basketball and volleyball court. The entire site is fully landscaped, and is protected by a perimeter fence with a security gate and intercom system. (CEF95)

The philosophy behind the decentralized housing network was entirely different from that of previous affordable housing programs. Before, amenities were kept sparse to discourage people from wanting to live in a government-subsidized project. In the later era, the projects were stocked with more amenities than comparable market-rate projects in a moderately successful effort to win approval for the project from the community (a way to defuse the not-in-my-backyard phenomenon).

In terms of what product type was built, the decentralized housing network had a sense-and-respond capability reminiscent of developers in the marketplace. San Jose, California, for example, had a shortage of large family projects downtown. This area was primarily Latino and had larger-than-average families. In response, one sponsor—the Ecumenical Association for Housing—responded by building bigger apartments with more bedrooms. In areas where land was inexpensive and construction costs low (Detroit, Cleveland), developers built single-family homes. In opposite circumstances (New York, San Francisco), there was more renovation of existing structures to keep costs low.

Variety of Clientele

Most projects were built with specific tenants in mind, targeting certain neighborhoods, ethnic and language groups, or tenants who needed specific social services—health care, psychological or substance abuse counseling, or special care for residents living with HIV/AIDS. An outstanding example of innovation on behalf of tenants was the Grand Families House in Boston. This $4.1 million project was specifically targeted to grandparents who were raising their grandchildren. The project had services aimed at youth: preschool activities, tutoring, day care, and other services. And it had amenities and services aimed at seniors: handicapped-accessible bathrooms, on-site medical checkups, and van service for doctor visits (NEF96).

Many projects in the sample tried to serve the homeless population in new and innovative ways. In Hartford, for instance, a project for homeless women and their children run by a nonprofit (My Sister's Place, Inc.) specialized in helping women transition out of homelessness. A project in Minneapolis specialized in helping "chronic inebriates," especially Native Americans. The project's sponsor, the American Indian Housing Corporation, was founded in 1992 "after the American Indian Task Force on Housing and Homelessness determined the needs of homeless Native Americans were not adequately addressed by existing organizations for the homeless" (Anishinabe Wakiagun MN NEF95). There were also dozens of projects for formerly homeless tenants that offered health, substance abuse, and psychological services along with meals, transportation, and job training.

The decentralized housing network played a small part in the move to relocate individuals with mental disorders from larger institutions to smaller community homes. Many sponsors of these types of projects had a history similar to that of Rubicon Programs, Inc., in Contra Costa County, California. Rubicon, founded as a service provider for the mentally ill, branched out into service-enriched housing in the late 1980s. The service-oriented projects had more participants than the typical project. The Fairfield Avenue project in Bridgeport, Connecticut, for example, involved the Central Connecticut Coast YMCA, the Corporation for Supportive Housing (a large nationwide nonprofit dedicated to supportive housing), and six state agencies. The project had "a consortium of local service providers to offer case management for each tenant. Services include alcohol and substance abuse counseling, medication assistance, money management, employment and education referral, transportation, and free YMCA gym membership" (NEF96).

Many sponsors cater to ethnic minority communities. Some were an outgrowth of locally based community action agencies in ghetto neighborhoods. Others were more focused on a language group like Spanish or Chinese and had a wider geographical spread. Chinatown Service Center, for example, was a nonprofit founded in Los Angeles in 1975 to serve "immigrants, refugees, and others who needed help in adjusting to

American life." It provided many of its services in multiple Asian languages. The Hispanic Housing and Education Corporation, established in 1991, developed housing and provided programs for Hispanic communities in Texas. The group used its developments as bases to provide job training, after-school tutoring, GED and ESL classes, recreation programs, and health services both for project tenants and residents of the surrounding neighborhoods," according to NEF. The Seattle-based Interim Community Development Association was founded in 1979 "to preserve and strengthen Asian and Pacific communities through neighborhood planning and advocacy and through the development of decent affordable housing." A community development corporation catering to Hassidic Jewish families built the Kiryas Joel Gardens and Heights project north of New York City (NEF96).

The decentralized network responded swiftly and creatively to the AIDS epidemic. Each project combined building-subsidy programs (tax credits and block grants) with support for operations and for services through programs like HUD's Housing Opportunities for People with AIDS. Many also sought to address the special needs of subpopulations suffering from this disease. The Hogar de Esperanza project in Philadelphia, for example, provided 20 units of affordable housing, in which all units are handicapped accessible, and offer residents "a comprehensive range of medical, social, and psychological services, in a bilingual setting" (NEF96). The project was built and operated by Asociación de Puertorriqueños en Marcha, a nonprofit social service provider and housing developer founded in 1970 to make comprehensive assistance and advocacy available for Latino newcomers to Philadelphia.

Variety of Sponsors

Many of the sponsors in the sample had undergone dramatic changes in the previous 10 years. More than 70 percent were either newly created, had shifted their emphasis from service delivery to building housing, or had merged with another organization within the previous 15 years. The dynamism of this sector tracked or mimicked the for-profit corporate mergers and acquisitions in the 1980s. These evolutionary changes suggest that community development corporations are capable of adapting to maintain effectiveness and are not ossifying tools of patronage.

Sponsors combined with other participants to create development teams. They also pooled resources in a neighborhood—several small nonprofits sponsored by churches, for example, joined to create a larger and more effective nonprofit for a larger community. Sometimes nonprofits would partner with for-profit developers to get the right combination of expertise. The Neighborhood in Partnership in Toledo, for example, was a merger of three Toledo community organizations. The new nonprofit teamed with a for-profit real estate developer, Vistula Development Group, to build the Museum Place project, a $7.3 million, 65-unit project (NEF95).

Church and Religious Groups. Scores of sponsors trace their founding to church and religious groups and have relied on their assistance. All Saints Episcopal Church in Pasadena, for example, founded a nonprofit to provide services and build housing in 1973. Five neighborhood churches in Chicago created the Resurrection Project, a nonprofit developer. The Resurrection Project, in turn, merged with another religion-associated nonprofit, Interfaith Community Organization, in 1995. The combined organization "works to restore resident confidence, improve and expand the area's affordable housing stock, increase home ownership opportunities, and safeguard the neighborhood from the speculative real estate market," according to NEF (Casa Guerrero NEF95).

Foundations. In addition to churches, many sponsors received material and technical support from foundations. The Technical Assistance Corporation for Housing in Chicago was created through a grant from the Ford Foundation in 1970 (Willard Square Apartments, Chicago NEF95). The Robert Wood Johnson Foundation made grants to sponsors such as the Asociación de Puertorriqueños en Marcha, to provide services through its five-year Grant Program on Chronic Mental Illness (Fourth Street ACCESS, Philadelphia NEF96).

Neighborhood-Specific Organizations. Many sponsors were created to help rehabilitate a particular neighborhood or area of a city. The most common example is the nonprofit charged specifically to rebuild and rehabilitate the downtown area of older cities. At times, these nonprofits were created from the top down—by a city trying to implement its vision for renewal or by a coalition of community leaders and businesses to try to arrest the decline of certain areas. In Richmond,

Virginia, for example, the Richmond Better Housing Coalition was established in 1988 by "public agencies, lending institutions, the business community, and grassroots neighborhood leadership," according to the NEF investor report.

Community Action Groups. Some neighborhood nonprofits were more clearly an outgrowth of community action and empowerment—in other words, created from the bottom up. For example, the inner-city Detroit-based Core City Neighborhoods, Inc., according to NEF,

> was founded in 1984 by four women who were determined to reverse the crime, poverty, unemployment, and housing deterioration that characterized their neighborhood. Since its founding, the group has renovated three multifamily developments, including a building that serves as transitional housing for battered women and their children.

NEF sold tax credits for the Core City Neighborhoods' new $10.3 million project that provided 120 units of high-quality housing on Detroit's southwest side: each amenity-rich unit was individually metered for electricity and gas and had a dishwasher, a frost-free refrigerator, central air conditioning, a washer and dryer, intrusion alarms, and a hook-up for cable TV (Alberta W. King Village Apartments NEF96).

Resident and Neighborhood Institutions. Similarly, the residents of the Cambria Apartments in Los Angeles created their own nonprofit corporation to buy their decrepit building. The group staged a rent strike, filed complaints with regulatory agencies for code violations, and bought the building from their landlord. The nonprofit, Communidad Cambria, based in Los Angeles, "hired security guards, began to oust squatters, made emergency repairs, and hired a responsible property management company." Their goal "was to preserve the Cambria Apartments for current and future low-income residents and to improve the socio-economic character of the surrounding neighborhood." They also hoped "to empower tenants of other buildings that are in similar conditions" (CEF95).

Often, too, older groups merged to create a more effective neighborhood-based institution to act as an agent for renewal. The Martindale-Brightwood Community Development Corporation in Indianapolis, for example, was the product of a merger of four neighborhood organizations. A national capacity-building program, the National Community Development Initiative, sponsored that project.

Several projects in the Bronx exemplified how communities could take control over their economic future. The list of the names of community development corporations working in the Bronx tells the story of locally based—even guerrilla—activism that helped turn that symbol of urban decay into a symbol of renewal: Mid Bronx Desperadoes, founded in 1974; Bronx Shepherds Restoration Project, founded in 1980; and Banana Kelly Community Improvement Association, organized in 1977 with the motto "Don't Move. Improve." A 1992 *Washington Post* article described the CDCs in the Bronx as a "postmodern miracle."[20]

The Urban Land Institute Sample, Mid-2000s

The Urban Land Institute is a nonprofit organization dedicated to promoting new approaches and best practices for the real estate industry. Its case studies serve as an instructive tool for its members. Since the mid-1980s, ULI has produced case studies of multifamily real estate developments, with a separate category for affordable multifamily developments. The following is a summary of four cases from the mid-2000s.[21]

Case Study 6: Montecito Vista

Montecito Vista is a 162-unit garden-style apartment complex in Irvine, a wealthy suburb 30 miles south of Los Angeles.[22] The Irvine Company, which created the master-planned city, is the major landowner and real estate developer in the city and is the entity that leased the seven-acre site to the sponsor. The project won an award from the National Association of Home Builders in 2004 as a model of "workforce" housing, that is, housing for the relatively low-paid professionals (nurses, teachers, and firefighters) who cannot afford the country's increasingly expensive real estate.

Irvine, along with the surrounding cities in Orange County, was once a bedroom community for Los Angeles. Today, this area is a job center in its own right. According to the ULI case study, the city and county have a ratio of 3.4 jobs for every residential unit. Finding affordable housing in the county can be a challenge. The California Association of

Realtors estimates that only 10 percent of Orange County households could afford to purchase the median-priced home. With such a mismatch of jobs to affordable housing, "thousands of residents of other communities commute into Irvine to work every day," according to the ULI report.

The project has relatively large two- and three-bedroom apartments. The apartment complex is in an amenity-rich environment—close to good schools and universities, job centers, parks, and shopping. The high-quality project, with its stucco exterior and tile roofs, blends in with neighboring luxury condominium and townhome projects. The project is built to high construction standards and is designed to withstand earthquakes with added plywood shear walls. Nearly a third of the apartments are built to the standards of the Americans with Disabilities Act.

The Sponsor

Jamboree Housing Corporation was founded in 1990 "to expand housing opportunities for low-income families and seniors."[23] In Jamboree's 2008 "Impact Report," the nonprofit corporation's president, Laura Archuleta, wrote: "More than 15,000 Californians in 46 communities call one of our properties home." She went on to praise the many effective relationships her organization has created in the public and private sectors, noting that

> Jamboree's incredible success is built on numerous partnerships. The work of community members; city, county and state staff; elected officials; lenders and investors; and our joint venture partners translates to thousands of affordable homes for families and seniors and countless hours of impactful resident services.

Services are also an important part of Jamboree's mission to help residents maintain their self-sufficiency. These services include computer learning centers with Internet access, after-school tutoring, budgeting and parenting skills classes, home-buying seminars, and referrals to local service agencies. Senior citizens also receive help with transportation and assistance with daily living activities, according to Archuleta (http://www.jamboreehousing.com/housingheart.html).

Who Was Served?

All the apartments are restricted by an agreement with the developer to low-income tenants who earn either less than 30 or 50 percent of the area median income. In other words, prospective tenants of Montecito must demonstrate that their income qualifies them for either an apartment reserved for those who earn less than 50 percent of the area median income, or one of the apartments that are even more discounted and available to tenants who earn less than 30 percent of area median income. As of 2007, the median gross rent in Irvine was nearly $1,272, and apartments at Montecito rented for $461 to $1,190.

Financing

After being sued in the 1970s for not building its fair share of affordable housing, the city of Irvine set a goal of having 10 percent of new residential development affordable to those who earn 80 percent or less of the area median income. The upshot is that both the city and Irvine Company have been highly motivated to find ways to increase affordable housing in the city. In this project, the city provided significant subsides with its HOME and CDBG funds. The Irvine Company provided the land through a long-term lease, purchased the tax credits, and provided a $250,000 predevelopment loan.

The project used tax-exempt bonds issued by the county for both its construction phase and its permanent financing. These bonds come with an automatic award of 4 percent LIHTC (table 4.6).

Table 4.6. Funding for Montecito Vista

Source	Amount ($)	Percentage of costs
Debt		
Tax-exempt bonds (county of Orange issued, placed by U.S. Bank)≈	10,000,000	46
City of Irvine (CDBG)	900,000	4
Orange County (HOME)	3,000,000	13.5
Equity		
Irvine Company (purchase of LIHTC)	8,000,000	36.5
Total	21,900,000	100
Total per unit	135,185	

Source: ULI Case Study.

Case Study 7: Sara Conner Court

What was once an abandoned infill site with contaminated soil along a busy street is now a beautiful environmentally friendly building and home to 57 low-income families.[24] Sara Conner Court, which is named after a long-standing low-income housing activist in the community, received a number of environmental awards for its successful remediation of a contaminated site and the use of "green building" elements that lessen the project's use of gas, electricity, and water. The dry cleaner formerly on the site left a significant residue of dangerous chemicals that required $650,000 in soil removal and other environmental remediation.[25] The project is now certified under a San Francisco Bay Area green building rating system known as GreenPoint.[26]

The site, about 30 miles southeast of San Francisco, is on a busy street once home to many small businesses. It was a difficult location to develop. "Developers are increasingly being asked to do infill projects on smaller sites, and Sara Conner Court is a model of how it can be done," said Linda Mandolini, Eden Housing's executive director (Kimura 2007).

An updated interpretation of the Craftsman style, the project comprises four buildings that create an interior courtyard with attractive landscaping, picnic and grill area, and a children's playground. The apartments are one- to three-bedroom units and range in size from 552 to 1,328 square feet. The project has a community room and a computer lab.

The financing for this project was complicated. It required close cooperation between the sponsor and the city of Hayward, Alameda County, state of California, Enterprise, Silicon Valley Bank, the California Community Reinvestment Corporation, and the tax credit investors (Enterprise Community Investment, Inc., and Bank of America).

The Sponsor

"Eden Housing was founded in May of 1968 by six community activists who were greatly concerned about the lack of non-discriminatory, affordable housing in Alameda County," according to Eden's web site. These pioneers, who first worked out of makeshift "offices" such as local coffee shops, took on their first affordable housing project with the rehabilitation of six older homes for first time homebuyers in Oakland. Since 1968, Eden has produced over 5,000 units of affordable housing and started two affiliates to provide management and tenant services.[27]

Who Was Served?

Rents were restricted to low-income tenants who earned either earned less and 30 or 60 percent of Alameda's median income. Rents were 20–60 percent below prevailing market rents (Kimura 2008).

Nearly half the tenants of the project are children. In addition to after-school and neighborhood watch programs, Eden contracts with outside service providers to bring financial literacy and home-buying classes onsite.

Financing

A close relationship between the sponsor and the city allowed Eden to move quickly with a site acquisition loan and to get the necessary zoning and planning approvals to start renovating the site. That work hit a significant obstacle, however, once the environmental report identified the need to remove the hazardous chemicals in the soil.

The bulk of the project's financing came from two loans from the city (30 percent of total) and proceeds from selling the tax credits (55 percent) (table 4.7). The 55-year city loans are paid out of residual receipts—the amount of cash flow the project generates after it has paid its first

Table 4.7. Funding for Sara Conner Court

Source	Amount ($)	Percentage of costs
Debt		
California Community Reinvestment Corporation	2,565,000	12
City of Hayward (HOME and CDBG)	4,786,273	23
City of Hayward Redevelopment Agency	1,858,038	9
Equity		
Enterprise Social Investment Corporation (sold to Bank of America)	11,478,000	55
Enterprise Foundation's Green Communities grant	50,000	0.2
Home Depot Foundation grant	25,000	0.1
Total	20,762,311	100
Total per unit	364,251	

Source: ULI Case Study.

mortgage and other operating expenses. A permanent loan from the California Community Reinvestment Corporation (a bank consortium sponsored by most California retail banks), sized to what the project could pay in debt service with its reduced rents, accounted for 12 percent of the total.

In the end, the project was expensive but largely because it was trying to accomplish much more than housing. It was revitalizing an area of a busy thoroughfare, which required a number of upgrades along the street front (sidewalks, landscaping, and a design that helped bridge the busy street to the lower-rise single-family homes behind the project). It also was trying to achieve long-term savings for the project and its tenants through its many environmentally sensitive elements (e.g., EnergyStar appliances, low-flow toilets, better insulated heating ducts, and other design innovations). Finally, removing the contaminated soil was costly.

Case Study 8: Solara Apartments

An aerial photo of this apartment complex tells a compelling story—all the roofs of the apartments and carports are topped with 170 shiny photovoltaic panels that provide all the electrical power to the 56 homes in this development.[28]

This project, located in a suburb 20 miles inland from San Diego, actually exports energy to the power grid; the residents have no electrical bills. The project was recognized by the state of California as the first project in its Zero Energy New Home program.

The complex consists of six two-story buildings built around the perimeter of the site, with a courtyard in the center. The project has a community center and space for public art onsite. The landscaping features native California plants, which require little watering and are drought resistant. A Meyer lemon tree grove provides fruit to the residents, and rosemary and sage plants provide cooking spices. A park is directly next to the project.

Solara is another example of infill development. Located on a busy commercial street abutting a large shopping center, the 2.5 acre site is within Poway's Redevelopment Project Area, a physically and economically distressed part of the city. Because the site had only a few abandoned structures and one attorney's office, the city was able to assemble the different parcels without the use of eminent domain. The city provided the site to the sponsor with a 99-year ground lease.

When local residents opposed the project at first, the sponsor worked with Housing Solutions, a public-private partnership that attempts to build support for affordable housing in the generally affluent city. The sponsor held multiple meetings with residents to respond to concerns and show architectural renderings.

The Sponsor

The sponsor, Community HousingWorks (CHW), coordinated all the early planning efforts with an interdepartmental planning team from the city of Poway. This approach facilitated many of the planning review and regulatory concessions that later made the project a success. The sponsor also brought in an outside expert on "green building," Global Green USA.

CHW has been building affordable housing for 25 years with 1,500 apartments in its portfolio. It has built four apartment complexes in Poway, which helps explain why CHW had such a positive working relationship with the city.

Who Was Served?

Rents were restricted to tenants who earn less than 30 and 60 percent of the area median income and range from $388 for a one-bedroom to $1,075 for a three-bedroom apartment.

CHW offers a number of outreach programs from its community room, including financial literacy, leadership training, home purchasing, and ownership counseling. As part of the lease, tenants are asked to live up to the environmentally friendly ethos of the project. To support this goal, CHW developed a program for Solara called 360 Green Curriculum. It has been so well received at Solara that the sponsor is beginning to offer it at all its apartment complexes.

Financing

The main source of financing for Solara (over $11 million) comes from the sale of low-income housing tax credits by the National Equity Fund (table 4.8). The project also received additional financing in exchange

Table 4.8. Funding for the Solara Apartments

Source	Amount ($)	Percentage of costs
Debt		
Union Bank of California	2,369,500	15
City of Poway Redevelopment Agency	775,000	5
County of San Diego (HOME)	1,000,000	6
Equity		
California Energy Commission, energy rebate	409,000	3
LIHTC (sold by NEF)	11,266,278	70
Investment tax credits (NEF)	208,011	1
Total	16,027,789	100
Total per unit	286,211	

Source: ULI Case Study.

for incorporating green building elements, which added nearly $400,000 in LIHTC to the project. In addition, the cost of installing the solar panels was offset by grants from the California Energy Commission and federal investment tax credits, which totaled over $600,000 in additional financing. Last, Union Bank gave additional support to cover costs of the solar panels by extending the amortization period of the first mortgage from 30 to 40 years. In all, these added resources effectively covered the $1.1 million cost of the solar panel system. Other funding came from familiar sources, including two residual receipts mortgages, one from the city and one from the county's HOME funds.

Case Study 9: Plaza Apartments

The nine-story Plaza Apartments provides 106 studio apartments to tenants who were formerly homeless in a busy, albeit struggling, section of San Francisco, close to city hall.[29] The project is a service-rich environment, with five case managers, a psychiatrist, and a physician's assistant all working onsite. The project has a large community room with a kitchen and a food bank. Each apartment is furnished with a dresser, bed, telephone, nightstand, kitchenette, and private bathroom.

The project has 2,000 square feet of retail space in addition to a 99-seat auditorium. It replaces a much smaller substandard single-room occupancy hotel. The new project contributes dramatically to the revitalization of a neglected area of San Francisco. Most of the neighboring properties are also SRO hotels, but in recent years the city has also tried to lure market-rate housing, and new restaurants and businesses to the area.

As with other ULI award winners, this project has a number of green building elements, including

- photovoltaic panels on the roof
- nontoxic paints, cabinet treatment, and flooring
- an overall silver rating under the LEED (Leadership in Energy and Environmental Design) Green Building guidelines

The Plaza, in the words of the ULI case study, was "a working laboratory" for the city on green building issues. These apartments "provided a platform for the SFRA [the San Francisco Redevelopment Agency] to see how difficult its requirements were from the developer's perspective." These insights inspired changes in the agency's green building program going forward. In an interesting example of how these insights could also help national programs, the sponsor also shared its findings with the Enterprise Green Communities Program. The sponsor requested that Enterprise "create a green maintenance manual, for building management, and a green homeowner's manual for each resident. Afterward, Enterprise stripped down these documents to a boilerplate and made them available for everyone to use on its web site," according to the ULI case study.

The Sponsor

The Plaza is the first project built by the Public Initiatives Development Corporation, a nonprofit subsidiary of the San Francisco Redevelopment Agency. According to the ULI case study, the corporation was created to "undertake projects that other developers are unable or unwilling to complete." Many municipalities have sponsored a 501(c)(3) nonprofit corporation to carry out the affordable housing needs of the city, but this development corporation was created relatively recently, in 2001.

Who Was Served?

This project offered an opportunity to combine services that target chronically homeless people, who are often the most difficult to house. The program aims to provide a stable home environment for a subpopulation that creates a tremendous drain on city resources because these individuals are high users of municipal services, including the jail, ambulance transportation, and the city-run San Francisco General Hospital. To be considered "chronically homeless," a tenant must have two of the following diagnoses: physical disability, mental disability, and a substance abuse problem.

"The first year the Plaza was open there was a holiday party and I remember looking around the room at the staff, volunteers, and residents that were busy putting out food, assembling the chairs—all seeming a bit hesitant to mingle at first. But then someone brought out the karaoke machine and the party started hopping," said Michele Mozelsio, an onsite physician's assistant. "People were laughing and cheering each other on. I remember thinking, this is more than an apartment building, it's a community. I think for most folks here, it's the first time they can feel like they're a part of something like that."[30]

Tenants pay 50 percent of their monthly income toward rent. The Department of Public Health pays the difference between the tenant's contribution and the actual rent. According to the ULI report, "The average tenant-paid rent is $410 and the average Department of Public Health subsidy is $341 per month."

Financing

The financing for this project is relatively simple. It is largely funded through sources available to the San Francisco Redevelopment Agency, which include CDBG and HOME funds (see table 4.9). The only other

Table 4.9. Funding for the Plaza Apartments

Source	Amount ($)	Percentage of costs
Debt		
San Francisco Redevelopment Agency	11,200,000	49.5
Equity		
LIHTC	11,400,000	50.4
Department of Public Health	15,896	0.1
Total	22,615,896	100
Total per unit	213,358	

Source: ULI Case Study.

major source comes from the proceeds of selling LIHTC to corporate investors.

Themes from the Recent Period

Many aspects of the recent period are immediately familiar: funding sources like CDBG, HOME, and LIHTC, for example, and collaboration among all levels of government and private and nonprofit firms. Similarly, the tenants tend to be the working poor, who make below 60, 50, or 30 percent of the area median income (except for tenants of the Plaza).

What also continues to be true is that these projects are more than just housing—they promote a number of other community goals:

- workforce housing for lower-paid skilled workers in high-cost areas
- examples of and inspiration for what can be achieved in environmentally friendly construction
- promotion of the social welfare objectives of a community struggling with a chronic homeless population

In fact, we see the old decentralized housing network solving a host of new problems, from how to build in infill areas of built-out communities to providing local communities with important amenities such as theater space.

Another familiar theme is that communities almost universally oppose the construction of affordable housing in their neighborhoods. Each case study has examples of how neighbors had to be won over. A tried and true strategy is to build beautiful buildings that enhance the area and possibly improve local property values. The photo gallery on the web site of the Tax Credit Coalition conveys a sense of the impressive diversity of the high-quality and beautiful apartment buildings being built today by the decentralized housing network (http://gallery.taxcreditcoalition.org).

Conclusion

The case studies demonstrate a wide variety of building types and populations served. Each project is unique. And yet the stability and consistency of this approach to building affordable housing are also striking. Unlike the story of how affordable housing fared in chapter 1, where every few years—every new administration—thinking and policy shifted dramatically. Since the late 1980s, the funding programs for the decentralized housing network (CDBG, HOME, and LIHTC) have been remarkably stable and predictable. Chapter 5 shows how these funding mechanisms, and the institution building that happened at the state and local levels, created the building blocks for a durable response to the affordable housing problem.

5

The Decentralized Housing Network and the Rise of a New Institution

Charles Jencks, in *The Language of Post-Modern Architecture*, dates the end of modernism precisely: 3:32 p.m. on July 15, 1972. That was the date and time when the federal government dynamited the Pruitt-Igoe low-income housing development in St. Louis. By the late 1960s Pruitt-Igoe, an award-winning modernist complex of high-rise apartment buildings, had become dangerous and uninhabitable for its low-income tenants (Harvey 2000, 39). Its demise, however, marked something more—a loss of faith in the modernist ideal that government bureaucracies were capable of solving social problems.

Thanks in part to decentralized funding mechanisms like tax credits and block grants, a new network for housing policy development and implementation had begun to grow in the 1970s and 1980s. In the 1980s, it seemed that Ronald Reagan's winning political coalition would stunt or kill the inchoate network by reducing or eliminating federal funds. Yet something unexpected happened. The federal cuts that threatened to choke off the decentralized housing network did the opposite: they spurred it on.

Response of Local Networks to Changing Policy Climate

In many respects, the decentralized housing network was a synthesis of the two prior eras of housing policy. In the 1960s and early 1970s, it

Figure 5.1. Pruitt-Igoe Demolition, 1972

appeared that Washington-based and bureaucracy-led efforts might solve the housing crisis. When this approach developed problems and lost political support, a subsequent policy regime led by President Reagan preached government retreat and the value of market-led efforts to solve the housing problem. An unforeseen response to this policy regime was the burgeoning efforts of nonprofits and housing activists, local government, and elements of the local private sector to build affordable housing without federal help.

It was in the third policy era (after 1986) that a *synthesis* emerged from the federal bureaucracy-led thesis and the market-led antithesis. In the third era, housing advocates and policymakers used federal resources to create a quasi market by providing tax incentives and block grants to promote low-income housing production. The local network responded to this inflow of new resources with vigor. It was market-like in that it had multiple actors responding to market signals (e.g., price of land and construction, tenants' ability to pay, and mortgage interest rates). But it was largely federally funded and represented an expansion of government policy and influence, too; the network became a hybrid governance structure that forged together federal and subnational government, housing activists, and the private sector into a new alliance.

Success made the program politically popular for both liberals and conservatives. Unlike narrowly defined programs, this new structure gave rise to a vibrant, adaptive institution for delivering affordable housing. The political debates over the decentralized approach to housing were much different from those of prior eras, when conservatives opposed federal government programs and liberals promoted them. In this third era, agreement between liberals and conservatives was more characteristic, at least in regard to housing. Part of this accord resulted from political necessity, playing "the hand that was dealt you," as Democratic Congressman Charles Rangel, obliged to work with a Republican administration, saw it. In later years, however, even ardent housing activists came to embrace the decentralized approach.

A Broadly Attractive Approach

The ecumenical ideology behind the new approach contributed to its political success, drawing adherents from across the political spectrum. The LIHTC program, for example, could be simultaneously billed as tax relief for conservatives, as an efficiency measure for moderates, and as empowerment of local activists with federal resources for liberals. It appeared to be "above the left-right debate," as Jack Kemp observed (U.S. Congress 1989).

Supporters also came from across the nation. Each state received an allocation of tax credits based on its population, in sharp contrast with the 1970s, when HUD funding declined and President Ford's HUD secretary, Carla Hills, concentrated increasingly scarce resources on cities with the worst housing conditions. As a result, more funds flowed to cities like Buffalo, Detroit, and Philadelphia, while money was taken away from western and southern cities (Bauman 2000). This shift did not win many political friends for housing from these faster-growing and increasingly politically powerful areas of the country.

The political coalition behind the new programs was broad, well organized, and effective. HUD, by contrast, was a massive federal bureaucracy whose biggest constituency was low-income tenants. Bureaucrats and the poor rarely make a winning lobbying team. The decentralized network, however, had many friends in both the public and the private sector. In the past, a few service providers would typically testify along with federal bureaucracies to protect funding and programs. What changed was that a whole social service complex—many more participants from all sectors of society and the economy—now had a stake in defending poverty programs. This new network drew strength from churches, union halls, local banks, community action agencies, city halls, state capitols, and Wall Street offices.

The political resilience of the decentralized programs grew, as budget and policy battles once fought in Washington, D.C., came to be fought at the local level. In the competition for political gain, communities across the country hammered out local compromises on policy and resource allocation. In communities where activists were strongly organized, they lobbied for housing for the very poor and those with special needs. In places where the business community was more organized, it pushed for more downtown redevelopment and shallow rent subsidies that went mostly to lower-middle-class tenants. The coalition that was strongest at the local level—nonprofits and housing activists in San Francisco or business leaders and downtown real estate interests in Richmond, Virginia, for example—used the programs to advance its interests. As a result, the local programs were popular—almost by definition— because they served the most organized and vocal interests of every community.

A Movement Matures into an Industry

In a remarkably short time, what started as a small-scale movement in the 1980s matured into a well-oiled industry. By the mid-2000s, the decentralized housing network had clearly achieved a great deal. One measure was the substantial number of high-quality affordable housing units the network had built. The exact number is hard to measure because there is no official count, and each funding source (HOME block grants, Community Development Block Grants, and LIHTC) claims credit for the same apartment even though each program provided only a portion of the financing. If we consider only the apartments funded under the LIHTC program, however, a survey by the National Council of State Housing Agencies estimated that there were more than 2 million affordable homes built with LIHTC from 1987 to 2006 (National Council of State Housing Finance Agencies 2008). "The Housing Credit induces about $6 billion of private investment each year to produce more than

115,000 apartments with rents affordable to low-income families," according to the council's web site. By way of comparison, as of 1999, only 2.75 million HUD-funded and public housing units had been built since the beginning of government affordable housing programs in 1937 (Bipartisan Millennial Housing Commission 2002, 95).[1] As part of the Community Renewal Tax Relief Act of 2000, Congress raised the cap on LIHTC 40 percent, and future allocations were to be indexed to inflation. HOME funds have also been an effective tool for building housing.[2] HUD estimated that by 2000 the HOME program had financed nearly 400,000 affordable housing units since its start in 1992, although it is hard to know how many of these apartments are also counted in the LIHTC totals.[3]

As the LIHTC, CDBG, and HOME budget numbers indicate, the federal government was putting important new resources into the decentralized housing network. It was also trying to play the role of catalyst in other ways. In a 1995 HUD report, *A Place to Live Is the Place to Start,* Bill Clinton wrote that in the past, "the proliferation of programs, complex regulations, and cumbersome bureaucratic procedures too often have stymied local innovation and limited the ability of communities to solve their own problems" (HUD 1995). Efforts to reinvent HUD, along with other federal efforts, could still play a positive role in struggling communities, however. Clinton argued that "economically distressed communities across our nation still need federal help to ensure that all Americans can find decent, affordable housing in safe, clean neighborhoods." A 1997 HUD report made this point explicit: "HUD is changing its role in communities to ensure that localities have the tools and resources they need to address these challenges—not with federal mandates or a one-size-fits-all formula, but with action plans written by local officials and tailored to local conditions" (HUD 1997, 19).

Strengthening CDCs

New federal resources and a more flexible HUD helped spark an increase in the capacity of community development corporations to produce housing. A survey by the National Congress for Community Economic Development estimated that by 2005 the total number of CDC-built affordable rental units was 848,000 (NCCED 1999). Thousands of new housing-related CDCs came into existence during the 1980s and 1990s. In 1969, for example, there were 112 CDCs building affordable housing. In 2005, there were over 4,600 CDCs. Almost all these CDCs received some federal funding, and most received the majority of their financial support from three federal programs: LIHTC, HOME, and CDBG (NCCED 1997).

The most ambitious effort to improve CDC capacity was the National Community Development Initiative, a 10-year, $250 million effort funded by a coalition of foundations, corporations, and government (Walker and Weinheimer 1998).[4] According to its 1999 report, future progress of the CDCs would require significantly more capital as well as "a long-term effort to strengthen these organizations and their ties to other community and citywide institutions." The believers in the CDC mechanism wanted to "give it a big boost" (Walker and Weinheimer 1998, 2).

The big boost included a series of programs in 23 cities aimed at improving staff expertise and organizational systems and procedures. The program also sought to provide CDCs with grants to support core operations so that they could become more financially stable. Finally, the initiative tried to make other elements of the decentralized housing network in the private and public sectors work more cooperatively and effectively with CDCs. In all, the National Community Development Initiative instituted five categories of capacity-building programs:

- basic organizational operating grants
- staff training
- specific grants to individual CDCs to develop new programs
- subsidies for taking on more ambitious projects—that is, learning by doing more
- promotion of CDC associations

To measure how much CDCs improved through these efforts, an Urban Institute study measured changes in three categories: consistently capable housing producers, top-tier CDCs, and CDC operating budgets. "Capable producers" were those that could consistently produce at least 10 units of housing per year. The number of CDCs that met this definition nearly doubled between 1991 and 1997, from an average of 4.5 to 8.3 per city. Top-tier producers "have strong boards and staffs, strong internal management systems, and diverse funding bases," according to the study. Local experts were asked to identify top-tier organizations operating in 1991 and 1997. Urban Institute researchers determined that the number of top-tier producers increased from 3.8 to 5.5 per city. The cities with dramatic increases in top-tier producers were Atlanta, Baltimore, Detroit, Los Angeles, Philadelphia, San Antonio, and St. Paul. Three cities—Indianapolis, Seattle, and Washington, D.C.—had a decline in top-tier groups. The operating budgets of CDCs also grew during the 1991–97 period by 60 percent (Walker and Weinheimer 1998, 28–29).[5]

By any measure, the 1990s represented a tremendous increase in the scale and scope of CDCs.[6] But because for-profit developers had to meet nonprofit benchmarks and standards for acceptable developer fees, risk taking (e.g., building in a high-crime neighborhood), and community involvement, the influence of these CDCs extended beyond the non-profit sector (Zigas 2004).[7] If the nonprofit CDCs were keeping the for-profit industry honest, the for-profits were helping the nonprofits work smarter. Nonprofits adopted many underwriting and accounting proce-dures from the private sector. Nonprofits also had to meet the efficiency standards set by for-profit firms.

State and local governments were also innovating. At the time of the Kaiser Report in 1969, no state had a housing finance agency capable of making low-interest loans or executing other subsidy programs for affordable housing developers. Now all 50 have them, along with Wash-ington, D.C., Puerto Rico, and the U.S. Virgin Islands. Cities and coun-ties have become more sophisticated, too, since they are now distributing block grants from Washington in addition to local funds from local taxes.

A Larger Role for the Private Sector

During this time, the private sector has also enhanced its ability to par-ticipate in affordable housing programs. All the major commercial banks, for example, developed community-lending departments that specialized in subsidized housing loans. They were motivated by busi-ness opportunities, public relations, and the requirements of the Com-munity Reinvestment Act of 1977.[8] Most major Wall Street firms along with public-purpose–oriented financial firms developed expertise in how to use the housing tax credit, tax-exempt bonds, and other financial tools for low-income housing transactions. For example, a secondary market emerged for low-income housing mortgages through organiza-tions such as the Local Initiatives Managed Assets Corporation, under the sponsorship of the Local Initiatives Support Council.[9]

The building and construction industry fully embraced public-private partnership programs in the 1990s. For example, the National Associa-tion of Home Builders sponsored the Housing Credit Group "as the leading private sector voice for the [LIHTC] program on Capitol Hill"

(*Multi-Housing News* 2002, 1a). One member of the committee, a real estate developer from Miami, praised subsidized federal housing programs: They matter, he argued, because "you're going to change a whole generation of children by building good homes. . . . You really change people's lives by doing this" (*Multi-Housing News* 2002, 1a). It appeared that even business executives could sound like housing activists, when their interests were properly aligned.

Capacity-building and consulting nonprofits continued to provide increasingly varied and sophisticated financial products. LISC and Enterprise Community Partners were joined by scores of similar smaller for-profit and nonprofit firms that operated locally or regionally.

As a participant in, and builder of, the early CDC movement, LISC was in a position to reflect on the history of housing policy of the prior 30 years. It was different in the 1970s, "long before today's steady streams of project capital—the Low Income Housing Tax Credit, the federal HOME program, the boom in bank community-lending programs, or the funding collaboration known as the National Community Development Initiative," according to the 2002 LISC report *The Whole Agenda: The Past and Future of Community Development.* In the early period, "CDCs had no choice but to view each new housing development as a unique and perilous adventure." Financing for development was stitched together from ad hoc sources—charity, volunteer labor, and "a hodgepodge of discretionary programs at the federal and local level." LISC and Enterprise eventually became billion-dollar empire builders, but they got their start with risky deals. Projects built by CDCs "somehow navigated the minefield of haphazard funding streams, reluctant lenders, and negligible technical support." That experience served as the kernel for what would become a multibillion-dollar industry and a mighty production system that built over a hundred thousand homes a year by the 1990s—a system "now so well-oiled that housing production is sometimes mistakenly perceived today as the 'easy' work in community development" (LISC 2002, 16–17). The idea that building housing for low-income tenants could be viewed as "easy" was a tribute to the new approach.

Weaknesses of the Decentralized Approach

The decentralized housing network has delivered high-quality services and remains robust politically, but it does have some serious drawbacks. The greatest weakness is that despite the efficiency of the system and the number of homes built, it has been unable to solve the housing problem for low-income Americans. HUD measures the number of families who pay more than 50 percent of their income in rent—a category they call "worst-case needs." In 1978, 5.1 percent of all households fell in this category; in 2001 it was also 5.1 percent (HUD 2003, xix, 7). Any subsidized housing program, however, would have struggled against three larger trends that contributed to increasing rent burdens during that period: the declining real wages of lower-income workers, increasing immigration of very low income people, and local efforts to limit the supply of all housing, but especially housing for low-income tenants. In spite of its popularity and effectiveness, the decentralized housing network was losing the battle to house the poorest Americans.

Affordable housing advocate Barry Zigas observed that the political right and left had reached consensus over the funding mechanism (tax credits and block grants) and the implementation of federal housing programs (nonprofit and for-profit real estate developers working with subnational government). What was missing, according to Zigas, was a tenfold increase in resources so that would enable the network to make a bigger dent in the housing crisis for low-income families. Cushing Dolbeare, who founded the National Low Income Housing Coalition in 1974 and was a senior scholar at the Joint Center for Housing Studies at Harvard University, was asked in a 2002 interview what the national housing policy should be. She agreed with Zigas: "Pretty much what it is," she said, "with more money" (Pitcoff 2002). Even housing advocates such as Dolbeare and Zigas did not suggest a return to the "good old days" of the 1960s and HUD leadership. They argued for more funding so that the decentralized housing network could make a greater impact, not a return to top-down bureaucratic leadership from Washington, D.C.-based institutions.

Decentralized housing programs also have the same problem of fairness that earlier housing programs confronted: only a fraction of eligible tenants get subsidized apartments. And apartments in the new programs are often targeted to the working poor, not those in most need. Those who are lucky enough to get an apartment enjoy a generous subsidy. Housing built by the decentralized network often has better construction quality than market-built units and more amenities. While these apartments are built cost-effectively, they are still expensive, averaging over $100,000 per apartment in the late 1990s in high-demand areas such as California, New York, and New England (Cummings and DiPasquale 1999, 272). As a result, significant subsidies have gone to only a fraction of those eligible.

Another problem is inconsistency. Local networks vary in their effectiveness, depending on local characteristics such as skill, drive, and organization. Some are energetic and effective, while others are parochial, myopic, poorly capitalized, and ineffective. Whether a community has access to quality low-income housing rests on the luck of the draw. Some areas—New England, the West Coast, and upper Great Lakes regions—tend to have more sophisticated and capable housing delivery networks. Some large communities, however, are seriously underrepresented in this policy environment. Las Vegas, for example, a metro area with more than 1.7 million residents, has a relatively underdeveloped community development infrastructure.

The city of Fresno is another example of a sizable community that has difficulty taking advantage of the new decentralized approach to affordable housing and community development. "Nonprofits here can't compete with [San Francisco] Bay Area organizations on funding proposals—the writing is not as sophisticated, and the applications aren't as strong," said one community advocate in a report by the Federal Reserve. In that report, Naomi Cytron, a researcher at the Federal Reserve Bank of San Francisco, writes,

> Community stakeholders noted that even if the neighborhood received a large infusion of capital, it might not be able to fully address its challenges. Interviewees cited gaps in technical skills among non-profits and community builders and fragmented leadership, as well as some lack of political will to work on changing the status quo—not to mention a lack of clarity on how to develop an action oriented strategy to improve current conditions.

As one Fresno resident said, "Even if Bill Gates wanted to give $1 billion to the neighborhood, could we use it?" (Community Affairs Offices 2008, 31).

The decentralized program also could be invisible. While in some instances that invisibility was a political advantage, it camouflaged the critical role of government as a problem solver. Even after 23 years of this approach to building affordable housing, there is still no one dataset that tracks the construction of all government-subsidized housing. HUD recently created a database of LIHTC projects, which captures the bulk of affordable housing produced but not all. Remarkably few Americans know that nearly every city in this country has high-quality, government-subsidized apartment buildings.[10] Because so few people know the extent of government-sponsored social programs, the misunderstanding of the relationship of citizens to their government and its programs continues to grow. It also makes it hard to rally voters around a program that remains in the shadows. In other words, it lacks the focus of FDR's fourth freedom—the freedom from want—that inspired voters and gave weight to the New Deal coalition's efforts to establish a more comprehensive welfare state based on the ideology of economic citizenship (Kennedy 1999, 469).

In earlier policy eras, if people disagreed with a government program, they could show their dissatisfaction by trying to punish or influence policymakers, for example, by marching on Washington, D.C., or protesting outside state capitols or city halls. Under the decentralized program, where does one go to demonstrate? Now there is nowhere to march.

The Rise of a New Institution

The decentralized housing network appears to correspond to larger trends in federal policy such as public-private partnerships and other market-oriented policies for social welfare. Government is relying less on its own bureaucracies and more on outside actors—nonprofit and for-profit firms—to achieve social welfare goals. *Governing by Network* (2004) by Stephen Goldsmith and William Eggers shows how a network approach is being used in policy areas beyond the provision of social services; the military and such agencies as the National Park Service, NASA, and the IRS have begun working with decentralized networks (Goldsmith and Eggers 2004). Several other books describe the how local governments, nonprofits, and for-profit entities in cooperate to provide social services (Kickert, Klijn, and Koopenjan 1997; Mandell 2001; Agranoff and McGuire 2003).

In contrast to the existing literature, I argue that the decentralized housing network is more than a public-private partnership or some form of collaborative management: It is a new type of institution. It is a decentralized institution comprised of a loosely knit network that includes the organizations that build and finance housing but, more important, also includes those that it is trying to help (e.g., low-income renters). This dense network is fluid. It has many participants with overlapping skills and capabilities. It is also more comprehensive than a simple public-private partnership; it comprises "multiple constellations of grassroots organizers; foundation program officers and centers; agency officials at local, state, and federal levels; university institutes and consulting firms; professional staff in banks, businesses, health systems, and newspapers; mainline civic associations; and social movement organizations," according to Carmen Sirianni and Lewis Friedland (2001, 22). Simply put, this new decentralized institution has a vast reach into both low-income communities *and* the communities of policymakers, finance, and research.

In the past, government approaches to affordable housing would "swing from loving to hostile," in the words of the 1982 McKenna Report. Since 1986, however, the decentralized housing network has been stable, growing in its capacity to serve low-income residents. By its very nature, though, it is a local and decentralized structure; conveying that its small but steady wins, year after year, amount to a very big accomplishment—a new policy regime—is very difficult. This aspect of how affordable housing gets built has been under the radar for most people and has contributed to an underestimation of what has been accomplished. Even those who are familiar with the program often do not understand how all the pieces fit together. To correct the underreporting of accomplishments and confusion over how the new approach works requires a shift in thinking: a deeper understanding of this new institution is essential to making the most of it going forward.

The decentralized housing network has gone beyond demonstrating its potential; its achievements have passed a threshold of scale and complexity that demands that we examine it in a new light. The network that has built affordable housing is not the market alone, or government bureaucracy alone, but rather an amalgam of organizations working together in a mutually supportive manner. It is this network that I describe as a decentralized institution.

I use the term *institution* in a broad sense; there is clearly no agency or building that houses it. As a whole, however, the decentralized housing network operates in a fashion similar to a formal institution or agency. But it also blurs some lines, especially with another institution—the market.

Understanding How the Decentralized Institution Operates

The specific components of the decentralized institution are a constantly changing configuration. They come together for a specific problem—building an apartment building, for example, or revitalizing a particular neighborhood, or lobbying for more federal resources—and then disband. The network can then reorganize into a new arrangement for a new project, which is one of its great advantages. For example, a city might be interested in revitalizing its downtown area by pairing its redevelopment agency with a local nonprofit and another anchor institution such as a university. This local development team could then tap the expertise of a national intermediary, such as LISC, and look for financing from the state housing finance agency, a state housing trust fund, and the proceeds from selling its LIHTCs to a Wall Street bank. When the project is finished, the group dissolves, but the individual participants continue to seek out new projects and new partners.

The process of coalescing and then disbanding to join again in a new configuration with new partners provides the opportunity to learn from mistakes. It guards against turf battles and the sclerosis that can set into traditional bureaucratic institutions. It allows flexibility in the response to a problem, so that if need arises for more expertise in a particular area such as education, health, or crime prevention, other groups or institutions with those skills or knowledge can join the network. For example, the nonprofit developer that built the all solar-powered apartment complex referenced in chapter 4 was not an expert on green building techniques; it partnered with another nonprofit that brought those skills to the development.

As the case studies show, many of the same individuals and organizations have come together to work on subsequent projects, though sometimes with different degrees of participation or responsibility. With each passing year, they have become more knowledgeable and comfortable with the new tools. Even more important, however, are the long-term relationships that characterize the network in many communities around the country. These relationships contribute to shared perspectives among participants, even though many of them have quite different goals and objectives.

It is hard to characterize these working relationships. The parties are independent, and yet their growing association keeps them together. Each participant is partly dependent on every other. Each party—the developer, the city, the equity investor, and others—share information because they are all analyzing the project simultaneously. The players influence each other, teach each other, and stretch each other's worldviews. This network seems to demonstrate what the sociologist Walter Powell (1990, 303) describes as "reciprocal, preferential, mutually supportive actions" that promote cooperation.

The process of combining and recombining participants in the decentralized housing network also performs a sort of check on any individual actor since almost anyone can be replaced. This aspect of the network provides an "exit" option—in the Albert Hirschman (2004) sense—for the development team.

An internal dynamic that keeps the decentralized network alive and developing as an institution, as it tries to increase its access to resources and learns through a process of policy feedback. This interpretation draws on a new institutional school of thought and argues the case, as Theda Skocpol does, that institutions matter and are an important variable in explaining how policies develop. "Not merely agents of other social interests," Skocpol writes, government officials and other individual actors in the network "are actors in their own right, enabled and constrained by the political organizations within which they operate" (1992, 41).

If we step back and view the effects of the network as a whole, rather than focusing on individual components, it is easier to see how low-income citizens are being served. As an example, some have criticized CDCs for being too market-oriented, for serving the interests of the middle and upper classes rather than their lower-class constituency. It is true that CDCs have a hard time behaving as their community action agency predecessors did—pressing too hard on demands is not a good way to make friends in city hall. But does that mean CDCs are less effective in promoting the interests of poor residents in neglected neighborhoods? Consider the example of the antipoverty activist and CDC Director Bill Edwards in Alabama, introduced in chapter 4. CDCs like his developed new practices to communicate with the local centers of economic and political power. In most cases, CDCs created citywide nonprofit coalitions that amplified their voices in city politics. In turn, city officials invited these coalitions into decisionmaking venues because they were knowledgeable, capable, and able to reach practical compromises. In other words, CDCs brought poor neighborhoods into the larger decentralized housing policy network as the case studies demonstrate. In Tuscaloosa, it was a coalition of local groups, led by Bill Edwards's CDC, that was able to mobilize support from the city council to raze and rebuild a slum of old sharecropper shacks.[11] In this example, if the CDC alone is analyzed, the larger picture of how the whole network is operating on behalf of low-income citizens is lost.

Lobbying Success

As an institution, the decentralized housing network has fought for its own survival. Richard Abrams writes in *The Nation Transformed* that the story of American politics is often confused as a struggle between the special interests and the people (Abrams 2006). It is better understood, he argues, as a struggle of special interests versus other special interests. The decentralized housing network, and the decentralized welfare state more generally, has now put poverty programs on a footing that may not be equal, but at least resembles, the lobbying efforts of other larger programs like defense and health. Unlike any other time in American history, powerful coalitions are now defending affordable housing policy.

An example from the 2006 federal budget makes the point. In January 2005, the *National Journal* reported that many Republicans believed that their party's first concern was to show "fiscal restraint" for its base (Bauman 2004). Early in the year's budget cycle, one program that appeared to be vulnerable was CDBG. The $4.7 billion program was slated to take a 50 percent reduction, according to congressional housing aides in a February 2005 article in the *Washington Post* (Weisman 2005, A1).[12] As soon as President Bush's budget was released with its proposed CDBG cuts, however, a coalition—made up of Wall Street bankers, tax-credit equity investors, lawyers, accountants and other consultants, governors, mayors, nonprofits, and housing and anti-poverty activists—successfully defended the program, sparing CDBG deep cuts in the 2006 budget.[13] It may be too early to talk about the social-service complex mirroring the military-industrial complex, but the decentralized housing network is developing an impressive track record of self-defense.

Paradox of the Welfare State

Too often, scholars see history of the welfare state history as simply a battle between the state and the market, rather than as a contest between competing interests. An understanding of this new decentralized institution corrects those misinterpretations. But it is paradoxical, too. While a decentralized approach is to some degree an abdication of responsibility— especially with regard to caring for the weakest in our society—the new institutions did not dismantle the welfare state; they simply changed its form. Some aspects of the welfare state have grown in capacity and political power. And that is the paradox: the trend toward the decentralized welfare state both weakens Marshallian universality *and* positively promotes the economic and social well-being of many low-income citizens, maybe even more than under more universalistic regimes. Older institutions had clear goals of universality, but they rarely achieved them. This new institution, while perhaps less aggressive and overt, is proving to be resilient, adaptive, and effective in the face of shifting political currents.

There is no doubt, of course, that over the past 40 years the welfare state has suffered setbacks and funding cuts, but it has not been dismantled, contrary to the claims of some studies. The decentralized version of the American welfare state has also maintained its harsh distinction between relatively generous subsidies for the middle class—social insurance programs, mortgage interest deduction, and the like—and miserly ones for the poor. The most dramatic change of the past 30 years, however, has not occurred in funding but in *how* and *to whom* welfare state services are delivered. The decentralized housing network is one example of how the lines between government, the private sector, and nonprofits have blurred. The result is a puzzle: in many ways, the welfare state is more present and harder to see.

What Has Influenced the Move to Decentralized Networks?

Understanding the history of how the affordable housing network has developed into a decentralized institution is important. But people still disagree on the root causes for this change. Much of the debate over what is driving this trend falls into two camps. Some have seen this development as the inevitable response to the shift in the economy, our politics, and technology. According to this view, the Washington, D.C.-based bureaucracies of the New Deal and Great Society welfare state were appropriate for the industrial era and its champions in the liberal-labor coalition of the Democratic Party. A decentralized approach to the welfare state, by contrast, was appropriate for the postindustrial economy and the rise of the type of free-market ideology promoted by the Republican Party. In this explanation, larger economic and political forces have shaped the evolution of the new approach for delivering social services.

The fact that other postindustrial economies have chosen to outsource the delivery of social services—especially to nonprofits—supports the argument that larger forces have encouraged decentralization. Even renowned welfare states like France, Germany, and Sweden are part of this trend (Johan Olsen 2003).[14]

Technology is another force moving us toward decentralization. With the advent of spreadsheet software, the cost of financial real estate underwriting has dropped precipitously. Spreadsheet software has made it possible for small shops like CDCs to analyze project feasibility under multiple scenarios. This is probably the most dramatic example of the many innovations in office productivity (fax machines, personal computers, e-mail) that have made smaller operations possible and lowered the transaction costs of multiparty projects like the ones characterizing the decentralized housing network. As the case studies in chapter 4 illustrate, every project has had complex development teams and many layers of financing, which, in total, have involved at least half a dozen entities in the simplest transaction. Without the ability to analyze quickly the financial and tax implications for a project from a number of angles and then share that information immediately, such complicated arrangements would not have been possible.

Others, however, have argued that it was not long-term trends but rather individuals playing the role of policy entrepreneur in the face of reduced budgets and a hostile political environment that brought about the shift to decentralization. In other words, individuals made the best of a bad situation. The decentralized approach to the welfare state, so the argument goes, was the only politically feasible option in a world that was increasingly hostile to government action on behalf of the poor—a decentralized welfare state was better than no welfare state at all. In this instance, it is hard to overestimate the contributions of activists like Dorothy Mae Richardson, Cushing Dolbeare, and Jim Rouse, who, through the sheer force of their determination, vision, and powers of persuasion changed the course of the history of affordable housing policy. This interpretation attributes more power to individuals in shaping the outcomes of politics than circumstances and larger trends (Clarke 2000, 203–204).

I think a more useful conceptualization, however, blends the two. A hybrid explanation treats shifts in larger forces like secular changes in politics, technology, and the economy as necessary but not sufficient conditions for the changes that led to the decentralized approach to housing and the decentralized welfare state. Within the framework of political and economic changes, a new institution was built—piece by piece—by multiple (and usually uncoordinated) individual actors. Individuals like Don Terner, Pat Clancy, and others were reshaping urban policy at the local level. At the same time, people such as Jim Rouse, Langley Keyes, Jack Kemp, and Senator George Mitchell were building new tools at a national level. These individual efforts started small, but as the case studies from chapter 4 demonstrate, they grew more ambitious and sophisticated over time. In the next chapter, I try to apply the insights gained from thinking like a network to current policy debates.

Table 5A.1. Stock of Federally Assisted Units by Funding Source, 1999

Federal program	Number of units
Inactive: Privately Owned, Project-Based	
Public housing	1,274,000
Inactive: Privately Owned, Project-Based	
Section 8 new construction/substantial rehabilitation	644,000
Section 202 elderly Housing direct loan	207,000
Section 236	60,000
Section 221(d)(3) below-market interest rate	71,000
Active: Privately Owned, Project-Based	
Section 202 supportive housing for the elderly	65,000
Section 811 supportive housing for persons with disabilities	18,000
Section 515 rural housing rental assistance	410,000
Total direct assistance	2,749,000

Source: Bipartisan Millennial Housing Commission 2002, 95.

Note: The apartments summarized here are from the development programs. The table excludes tenant-based Section 8 certificates and vouchers, which numbered 1,581,000 in 1999. I also excluded rural housing that is administered in partnership with the Department of Agriculture (410,000 units in 1999).

6

How Does Thinking Like a Network Change Our Approach to Public Policy?

An argument can be made that the essential ingredients of improved public performance in the twenty-first century are not so much strengthened internal workings of agencies, but rather improvements in how agencies collaborate and interact with other organizations through networks to achieve results. The point of all of this is that the transformations that are needed and underway in federal agencies generally need to be directed to a very specific end—to provide the agency with the capacity needed to understand the governance environment in which it operates and to contribute effectively to results within that environment.

—J. Christopher Mihm (2006, 36)

How we think about institutions has been powerfully shaped by the work of Ronald Coase, who in his seminal 1937 article asked a simple question, Why do we have large corporations organizing much of our economic life, when markets are supposed to be more efficient? Alfred Chandler (1977) gave historical weight to Coase's observations when he showed how information and strategic raw materials for the new mass production industries were more efficiently organized through integrated firms (hierarchy) rather than in spot markets for materials, labor, transportation, and the like. Such efficiency encouraged corporations to develop vertically and horizontally as modern business enterprises.

In the 1970s, Oliver Williamson (2000) reignited economists' thinking about the market-firm dichotomy. He argued that the main function of the firm was to reduce transaction costs that can be driven up by lack of information, uncooperative behavior by partners with strategic resources, or the risk of a product's reputation among consumers. Without the proper incentives, actors along the production process—from raw material to distribution—could create problems and add cost. The solution to this problem for Coase and Chandler was the firm. Williamson argued for a third possibility "located between market and hierarchy" that tends to be characterized by independent economic actors loosely coordinated through long-term relationships. "The economics of governance makes three basic governance structure distinctions: classical markets (simple spot market exchange), hybrid contracting (of a long-term kind), and hierarchies (firms, bureaus)," he wrote (2005, 7).

Mark Granovetter (1985) posits that Williamson's hybrid contracting, or network relationships, can have even greater stability than other arrangements because they are embedded in social and economic relationships where reputation and the desire for repeat transactions are of high concern to the participants. Empirical evidence shows, Granovetter argues, that "even with complex transactions, a high level of order can often be found in the 'market'—that is, across firm boundaries—and a correspondingly high level of disorder within the firm" (502).

But for our purposes, analyzing a policy network in ways outlined by Williamson and Granovetter has generated an important shift in our conceptual framework.[1] In the 1980s and 1990s, a group of theorists described these new organizational structures as *virtual* (Chesbrough and Treece 1996), *network* (Powell and Smith-Doerr 1994), or *flexible specialization* (Piore and Sabel 1984). This school of thought provides a deeper theoretical grounding in the origins and workings of decentralized policy-implementing networks like the one that builds affordable housing. And our ability to model and understand the detailed workings of networks in social and economic life continues to improve. An excellent introduction to the state of the art, for example, can be found in Matthew O. Jackson's *Social and Economic Networks* (2008). Viewing the affordable housing network as a dynamic institution rather than as an isolated program or series of programs raises a number of questions and concerns. It also offers insights into the delivery of other social services.

Implications for Public Policy Going Forward

Thinking about housing policy—or any policy—as a system or network, rather than as a program, prompts us to think differently about (1) the network as a whole system, (2) each node in the network and how the different components fit together, and (3) the ability of the system to adapt to changing circumstances.

Analyzing the Whole System

Evaluating the health of the entire system requires a perspective broad enough to determine whether all available money, ideas, and experience are being used to their maximum effectiveness. In the case of affordable housing, currently no single entity plays that oversight role. The IRS, HUD, the National Association of Housing Finance Agencies, and private companies, like law and accounting firms, perform specific functions but are not empowered to ensure that this system functions at its optimal level.

Who, for example, is in a position to correct things if they go wrong? So far, the system has been robust and has not needed a major intervention. But the current credit crunch, combined with the mortgage market problems that triggered the federal government's takeover of Fannie Mae and Freddie Mac (both significant LIHTC purchasers) has created one of the most serious downturns in the LIHTC market since its inception.[2] In an effort to shore up this market, Congress and President Obama provided $2.25 billion from the American Recovery and Reinvestment Act of 2009. These funds will be used to help fund LIHTC projects that were unable to sell their tax credits.[3]

The market for LIHTC will likely rebound eventually, but mounting anecdotal evidence suggests that affordable housing projects are not being built because developers cannot raise sufficient tax credit equity to make them feasible. In this instance, it would be helpful to have an entity that works the way the Federal Reserve System did during the financial meltdown in 2008–2009.

A lead organization (or collection of organizations) would also help bring better coordination.[4] The current system contains too much overlap in some places and has gaps in others. A network perspective forces us to look differently at how components of the system should operate. Today, we do not have the appropriate data collection or measures to gauge how well the network is functioning. It is surprising, for example, that we are still unable to get a completely accurate count of subsidized apartments built in a given year, much less some other measures that gauge efficiency over time.

A lead entity would also be concerned with how each node of the network is operating and contributing to the system. Each part should operate with greater transparency and better explain how it promotes the activity of the network. The first step to achieving this clarity is collecting, analyzing, and sharing relevant data at the level of the institution. Multi-divisional corporations, for example, will often use the accounting measure of the internal rate of return on investment, or IRR. What is the IRR for a decentralized network?

Beyond helping organize the network, better data would strengthen the capabilities of the network in multiple ways. It would help each part of the network play its part better. If individual parts know how they fit into the system, they can stop duplicating efforts that are better performed by others. Some duplication is probably healthy from a competition standpoint, but it would be helpful to know when another member of the network is better suited for a particular function. Then, as more data are collected over time, investors and rating agencies could start building more sophisticated risk-return financial models. With a greater understanding of how the underlying assets perform, certain investments, such as affordable housing apartment buildings, would no longer have to pay the risk premium they do now, even though they are very safe investments. As Annie Donovan from NCB Capital Impact said at a Federal Reserve conference in September 2006, "We believe we have something tantamount to a 'AA' risk and we're not necessarily getting 'AA' pricing right now" (Erickson 2006a).

Analyzing the Parts and How They Fit into the Whole

Having a better understanding of the parts and the whole of the system also will help us with many of the contentious issues facing community development organizations today. Many have suggested that nonprofits should scale up their operations to achieve operational efficiencies. The "Going to Scale" project at the Harvard Business School, for example, is looking for ways to increase the reach of nonprofits (Letts, Ryan, and Grossman 1999). The Aspen Institute, sponsored by many within the community development industry, has also been exploring this issue.[5]

The danger, of course, is that as organizations become larger and presumably more efficient, they run the risk of losing their specialized focus in a particular area or neighborhood (such as with locally based CDCs) or specialized services or clientele like the Peter Claver community described in chapter 4 that specializes in housing tenants with AIDS. Getting bigger has problems, since it invites mission creep and the loss of key advantages such as local knowledge.[6] Using corporations and the

...ing, and sharing relevant data at the level of the institution. Multi-
...onal corporations, for example, will often use the accounting mea-
...f the internal rate of return on investment, or IRR. What is the IRR
...decentralized network?

...yond helping organize the network, better data would strengthen
...pabilities of the network in multiple ways. It would help each part
...network play its part better. If individual parts know how they fit
...he system, they can stop duplicating efforts that are better per-
...ed by others. Some duplication is probably healthy from a compe-
...standpoint, but it would be helpful to know when another member
...network is better suited for a particular function. Then, as more
...are collected over time, investors and rating agencies could start
...ing more sophisticated risk-return financial models. With a greater
...erstanding of how the underlying assets perform, certain invest-
...ts, such as affordable housing apartment buildings, would no longer
...to pay the risk premium they do now, even though they are very safe
...stments. As Annie Donovan from NCB Capital Impact said at a Fed-
...Reserve conference in September 2006, "We believe we have some-
...g tantamount to a 'AA' risk and we're not necessarily getting 'AA'
...ing right now" (Erickson 2006a).

...lyzing the Parts and How They Fit into the Whole

...ing a better understanding of the parts and the whole of the sys-
...also will help us with many of the contentious issues facing com-
...nity development organizations today. Many have suggested that
...profits should scale up their operations to achieve operational
...ciencies. The "Going to Scale" project at the Harvard Business
...ool, for example, is looking for ways to increase the reach of non-
...fits (Letts, Ryan, and Grossman 1999). The Aspen Institute, spon-
...ed by many within the community development industry, has also
...n exploring this issue.[5]
...The danger, of course, is that as organizations become larger and pre-
...nably more efficient, they run the risk of losing their specialized focus
...a particular area or neighborhood (such as with locally based CDCs)
...specialized services or clientele like the Peter Claver community
...scribed in chapter 4 that specializes in housing tenants with AIDS.
...tting bigger has problems, since it invites mission creep and the loss
...key advantages such as local knowledge.[6] Using corporations and the

6

How Does Thinking Like a Network Change Our Approach to Public Policy?

An argument can be made that the essential ingredients of improved public performance in the twenty-first century are not so much strengthened internal workings of agencies, but rather improvements in how agencies collaborate and interact
with other organizations through networks to achieve results. The point of all of
this is that the transformations that are needed and underway in federal agencies
generally need to be directed to a very specific end—to provide the agency with the
capacity needed to understand the governance environment in which it operates
and to contribute effectively to results within that environment.

—J. Christopher Mihm (2006, 36)

How we think about institutions has been powerfully shaped by the work of Ronald Coase, who in his seminal 1937 article asked a simple question, Why do we have large corporations organizing much of our economic life, when markets are supposed to be more efficient? Alfred Chandler (1977) gave historical weight to Coase's observations when he showed how information and strategic raw materials for the new mass production industries were more efficiently organized through inte-grated firms (hierarchy) rather than in spot markets for materials, labor, transportation, and the like. Such efficiency encouraged corporations to develop vertically and horizontally as modern business enterprises.

In the 1970s, Oliver Williamson (2000) reignited economists' thinking about the market-firm dichotomy. He argued that the main function of the firm was to reduce transaction costs that can be driven up by lack of information, uncooperative behavior by partners with strategic resources, or the risk of a product's reputation among consumers. Without the proper incentives, actors along the production process—from raw mate-rial to distribution—could create problems and add cost. The solution to this problem for Coase and Chandler was the firm. Williamson argued for a third possibility "located between market and hierarchy" that tends to be characterized by independent economic actors loosely coordinated through long-term relationships. "The economics of governance makes three basic governance structure distinctions: classical markets (simple spot market exchange), hybrid contracting (of a long-term kind), and hierarchies (firms, bureaus)," he wrote (2005, 7).

Mark Granovetter (1985) posits that Williamson's hybrid contracting, or network relationships, can have even greater stability than other arrangements because they are embedded in social and economic relationships where reputation and the desire for repeat transactions are of high concern to the participants. Empirical evidence shows, Granovetter argues, that "even with complex transactions, a high level of order can often be found in the 'market'—that is, across firm boundaries—and a correspondingly high level of disorder within the firm" (502).

But for our purposes, analyzing a policy network in ways outlined by Williamson and Granovetter has generated an important shift in our conceptual framework.[1] In the 1980s and 1990s, a group of theorists described these new organizational structures as *virtual* (Chesbrough and Treece 1996), *network* (Powell and Smith-Doerr 1994), or *flexible specialization* (Piore and Sabel 1984). This school of thought provides a deeper theoretical grounding in the origins and workings of decentralized policy-implementing networks like the one that builds affordable housing. And our ability to model and understand the detailed workings of networks in social and economic life continues to improve. An excellent introduction to the state of the art, for example, can be found in Matthew O. Jackson's *Social and Economic Networks* (2008). Viewing the affordable housing network as a dynamic institution rather than as an isolated program or series of programs raises a number of questions and concerns. It also offers insights into the delivery of other social services.

Implications for Public Policy Going Forward

Thinking about housing policy—or any policy—as a system or network, rather than as a program, prompts us to think differently about (1) the network as a whole system, (2) each node in the network and how the different components fit together, and (3) the ability of the system to adapt to changing circumstances.

Analyzing the Whole System

Evaluating the health of the entire system requir enough to determine whether all available money are being used to their maximum effectiveness. Ir housing, currently no single entity plays that ov HUD, the National Association of Housing Finar vate companies, like law and accounting firms, p tions but are not empowered to ensure that this s optimal level.

Who, for example, is in a position to correct thi So far, the system has been robust and has not neec tion. But the current credit crunch, combined with problems that triggered the federal government's tal and Freddie Mac (both significant LIHTC purchasei the most serious downturns in the LIHTC market si an effort to shore up this market, Congress and Pre vided $2.25 billion from the American Recovery and 2009. These funds will be used to help fund LIHT(unable to sell their tax credits.[3]

The market for LIHTC will likely rebound eventu anecdotal evidence suggests that affordable housir being built because developers cannot raise sufficient make them feasible. In this instance, it would be helpf that works the way the Federal Reserve System did d meltdown in 2008–2009.

A lead organization (or collection of organization: bring better coordination.[4] The current system contai lap in some places and has gaps in others. A network us to look differently at how components of the systei Today, we do not have the appropriate data collectio gauge how well the network is functioning. It is surpri: that we are still unable to get a completely accurate co apartments built in a given year, much less some oth gauge efficiency over time.

A lead entity would also be concerned with how each work is operating and contributing to the system. Each p ate with greater transparency and better explain how activity of the network. The first step to achieving this cla market to help communities that have been overlooked by corporations and the market is very difficult. In this case, it seems to be a potential mistake for local nonprofits to start acting more like for-profits.[7]

Perhaps a better approach is to specialize even further to capitalize on the nimbleness demonstrated by local participants in the case studies. In a study of high-performing nonprofits, Heather McLeod Grant and Leslie Crutchfield wrote in the *Stanford Social Innovation Review* (2007):

> We learned that becoming a high-impact nonprofit is not just about building a great organization and then expanding it to reach more people. Rather, high-impact nonprofits work with and through organizations and individuals *outside themselves* to create more impact than they ever could have achieved alone. They build social movements and fields; they transform business, government, other nonprofits, and individuals; and they change the world around them.[8]

Grant and Crutchfield's conclusion squares with the experience of the decentralized housing network and appears to reinforce the notion that one of the best ways for an organization to maximize its impact is to participate in, and try to influence, a network.

A conference on community development finance sponsored by the Federal Reserve Board of Governors in 2006 explored the idea of growing together as a network. Discussion also focused on how multiple organizations, playing specialized roles in a transaction, could expand their capacity together. Many conferees referred to this as a network approach to achieving scale for the community development industry. Frank Altman, from the Community Reinvestment Fund, said,

> Our biggest problem, in my view, is getting the whole industry to scale to achieve specialization or differentiation so that we view ourselves as a network that works together with highly specialized organizations that can originate, can service, can securitize. Then we build on that network and on the specialization that these different entities have to create something that is bigger and better than what we have if we're each operating individually. (Erickson 2006a, 20–21)

Altman counseled that "rather than building vertical organizations," nonprofits could specialize "whether it be LIIF [Low Income Investment Fund] in its capacity with child-care loans or New Hampshire [Community Loan Fund]'s ability to make mobile-home loans." Specialization, according to Altman, would reduce overlap and drive down transaction costs. "We need to find ways of applying technology and systems across the industry," he said, "that will allow the industry to become more efficient because then we'll need less subsidy" (Erickson 2006a, 21).

Adapting to Changing Circumstances

Viewing the decentralized housing network as a system also raises questions about adaptability and innovation. The ability to sense and respond to problems and opportunities is essential if the decentralized housing network is to tackle the many challenges it faces. Not only is the problem of housing the country's neediest individuals and families overwhelming, but also the very nature of that problem is changing in profound ways.

The demographics of those served by low-income housing, for instance, are undergoing considerable change. For one thing, that population is increasingly foreign born, and those individuals require institutions that are culturally sensitive, including being multilingual. For another, the challenge of an aging population will put increasing demands on affordable housing as many of these elderly tenants age in place.

Where poor people live is changing dramatically, too. Increasingly, the areas of growing poverty are the suburbs. A study by the Brookings Metropolitan Policy Program found that "in 1999 large cities and their suburbs had nearly equal numbers of poor individuals, but by 2005 the suburban poor outnumbered their city counterparts by at least 1 million" (Berube and Kneebone 2006, 4). Not so long ago Kurt Russell played a movie role in which his character was trying to escape from a futuristic Manhattan that had become an abandoned prison. Now, people complain that Manhattan has become a Disneyland for the rich. What happens to community development when downtowns are rich and suburbs are poor (Leinberger 2008)? If inner-city blight is bad, with all the anchor institutions in major cities—city halls, universities, hospitals, opera houses, foundations, office towers, and the like—what will happen to old inner-ring suburbs when money and investment leak away? Will the network have the tools to revitalize those areas?

Thinking as a Network

Going forward, therefore, we need to consider the ability of the entire system to use available inputs such as information and subsidies to produce better results. This shift in thinking from the program model to the systems model leads to a clearer perception of how affordable housing gets built at the same time that it brings us to a more comprehensive understanding of the economic health of low-income communities. No one is served by an obsession over the number of apartments built as opposed to the greater goal of improving economic conditions for low-income people and communities. Affordable housing is a means to an end; it has value because it promotes the housing stock in a neighborhood *and* provides a stable base for families where they can build wealth, keep their children in the same schools, and provide the peace of mind and dignity that come from living in desirable surroundings.

The Decentralized Housing Network as a Model for Small Business and Education Programs

The success of the decentralized housing network has inspired other programs, particularly small business development and charter schools. Perhaps the most striking example concerns small business development—and community development generally—with the New Markets Tax Credit (NMTC) program.[9] The NMTC program is a shallow subsidy to encourage investment in low-income neighborhoods. These tax credits are allocated by the Community Development Financial Institution Fund of the U.S. Treasury (CDFI Fund). In six rounds of NMTC awards between 2001 and 2008, the CDFI Fund has awarded $19.5 billion in tax credits (GAO 2007, 14). These transactions are often even more complicated than their low-income housing tax credit cousins, employing a number of consultants, intermediaries, and community groups.

The NMTC network looks very much like the LIHTC network. Some players operate much as housing community development corporations do in the decentralized housing network. These mission-driven community development financial institutions (CDFIs) push the envelope of what is possible in providing mission-oriented investments in difficult markets. They resemble community banks in that they tend to be small and attentive to local needs. They also resemble CDCs in the affordable housing world because their mission is to provide access to credit and financial services to low-income communities and individuals. They are in the businesses of "making a market" where one does not currently exist (Donovan 2008). For-profit firms also participate in the program, and, as in the affordable housing example, nonprofits set goals for the mission and for-profits set standards for efficiency.

Many of the organizations on the periphery of the decentralized housing network also operate in the NMTC network. Most big Wall Street banks, for example, are involved in the program. While it is not their main line of business, of course, these for-profit financial firms provide services to CDFIs in structuring transactions and selling tax credits.[10] Commercial banks, such as Wells Fargo or Bank of America, also play a role in providing loans and investments to NMTC transactions. This program has the support of state and local governments, although states are less invested in the process since they do not allocate the tax credits. These players even have their own trade association, the New Markets Tax Credit Coalition, which mirrors the work of pro-LIHTC lobbying organizations.[11]

Investments in NMTC projects must have underlying market viability. In other words, an investor considering putting money in a tortilla factory in a low-income neighborhood must know that this is a smart business decision and that demand for tortillas is sufficient in that local market. The tax subsidy is not enough to support a business that loses money, but it is often just enough to tip the scales in favor of investing in what some term "near bankable" deals.[12]

Bill Clinton promoted the idea of the New Markets Tax Credit by touring many of the same sites that Robert Kennedy and Lyndon Johnson visited in promoting the War on Poverty 30 years earlier.[13] The pilot program was part of the Riegle Community Development and Regulatory Improvement Act of 1994, which passed with overwhelming support from both Republicans and Democrats.[14] Benson Roberts, vice president for policy at the Local Initiatives Support Corporation, makes the observation that the program's

> appeal is actually more than bipartisan; it has managed to span the ideological and policy differences within both parties. Within the Republican Party, New Markets appealed to both 'opportunity society' and business-oriented members, and to both rural and urban representatives. Among Democrats, both traditional liberals and more centrist 'New Democrats' supported New Markets. (Benson F. Roberts 2005, 21)

That sort of consensus, which we saw in the debates over the LIHTC program, is another indicator that this approach to public policy is here to stay.[15]

Bill Clinton, too, noted that the New Markets initiative was popular with liberals and conservatives "What is magic about this notion," Clinton said, "it's not charity. It's a hand up and not a hand out." The second reason he gave for its popularity was the potential for profit: "We're not asking anybody to do anything that isn't a good business decision."[16] Both these reasons deserve more attention. Something about giving local communities tools to help themselves is wildly popular with liberals and conservatives alike. We saw this during the debates over the HOME and LIHTC programs, too. But perhaps even more important, making this work profitable to individuals brings out talented problem solvers who might stay on the sidelines if these programs were not lucrative. For purists in either liberal or conservative camps, this melding of interests and motivations is distasteful. But it is a mix that appears to yield both good policy and good politics.

Charter Schools and Neighborhood Improvement

Community development professionals are also increasingly interested in using schools as the key institutions for promoting positive neighborhood change. As a 2004 report from Abt Associates observed:

> At this time, the concept of integrating school reform and neighborhood revitalization strategies is still at an early stage of development. We know that coordinated investment in neighborhoods and schools can produce better outcomes in low-income neighborhoods than investment in either schools or neighborhoods alone (Turnham and Khadduri 2004, 27).

Many types of approaches to school reform can play a role in revitalizing a neighborhood, but a particularly interesting one is the charter school movement.

Charter schools are an alternative to failing public schools; they are state sponsored and receive per pupil state funding. In exchange for increased autonomy, charter schools must submit to rigorous testing and monitoring requirements. Although only a few charter schools were in existence in the early 1990s, now just under 4,000 serve 1.16 million children in 40 states and the District of Columbia (Consoletti and Allen 2007, 5). These schools often teach in some of the most challenging environments.[17]

Charter schools are also developing their own network, one that is similar to the decentralized housing network. In fact, many of the same players (LISC, Enterprise, and CDFIs) are finding innovative ways to use scarce subsidies to build and operate these schools.

There is no charter school tax credit, but a growing network is now building and operating charter schools. This growth has been fueled by the NMTC program, tax-exempt bonds, and an innovative facilities-loan credit enhancement program offered by the Department of Education.[18] "The Department of Education Credit Enhancement Program provides full or partial guarantees (of principal and interest) to lenders whose funds are used to finance the construction or renovation of facilities for charter schools," according to Jonathan Kivell (2008), in a Center for Community Development Investments working paper.[19] From 2002 through 2006, the credit enhancement has helped 138 charter schools leverage $407 million in facilities financing.[20]

The network building charter schools looks very much like the decentralized housing network, with mission-driven nonprofits, larger for-profit firms, banks, and state and local government. This network even has an equivalent to CDCs and CDFIs—the charter management organizations and development intermediaries that help schools build their facilities and manage their operations.[21] David Umansky, cofounder and CEO of Civic Builders, Inc., a nonprofit organization that acts as a real estate developer for charter schools, stated his organization's general premise: "Charter schools should not be in the real estate business. Schools have financing and management challenges in dealing with real estate, which include managing, developing, and owning properties" (Kivell 2008, 11). His firm is a specialized node in the growing charter school network that echoes Frank Altman's sentiments on specialization.

Other Examples

The environment and health are other areas that show promise for the use of a decentralized network with mission-oriented and community-based organizations and capacity-building intermediaries.[22] The green nonprofit could work both on remediating potential environmental hazards, such as lead-based paint, and on promoting green building techniques for new development and more effective recycling programs. A green community might also involve energy conservation and, potentially, energy production.[23] Finally, it could help create higher-paying "green collar" jobs for low-income workers.[24]

Local mission-oriented health nonprofits could focus on improving the human capital of a low-income community by promoting healthier living. Some low-income communities have a shockingly high percentage of residents on disability, and the negative health effects of living in low-income communities are well-researched and understood (Deborah Cohen et al. 2003). Better health could potentially help individuals who want to participate in the larger economy, as well as save substantial public resources from Medicare or emergency room visits.[25] In addition, "the development of health centers improves real property, generates construction jobs, and produces permanent community assets," according to community health care advocate Ronda Kotelchuck (2008, 83). "It also creates new, varied, stable, and well-paying employment opportunities."

Four Stages for Building Out the Network

We are only scratching the surface of what a fully connected and informed network can accomplish—both in innovation (new approaches and new products) and in new areas (unserved areas and communities). Within the next five years, I see four important developments affecting community development policy:

- horizontal integration of individual policy networks to create problem-solving communities
- vertical integration of those networks into the communities that use *and* provide capital
- growth of the network into underserved communities
- better coordination of overlapping networks in related policy areas (e.g., economic development, health, education, the environment, and public safety)

Creating a Problem-Solving Community

In an effort to increase the effectiveness of the network, we must first create a strong problem-solving community. In the community development field today, good ideas are shared with friends at conferences, in trade journals, and on some email listservs and Internet sites, but there is still no efficient way to connect the many players in the network in an ongoing and meaningful exchange. Success in this task would require connecting all community development practitioners together in a way that allows them to share ideas and best practices. With those comprehensive connections in place, they could work as a community to produce new products or ideas in a peer production arrangement.[26]

Technology is poised to play a major role in promoting horizontal integration. In the way that it took fax machines and personal computers to help make small CDCs viable in the 1980s and 1990s, the rise of web technology—particularly web-based social network and collaboration software—will likely help connect disparate groups interested in working together. Using the Internet to connect like-minded people the way that social networks have done, through web sites such as LinkedIn, MySpace, and Facebook, will be a powerful tool in creating effective problem-solving communities.[27] Those who think these sites do little more than provide a forum for gossip might be surprised to know that many large corporations are now using similar platforms to boost productivity (*Economist* 2007).[28]

The open source software movement has also demonstrated that the efforts of disparate groups and individuals can be captured and incorporated into a work product that rivals the titans of the corporate order. On this point, see the discussion of the Linux operating system versus Microsoft's Windows in *Wikinomics: How Mass Collaboration Changes Everything* (Tapscott and Williams 2006). Another excellent source that explains the potential of peer production is Yochai Benkler's book, *The Wealth of Networks: How Social Production Transforms Markets and Freedoms* (2006). Peer production platforms will be made even stronger with new developments in collaboration-enhancing software, such as information markets and dynamic polling tools.[29]

The Federal Reserve Bank of San Francisco is experimenting with a dynamic polling application from a technology start-up company (eJones) on its web site for community development finance professionals. This tool provides an efficient means for taking the pulse of the community development finance community on such issues as how to increase liquidity for community development loans by fostering a secondary market. People increasingly recognize that harnessing the ideas of those from different nodes in the network can more accurately and efficiently find solutions to problems—a concept embodied in the popular phrase, "we is smarter than me."[30]

What is also needed in the information realm is something like a Google search engine that can better match problem-solving ideas and practices to specific problems. Today, the idea of sharing so-called best practices is a crude effort at best. For example, one of the long-standing problems is that the goods and services available in low-income neighborhoods are of lower quality and higher priced than those in wealthy suburbs (Fellowes 2006). In most cases, it is more expensive to buy an apple in a low-income neighborhood than in a wealthy suburb. A high-quality supermarket in the low-income neighborhood could help address this problem by providing high-quality food to residents at a competitive cost. The problem is that supermarkets stay away from low-income neighborhoods for a variety of reasons—too far from established supply routes (a problem for rural areas), high security costs (a problem in inner-city locations), too rapid increase in rents (a problem for poor neighborhoods undergoing gentrification), and lack of ethnic foods (a problem in immigrant gateway communities). Who has overcome these obstacles, and how did they do it? Having access to a sophisticated search capability to match very narrowly targeted solutions to specific problems would be a great resource for community development.

Connecting the Providers and Users of Capital

The next phase in building out the network is vertical integration—that is, connecting to low-income individuals and communities in one direction and to the world of investors (particularly foundations and the socially responsible investment community) in the other. In this effort, low-income neighborhood residents will play a bigger role in identifying investment opportunities. A number of recent articles have envisioned the role that citizens can play in areas formerly reserved for professionals with the backing of powerful institutions. Journalism, for example, was once the purview of highly trained specialists operating at the direction of mostly for-profit news-gathering organizations. With today's technology of small digital cameras and blogs, everyone has an opportunity to become a citizen-journalist (Noam Cohen 2008). The decentralized community development network will be much stronger when it has thousands of citizen–community development investment analysts roaming their own neighborhoods and highlighting opportunities for making a small business loan to a savvy entrepreneur, designing an affordable housing project, or building a facility such as a charter school that meets particular community needs.

The current method of matching suppliers of capital to users is primitive. On the borrowing side of the equation, we should have a way to gather and analyze information about potential investments continuously. The information could be contributed from multiple sources—from residents of a neighborhood, self-appointed citizen–investment analysts armed with a few tools to evaluate projects, local entrepreneurs, and institutions such as foundations looking to seed promising investments in distressed areas.

On the lending and investing side of the equation, we need a central information clearinghouse where individuals, governments, institutional investors (banks, foundations, and universities) can indicate what their appetite is for particular types of investments. Investor clusters could form around certain investment types (charter schools, specific neighborhoods, inner-city entrepreneurs, women-owned businesses) and look for ways to connect themselves to emerging investment opportunities.

One focus of this book has been on community development corporations and how they have marshaled resources to make viable investments in low-income communities. But an equally exciting transformation is happening among investors. In the past, there have been those who were willing to take a less-than-market-rate return in exchange for some greater social good (government and philanthropies) and those who wanted a market-rate return (banks, ordinary investors). Today, that world is splintering into many communities. Foundations, for example, used to make money off their endowments to fund grants to mission-related activities. At times, the investments could even be in industries that undermined that same foundation's mission (e.g., a foundation that was trying to promote health but invested in tobacco companies for the high rates of return). Increasingly, there is a trend toward program-related investments (PRIs) that is breaking down the wall between the investment and the grant-making sides of the foundation house. PRIs achieve a financial return, although a usually below-market one, while also promoting the goals of the foundation. Foundations are exploring even deeper efforts that put more of their core capital, the corpus, at risk in mission-related investments (MRIs) (Shaw 2007). In sum, foundations now have a range of investment and social-return options. Individual investors have also had more choices with the advent of socially responsible investing options (Mincer 2008, R5).[31]

One promising strategy to connect investors with exactly the kind of risk, return, and mission objectives of their investment is to use securitization techniques. Community development institutions had been making inroads into using securitization tools to tap capital markets before the recent calamity in the structured finance market (Erickson 2006b). Securitization—done properly—takes an investment and divides it into layers of risk. In any given project, or more likely a pool of projects, investors can pick and choose where they want to be on a wide spectrum between pure market return and pure public-purpose grants.[32] Once the problems with securitization, such as the principal-agent issue that led to much of the bad behavior with subprime mortgage securitizations, are resolved, this could become an important tool again for community development finance. Securitization done right will allow users of capital to provide products that meet the needs of an increasingly complex and engaged investment community.

Another way of connecting users and providers of capital could be an online auction house—a sort of eBay of capital model.[33] Already there are many examples of connecting lenders to borrowers online—Prosper.com and Lending Club for peer-to-peer lending and eBay's Microplace and Kiva.org for international microfinance loans and donations (Choi 2007).

Ultimately, however, the way to expand on innovations like the ones achieved by the decentralized housing network is to create more carrots and sticks to encourage capital to flow toward community revitalization. The affordable housing experience demonstrates that when the money flows, nascent organizations grow, innovate, and link up with partners. When the carrots of tax credits and block grants were combined with sticks like the Community Reinvestment Act, the additional resources catalyzed the community potential hidden just below the surface. New programs, or the expansion of existing ones, could make even more dramatic breakthroughs for solving problems for struggling communities.

Promoting Growth in Underserved Areas

After a public policy network has completed the first step (creating a problem-solving community) and the second step (better connecting the users and providers of capital), the network is ready for the third step—promoting its growth in unserved or underserved areas.

In chapter 5, I highlighted the two large underserved communities of Las Vegas and Fresno. I propose two early responses to this problem. First, the government should not sit back and wait for communities to petition for help. As chapters 1–3 have shown, while good historical reasons explain why government has been reactive instead of proactive in this area of social policy, we have achieved most of the gains that this system can deliver. This process must be turned inside out. Instead of waiting for calls for help that may never come, multidivisional teams should converge on areas of high need and triage what services can be provided there. For example, in California a team from Sacramento from the California Housing Finance Agency and the Department of Housing and Community Development could join bankers and a high-performing regional CDC, such as Mercy Housing, in a neighborhood like West Fresno and identify what programs could help that low-income community. The United States is riddled with economically underperforming communities that exert a significant drain on resources.[34] A face-to-face meeting between a multiparty team of experts and local stakeholders for a discussion of policy options is an important first step in boosting that community into a higher economic orbit.

Sustainable change is not possible in these overlooked communities, however, until there are stronger local partners. As part of the triage by outside teams, an effort should be made to identify local leaders and stakeholders (from government, nonprofits, civic organizations, and for-profit corporations, for example) that show promise of having the capacity to tackle complex projects. Once candidates are identified, a number of capacity-building strategies can be employed, such as leadership training programs offered by groups like the Coro Foundation or the W.K. Kellogg Foundation in rural areas.[35]

In the end, however, more talented human capital may have to be recruited to these regions and neighborhoods. To attract that talent, we may need to create strong incentives like forgiveness of student loans or cash awards for these highly trained professionals to go into underserved areas—a sort of Peace Corps or VISTA program for community development.

Optimal Cooperation of Networks

In the fourth stage of development, each network works in concert with other policy networks to attain the best possible outcomes for communities. For example, a community development team working in a particular neighborhood could simultaneously share information, strategy, and effort with overlapping networks in education and youth issues, crime and public safety, health, asset building, public transportation, and recreation. As an example, the police department's community policing efforts could run in parallel with charter school development, new affordable housing projects, and public health efforts—all designed to promote growth in a distressed neighborhood. When all the policy networks are fully integrated, standing shoulder to shoulder, and working together, progress will be tremendous.

A useful but potentially painful exercise involves self-analysis on the part of the affordable housing network. Does the work of the network fit into the larger goal of building economically viable communities? It may be the case that more affordable housing is counterproductive, for example, if it results in further concentration of low-income families in communities where services and opportunities are weak. Perhaps the more pressing intervention in some of these communities is to improve schools or create well-paying jobs. In stronger economic markets, the work of mission-oriented CDCs might contribute to the gentrification pressures that are hurting the existing residents of a low-income community. The true test of flexibility and adaptability in that context, therefore, could mean standing aside to let other institutional players have access public resources for community revitalization.

Conclusion

The decentralized housing network is not cheap. It requires billions of dollars to keep it running and to keep it leveraging the input from subnational government and the private and not-for-profit sectors. In future discussions over these federal expenditures, the network should be more explicit about the benefits it generates for that public investment—what do we get for what we pay? This should be an expansive conversation because many positive benefits flow to individuals and neighboring communities from a neighborhood that has been returned to economic viability.

Some expensive negative consequences might also be avoided by funding initiatives like the decentralized housing network. In a "do nothing" environment, "savings" from scaling back social programs could be offset by the increased costs of social dysfunction, including higher costs for law enforcement, incarceration, emergency room visits, and the forgone contributions of undereducated, low-skilled workers. Richard Abrams suggests that underfunding social programs contributes to "antisocial temptations and incentives." He writes, "In the last quarter century, the prison population soared to almost 2 million, including almost 2 percent of the adult male population—at an average cost of $40,000 per prisoner per year. That came to about $80 billion per year, or more than the government spent on Medicaid ($57 billion) and Head Start ($5 billion) combined in 2000" (Abrams 2006, 252). Doing nothing is expensive, too.

This book has covered a long arc of history, from the idealism and optimism of the Great Society through an era when government, it seemed, had no answers. I have argued that this evolution is more complicated than it appears. But as we go through a period when even die-hard free market conservatives have embraced government bailouts and rescue plans for the economy, we may be on verge of yet another era—one where government and markets blend to create better outcomes for society. "It's the beginning of the end of the era of infatuation with the free market," said Steve Fraser, author of *Wall Street: America's Dream Palace*. "It's the end of the era where Wall Street carries high degrees of power and prestige. And it's the end of the era of conspicuous displays of wealth. We are entering a new chapter in our history."[36] If this is true, it might be worthwhile to look back to the beginning of this story. The term *Great Society* comes from a speech President Johnson gave at the University of Michigan in May 1964. He said: "We have the opportunity to move not only toward the rich society and the powerful society, but upward to the Great Society." That was "where the city of man serves not only the needs of the body and the demands of commerce but the desire for beauty and the hunger for community" (Patterson 1996, 562).

In a series of interviews in the Mississippi Delta, Valerie Hunt found that individuals were often intimidated by formal forums for citizen input, such as city council meetings, but found it less threatening to interact informally with staff of a local community development corporation. One CDC director said the most important resident input he gets is from informal settings:

> You go to the grocery store, and you know, they see you in your sweats, in your tennis shoes and you become one of them and that's when they open up and talk to you. My best conversations happen there . . . everything from church, bills, and school to our programs and board members. They will talk to you about anything, maybe even come to the office, but not without the initial conversation. Yeah, we cover a lot of ground in the grocery store. (Hunt 2007, 19)

The promise of the decentralized network is that it empowers a local CDC director who meets his or her neighbor in the grocery store to tackle a problem or idea—not alone, but backed up by a network made strong because it can deliver access both to the universe of problem-solving ideas and to government subsidy and global capital. When that promise is made real, we will see university researchers, Wall Street bankers, and government and nonprofit experts bringing their skills and resources to bear to solve problems in line at the grocery store.

Notes

Chapter 1. Directions in Housing Policy from Lyndon Johnson to Ronald Reagan, 1964–86

1. George Wallace, a champion of racial segregation, won 13.5 percent of the popular vote in his 1968 run for president (Brinkley 2004, 838).

2. At the 1964 Republican Convention, Goldwater famously reminded his supporters that "extremism in the defense of liberty is no vice." (Full text and audio of the speech is available at http://www.americanrhetoric.com/speeches/barrygoldwater1964rnc.htm.)

3. The term "Great Society" comes from a speech Johnson gave at the University of Michigan in May 1964. He said, "We have the opportunity to move not only toward the rich society and the powerful society, but upward to the Great Society." That was "where the city of man serves not only the needs of the body and the demands of commerce but the desire for beauty and the hunger for community" (Patterson 1996, 562).

4. Lyndon B. Johnson, Remarks at the Johnson County Courthouse, Paintsville, Kentucky, 1964. The American Presidency Project at the University of California, Santa Barbara, available at http://www.presidency.ucsb.edu/ws/?pid=26190.

5. Address to a convention of the National League of Cities by HUD Secretary Robert Weaver, March 30, 1966. Record Group 207, Federal Archives, College Park, MD.

6. Economic Opportunity Act of 1964: Hearings before the Subcommittee on the War on Poverty Program of the Committee on Education and Labor, House of Representatives, 88th Congress, 2d sess., March 17–20 and April 7–14, 1964. Also see Public Law 88-452, Title II, Pt. A, sec. 202, 88th Cong., 2d sess., 1964 U.S. Code *Congressional and Administrative News,* 595–96.

7. Economic Opportunity Act of 1964, 305.

8. Much of this thinking was inspired by the Chicago political activist, Saul Alinsky. For background on Alinsky's neighborhood-by-neighborhood style of political organizing, see Sanders (1970).

9. Interestingly, Taft was a supporter of the federally subsidized housing goals of the Housing Act of 1949 (Orlebeke 2000, 493).

10. Economic Opportunity Act of 1964, 334.

11. "[Congressman] Martin: 'many of our citizens want to take care of these problems at the local level through private initiative and through local initiative and not have the federal government get into it. I also think that poverty should be dealt with on the local level, not by the federal government setting up massive programs that will start off at almost a billion dollars a year.'

"The Attorney General [Robert Kennedy]. 'Congressman, I am entirely in agreement with that. I do not disagree with anything that you say, up to the last few sentences. I think first you have to decide whether you have a problem, and I do not think you can travel around the United States, or just around the District of Columbia . . . and not reach the conclusion we have a problem. It is a problem. The second question is whether they can do something about it at the local level. In many of these areas they cannot do something about it. They are citizens of West Virginia, or Kentucky, of Alaska, and they are also citizens of the United States. This is fundamental" (Economic Opportunity Act of 1964, 330).

12. Public Law 88-452, 78 Stat. 508, 42 U.S.C. § 2701.

13. Public Law 88-452, Title II, Pt. A, sec. 202, 88th Cong., 2d Sess., 1964 U.S. Code *Congressional and Administrative News*, 595–96.

14. The Ford Foundation helped develop the thinking behind the Community Action Plans and Community Action Agencies through its 1961–1962 Gray Areas Program.

15. Economic Opportunity Act of 1964, Amendment of 1970, Part I, 91st Congress, 2d sess., 1970, 620.

16. There was a brief period when the federal government built housing for war industry workers during World War I. See Radford (1996, 16–17).

17. For an excellent overview of the history of public housing, see Vale (2000, 2003).

18. Although public housing is often associated with the worst of affordable housing, "since 1995, about 200,000 public housing units, including the great majority of 'high rises,' have been torn down" (Sard and Fischer 2008, 6).

19. "As enacted, Section 235 established a homeownership program providing special mortgage insurance and cash payments to help low- and moderate-income home purchasers meet mortgage payments by subsidizing debt service costs in excess of an amortization at one percent interest. Under this program, an eligible buyer may purchase a private home with an FHA-insured mortgage, bearing the prevailing rate of interest, and the federal government makes a monthly assistance payment to the lender on his behalf. Provided the purchaser is applying at least 20 percent of his monthly income to the mortgage payments, he could pay each month as much as the same amount he would pay if the mortgage loan provided for only 1 percent interest. The federal government pays the rest. Another significant addition to subsidy programs was the Section 236 multifamily rental housing program also enacted in the 1968 Act. This program provides a subsidy formula similar to that under Section 235, although the mechanics of the Section 236 subsidy payment are geared to rental housing" (U.S. Congress 1972, 28).

20. "Under present law, as many as 25 million American households—40 percent of the total population—are eligible for the major subsidy programs" (U.S. Congress 1971, 23).

21. HUD had already been experimenting with vouchers since 1970 with the Experimental Housing Allowance Program. In the Housing and Urban Development Act of 1970, the Congress directed HUD to "undertake on an experimental basis a program to demonstrate the feasibility of providing families of low income with housing allowances to assist them in obtaining rental housing of their choice in existing standard housing units." Section 8 served 1.4 million families with vouchers in 2000 (U.S. Department of Housing and Urban Development 2000).

22. Calculated from information from the U.S. Bureau of Labor Statistics web page at http://www.bls.gov/cps/prev_yrs.htm#content.

23. U.S. Census, "Historic Tables: Table 13. Number of Families below the Poverty Level and Poverty Rate: 1959 to 2002," http://www.census.gov/hhes/poverty/histpov/hstpov13.html.

24. Despite this general trend of nonsupport, it is important to remember that most voters historically have expressed hostility toward government while simultaneously supporting government services. A 1992 National Election Survey asked, "Should the government provide fewer services, even in such areas as health and education, in order to reduce spending" or should government "provide many more services, even if it means an increase in spending?" In that poll, 39 percent wanted more services, 31 percent fewer, and 30 percent chose the middle option between the two extremes. And business, which does not want to pay high taxes or high wages, may oppose social programs that bring these things about. Yet, here too, there is enthusiastic support for government contracts, federal efforts to maintain aggregate demand in the economy, and federal programs that regulate and restore confidence in financial markets (National Election Studies 2000).

25. College graduates were 8 percent of the adult population in 1960 but 27 percent in 2003, while the proportion of people without high school diplomas declined from 59 to 15 percent over that period (U.S. Census Bureau, Statistical Abstract of the United States: 2004–2005, table 212).

26. After 1980, more families fell out of the middle class and fewer from the lower class made their way into the middle. For example, before 1980, 35.5 percent of low-income individuals moved into middle-income groups. After 1980, only 30.4 percent did so, a 14.4 percent decline in upward mobility. Falling out of the middle class was 37.1 percent more likely after 1980 (6.2 percent from 1967 to 1980 and 8.5 percent after 1980) (Peterson 1995).

27. Janet L. Yellen, Speech to the Center for the Study of Democracy, University of California, Irvine, November 6, 2006. http://www.frbsf.org/news/speeches/2006/1106.html.

28. Jeffrey Schmalz, "The 1992 Campaign: Candidate's Record; Brown Firm on What He Believes, but What He Believes Often Shifts," *The New York Times,* March 30, 1992.

29. Often credited for launching the "middle class tax revolt," California's Proposition 13 significantly reduced public investment in education, services, and infrastructure. On June 6, 1978, California voters approved the proposition by a two-to-one vote. Proposition 13 reduced local property tax collections by more than 50 percent (California Legislative Analyst 1979). California ranked fourth among the states for total state and local government tax revenue per $1,000 of personal income in fiscal year 1977–78. A year later, Californians dropped to 23rd. In one year, property taxes fell from 52 percent above to 35 percent below the national average (Sears and Citrin 1982).

30. See excerpts from the "Port Huron Statement," in Chafe and Sitkoff (1991, 345–50). Richard Abrams, who was a professor at Berkeley in the 1960s wrote, "For the impatient young insurgents such as those who triggered the Free Speech movement at the University of California, Berkeley, in 1964, liberals were too compromising, too slow, too committed to incremental rather than radical change, and too feckless on behalf of their own ideals" (Abrams 2006, 210).

31. I heard this comment at a lecture Theodore Lowi gave at the 2001 Cornell Reunion, June 11, 2001.

32. "Aid for Housing and Communities Frozen by Nixon: Romney Verifies Moratorium," *Wall Street Journal,* January 9, 1973, 3.

33. House of Representatives, "Housing and Community Development Legislation— 1973," Part 3, 2096.

34. Priscilla S. Meyer, "Housing Study Shows 23 Million Unit Need in U.S. During Decade: Harvard, MIT Center Estimates 13 Million Persons 'Deprived' of Adequate Homes in 1970." *Wall Street Journal,* December 12, 1973, 12.

35. The "early growth of such CDCs should be supported by a 'development support institution' able to provide grants for administration and project activities; equity and debt capital on subsidy terms, particularly for projects of scale; and technical and managerial assistance" (Ford Foundation 1973, 8).

36. "Nixon Housing Plan Proposes Tax Credit for Lenders and Cash for the Elderly Poor: Lender Tax Credit, Cash for Poor Backed in Nixon Housing Plan," *Wall Street Journal,* September 20, 1973, 3.

37. "Nixon Housing Plan," *Wall Street Journal,* September 20, 1973, 3.

38. "Housing Paradox," *New York Times,* March 10, 1973, 30.

39. "HUD Chief Runs into Hostile Senate Unit on Nixon's New Housing Policy Proposals," *Wall Street Journal,* October 3, 1973, 8.

40. "HUD Chief," *Wall Street Journal,* October 3, 1973, 8.

41. "U.S. Housing Subsidy Programs Mismanaged, Some in Congress Say Democratic Majority on Panel Urges Overhaul; Republicans Protest Hearings During Recess," *Wall Street Journal,* March 5, 1973, 3.

42. "U.S. Housing Subsidy Programs Mismanaged," *Wall Street Journal,* March 5, 1973, 3.

43. "A Promise of a Mouse," *Wall Street Journal,* October 2, 1973, 20.

44. "A Promise of a Mouse," *Wall Street Journal,* October 2, 1973, 20.

45. Interview with David Garrison, senior fellow and deputy director, Greater Washington Research Program, Brookings Institution, August 15, 2003.

46. Garrison interview.

47. "The Cost of a Housing Act," *The New York Times,* July 2, 1974, 34.

48. Lynn told the Subcommittee on Housing of the House Banking and Currency Committee, "First, and most fundamental, we seem agreed on the concept of special revenue sharing or block grants—whichever term you prefer—which provides formula-calculated entitlements based on objective factors producing sums certain year after year to local governments for community development needs." The program that had the federal government engaged in a project-by-project approval process created a housing-

production bottleneck in Washington, D.C. But if more money and authority devolved to local government, local officials would have to take more responsibility. According to Lynn, local government would no longer have "the federal bureaucracy to blame when anything goes wrong" (U.S. Congress 1974, 203).

49. House of Representatives, "Housing and Community Development Legislation—1973," Part 3, 1681.

50. It would be interesting to study this shift in more detail. Perhaps the Voting Rights Act of 1965 or other changes at the local level contributed to a more responsive and fair city governance.

51. Harvey said, "Housing is more than physical shelter. To those who have suffered discrimination and the dehumanization of life in overcrowded, rat infested slums, it has meant the perpetuation of second class status and even as the Supreme Court in *Jones v. Mayer* said 'it is a relic of slavery'" (U.S. Congress 1973, 1204).

52. "Ford Signs $11 Billion Housing-Aid Bill Giving Localities More Control of Funds," *Wall Street Journal,* August 23, 1974, 11.

53. Edward Burks, "Ford Signs Bill to Aid Housing," *New York Times,* August, 23, 1974, 9.

54. Burks, "Ford Signs Bill to Aid Housing," 9.

55. "The Housing and Community Development Act of 1974 combined seven categorical programs to form the CDBG program. The objective of the program is to develop viable urban communities by providing decent housing and a suitable living environment and expanding economic opportunities, principally for persons of low and moderate income. Program funds can be used on housing, economic development, neighborhood revitalization, and other community development activities," according to the U.S. Government Accountability Office (2006, 5).

56. Besides the Bipartisan Millennial Housing Commission report, another good source on the later years of CDBG is the U.S. Government Accountability Office (2006).

57. "The CDBG program receives widespread political support for providing local flexibility in community development" (Bipartisan Millennial Housing Commission 2002, 113).

58. Jimmy Carter, while sympathetic to the needs of the poor, was certainly subject to the theory that government had to come to grips with an era of limits. In an address to Congress, Carter said government could not "solve our problems. . . . It cannot eliminate poverty, or provide a bountiful economy, or reduce inflation, or save our cities, or cure illiteracy, or provide energy" (Bauman 2000, 247).

59. Years later, this unregulated Savings and Loan industry required a federal bailout that was conservatively estimated to cost $325 billion in addition to other incalculable depositor losses ("Resolving the Savings and Loan Crisis: Billions More and Additional Reforms Needed," by Charles A. Bowsher, Comptroller General of the United States, before the Senate Committee on Banking, Housing and Urban Affairs).

60. Bradford Hunt, an urban historian with a substantial background in the budgetary process, warns against confusing budget authority (an authorization by Congress to pay) and outlay (actual government payments). So, on the one hand, the budget authority—the money that had been promised by Congress to further affordable housing goals—was cut dramatically. On the other, however, the amount of money spent on affordable housing each year (outlays) kept rising slowly throughout the 1980s.

Chapter 2. Building the Decentralized Housing Network

1. One of the most well-known neighborhood organizers is Saul Alinsky, but strong community organizing continues today. For more information on Alinsky, see Horwitt (1989).

2. NeighborWorks "2005 Dorothy Richardson Awards for Resident Leadership," brochure, August 22, 2005, 2, http://www.nw.org/network/neighborworksProgs/awards/resident/documents/drAwards2005.pdf.

3. The term CDC can be confusing. Technically it refers to a community-based organization. However, it is often used interchangeably for other nonprofit developers, such as BRIDGE Housing in San Francisco, that are *regional* housing developers. Many of the largest regional housing developers are members of the Housing Partnership Network: http://housingpartnership.net/.

4. $440,129 from the Community Services Administration, a Great Society holdover, and $30,000 from CDBG (Pierce and Steinbach 1987, 56).

5. Nonprofits have certain built-in advantages in the decentralized funding programs. They are required by statute to receive 15 percent of their federal HOME, state LIHTC allocating agencies must set aside at least 10 percent of their annual allotment for nonprofits, and nonprofits are priority purchasers of properties formerly held by distressed savings and loan associations and failed commercial banks.

6. Author's interview with Barry Zigas, August 12, 2004.

7. See Stinchcombe (1990, 15–16): "Many of the sources of untrustworthiness of information are faults in the incentive system for providing accurate information and accurate estimates of how likely one is to be wrong. These are generally dealt with theoretically under the heading of 'agency theory,' which deals with the broad class of problems in which the agent has more information—later or better news—than the principal about the uncertainties involved in a decision that the principal has to take (or that the agent has to take on the principal's behalf)."

8. Putnam refers to this as glue and bridges—glue to hold the community together and bridges to make connections to outside groups and institutions.

9. Local housing authorities had some experience but were not dynamic institutions that could innovate or take advantage of new policies.

10. Richard Nathan and Martha Derthick, *The New York Times,* December 18, 1987, A39. Also see Derthick's chapter regarding the activism of state and local government as a response to Reagan's cuts in *Building Foundations: Housing and Federal Policy* (DiPasquale and Keyes 1990).

11. The magazine *Affordable Housing Finance* does an annual survey of affordable housing production. For a list of the top 50 affordable housing owners, see http://www.housingfinance.com/ahf/articles/2008/may/AHF50TOPOWNERS010508.htm.

12. Tax-exempt bonds are sold under the authority of Section 11b (a 1974 amendment to the 1937 National Housing Act) (Case 1991).

13. This continues to be a problem for CDCs—most funding is project based. There is a serious lack of operations and overhead subsidy for CDCs.

14. The report was prepared by Stuart Hershey, who was himself an interesting example of the new approach to housing; he was president of a housing development consulting firm, on the board of a Baltimore-based CDC (Southeast Community Organization), and worked for the Maryland Department of Economic and Community Development.

15. For an extensive list, with descriptions, see Hecht (1994).

16. http://www.lisc.org/

17. For a tremendous amount of detail on this important figure, see Olsen (2003) and Bloom (2008).

18. Rouse is credited with coining the terms "shopping mall" and "festival market place."

19. "The History of NeighborWorks America and the NeighborWorks Network," http://www.nw.org/network/aboutUs/history/default.asp.

20. "The History of NeighborWorks America and the NeighborWorks Network," http://www.nw.org/network/aboutUs/history/default.asp.

21. The Community Builders, Inc., "History," http://www.tcbinc.org/who_we_are/history.htm.

22. The notable exception to this observation was the high number of for-profits that participated in the Section 8 New Construction and Rehabilitation programs.

23. Because private banks have been so involved in the decentralized housing network, they organized a trade association, the National Association of Affordable Housing Lenders (NAAHL). Financial institution executives working in affordable housing created this group in 1988. General members of this organization therefore are involved in housing finance—banks, insurance companies, savings and loans, secondary market organizations (e.g., FNMA), and nonprofit intermediaries. There are also associate members who are not making loans directly but are party to these transactions—for-profit and nonprofit housing builders, government agencies, and professionals, including lawyers, consultants, appraisers, and accountants. NAAHL is an industry group that seeks to lobby for sound affordable housing policy that provides for the maximum participation of private investment (http://www.ffhsj.com/fairlend/naahl.htm).

24. The Community Reinvestment Act (CRA), enacted by Congress in 1977 (12 U.S.C. 2901) and implemented by Regulations 12 CFR parts 25, 228, 345, and 563e. (For more information on CRA, see the Federal Financial Institutions Examination Council's web site: http://www.ffiec.gov/cra/.) To read some of the debates during its passage, see U.S. Congress (1977). The most comprehensive and up-to-date source on CRA is a joint publication from the Federal Reserve Banks of Boston and San Francisco, "Revisiting the CRA: Perspectives on the Future of the Community Reinvestment Act" (Boston and San Francisco: Federal Reserve Banks of Boston and San Francisco, 2009). It is available at http://frbsf.org/publications/community/cra/index.html.

25. A good overview of the CRA is available from the Federal Reserve Board of Governors' web site at http://www.federalreserve.gov/dcca/cra/.

26. The Treasury report is available at http://www.treas.gov/press/releases/docs/crareport.pdf.

27. "A qualified investment is one that has community development as its primary purpose, and may include an investment, deposit, membership share, or grant in or to a variety of financial intermediaries or organizations" (Joint Center for Housing Studies 2002, 26).

28. The entity making the investment is the United Methodist Church General Board of Pension and Health Benefits. For an example, see Erickson (2006).

Chapter 3. Fighting for Federal Resources for the Decentralized Housing Network

1. See especially the chapter titled, "War on Poverty: The Failure of the Welfare State."

2. Gilbert argues that the effort to use nongovernment participants from the nonprofit and private sectors to promote social welfare amounts to a new era that he calls "the enabling state," which appears to be turning its back on the older conception—popularized by the British thinker T.H. Marshall—of economic citizenship as something universal and guaranteed by the state. Along these same lines, see Marwell (2004), Myles and Quadagno (2000), Huber and Stephens (2001), and Gottschalk (2000).

3. For Marshall's ideas on a universal welfare state, see Marshall (1950).

4. The Joint Committee on Taxation tracks tax expenditures. For a current overview, see Hungerford (2006).

5. That said, most policymakers are not fooled by the complexities of the system. The powerful chairman of the Senate Finance Committee, Russell Long, made this clear when he described tax expenditures, "that label don't bother me. . . . I've never been confused about it. I've always known that what we're doing is giving government money away" (Howard 1997, 4).

6. 2004 U.S. Federal Budget, Historic Tables, Table 3.1—Outlays by Superfunction and Function: 1940–2003.

7. A related idea to the housing network is Zelizer's concept of policy communities. Zelizer argues that a policy community developed around tax policy: Congress's committee structure "created an insulated arena for representatives from both parties and from competing regions to achieve difficult compromises without public scrutiny." These committees were often led by powerful chairs who served for long periods and were effective in mastering technical aspects of specific policies. They also helped connect Congressional decisionmakers with a larger policy community that included bureaucrats, academics, advocacy and industry groups, and specialized policy media.

To explain these developing connections, Zelizer draws on John Kingdon's idea of a policy community that "hums along on its own, independent of such political events as changes of administration and pressure from legislators' constituencies" (Kingdon 1995). In particular, Zelizer focuses on the tax policy community that included, "political party officials, leaders and experts from umbrella business and financial associations (such as the Chamber of Commerce), staff members of the executive and congressional branch, bureaucrats and administrators, university professors, independent specialists, editors and writers of the specialized policy media, and participants in think tanks" (Zelizer 1998, 8).

8. Also important in the Task Force's evaluation was a series of 20 draft reports prepared by scholars and practitioners under the direction of Professors Langley Keyes and Denise DiPasquale of the Massachusetts Institute of Technology. Each paper was examined and several authors appeared as speakers before the task force. That collection

of papers was made into a book, *Building Foundations: Housing and Federal Policy* (DiPasquale and Keyes 1990).

9. HOME is authorized under Title II of the Cranston-Gonzalez National Affordable Housing Act, as amended. Program regulations are at 24 CFR Part 92. More information is available at http://www.hud.gov/offices/cpd/affordablehousing/programs/home/index.cfm.

10. The behind-closed-doors negotiations were designed to facilitate the tough decisions on spending reductions and tax increases needed to balance the federal budget, and this cast a shadow over the NAHA debates. The "money we are going to have to spend on housing ultimately, apparently, is going to be determined by our colleagues and those in the administration who are in the budget summit," according to Senator Kit Bond (R-MO) (*Congressional Record,* 100th Congress, 2d session, 1988, S8198). Interestingly, there was considerable discussion on direct expenditures and their budgetary effect in this debate, but almost no discussion of the fiscal impact of indirect expenditures, such as tax credits (e.g., the LIHTC program). The Senators made it sound as though tax credits were free money. Even though my research of the Senate debates over tax incentives for housing seemed to reveal a tremendous amount of ignorance in how tax expenditure worked, some members of Congress knew exactly what they were (see Howard 1997).

11. For more information on the National Housing Conference, see its web site at http://www.nhc.org/housing/about-overview.

12. St. Paul Mayor George Latimer represented the National League of Cities. He said, "let me reaffirm what Mr. Rouse said to you and what you yourself have said many times, and that is with the greatest energy and innovation in the world on the part of local not-for-profits and local governments, it is critical that the federal government reaffirm its commitment to housing" (U.S. Congress 1988c, 273). State and local government witnesses wanted the Senators to know that their agencies had new capacity and could be viable partners of the federal government. State and local governments, for example, were claiming that their experience of innovation during a time of federal cutbacks had prepared them to be more effective and entrepreneurial. Cities, for their part, also had a proven track record of doing something about housing without federal help. For example, a 1989 study by the Community Development Research Center of the New School for Social Research reported that nearly half of the nation's 51 largest cities were raising local funds to subsidize affordable housing construction by drawing on general fund revenues, local taxes, fees, and city-issued bonds (*Housing and Development Reporter* 1989, 246).

13. Another NCSHA witness, Henry Huckaby, suggested that housing finance agencies had graduated to the point where they could be highly effective partners in national housing policy programs. "Five years ago our agencies were financiers-conduits of tax-exempt capital originated at Wall Street," he said. "Today, we are truly housing finance agencies, active across the broad range of housing needs—setting policy, allocating resources, and designing and implementing programs." But he warned that without federal leadership, "we risk a Balkan-like array of programs that amounts to little more than a scattergun approach" to the problem" (U.S. Congress 1988b, 192–93).

14. Dale Stuard, president of the National Association of Home Builders, said "This report should be on the required reading list for all Americans, especially those with the power to make changes." In a subsequent hearing, Stuard said, "We believe the idea of a National Affordable Housing Act is an idea whose time has come" (U.S. Congress 1988b, 103).

15. Luallen of NCSHA, along with many other witnesses, explained that any reforms on the federal direct expenditure side of the housing equation would have to be matched by reforms on federal tax expenditures—both LIHTC and tax-exempt bonds. "The low-income housing tax credit must be improved and extended, and such efforts must be accompanied by changes in tax exempt multifamily bond financing that restores the viability of this low income financing vehicle," he said (U.S. Congress 1988b).

16. IDA member organizations had a positive working relationship with "community foundations, national nonprofit organizations such as Neighborhood Housing Services of America, the Enterprise Community Partners, the Local Initiatives Support Corporation, community development corporations, and banks and insurance companies as well as other corporations making socially responsive investments" (U.S. Congress 1988b, 655–56).

17. Senator Bob Graham (R-TX) agreed: "Most important, Mr. President, is the recognition in the structure of the bill that each and every community in America has different needs, different resources, and different populations to serve. No longer will the federal government mandate its solution to the perceived problems of states and localities" (U.S. Congress 1992, S8872). Bond's web site says that he believes "government and taxes should be no bigger than necessary" (http://bond.senate.gov/biography/history.cfm).

18. Joe Davidson, "House Clears Bill That Would Result in Big Boost in U.S. Housing Support," *Wall Street Journal,* October 26, 1990, A16.

19. Denise DiPasquale and Jean L. Cummings (1992, 87) made the following comparison of these three eras of tax law: "In the pre-ERTA years before 1981, with the DDB [double declining balance] method of depreciation and the long tax life, 61 percent of historic costs were depreciated by year 13. Under ERTA, with the DDB method of depreciation and a very short tax life, 88 percent of historic costs were depreciated. Under Tax Reform [TRA 86], with SL [straight line] depreciation and a longer tax life, 47 percent of historic costs were depreciated."

20. U.S. Senate Tax Reform Proposals: XIV (Housing, Real Estate, and Rehabilitation), July 16, 1985, 496.

21. U.S. Senate Tax Reform Proposals: XIV, 169.

22. U.S. Senate Tax Reform Proposals: XIV, 519.

23. U.S. Senate Tax Reform Proposals: XIV, 190, and an interview with Barry Zigas, August 12, 2004. On TRA 86, see Martin (1991, 159). TRA 86 was an attempt by Congress to expand the base of taxpayers, reduce the number of tax expenditures and loopholes, and lower tax rates for all income groups and corporations.

24. Zigas interview.

25. Tax Reform Act of 1986. Public Law (PL) 99-514. 100 Stat. 2085, HR 3838, 99th Congress, 2nd Session (October 22, 1986). Low Income Housing Tax Credit provisions are outline in Section 42 of the Internal Revenue Code.

26. The tax credit mechanism is actually much more complicated in how it works, but the coupon analogy is sufficient to understand the argument. In practice, tax credit investors become the limited partner in a legal partnership that owns the apartment building. In most cases, the lion's share ownership, 99 percent and above, rests with the limited partner so it can receive most of the tax credits and the tax benefits that come from operational losses and depreciation. The real estate developer is the man-

aging general partner, even though the developer's share of ownership may be one percent or less.

27. For a good brief overview of the Low Income Housing Tax Credit, see Novogradac and Company's web page: http://www.novoco.com/low_income_housing/resources/program_summary.php.

28. Zigas interview.

29. Iver Peterson, "Prospects Rise for Housing Legislation: Federal Measure Seeks to Help Home Buyers," *The New York Times,* June 11, 1989, R1.

30. *The New York Times,* editorial, "Best Vehicle for Affordable Housing," Nov 18, 1989, A26.

31. See Technical and Miscellaneous Revenue Act of 1988 (PL 100-647), Omnibus Budget Reconciliation Act of 1989 (PL 101-239), and Omnibus Reconciliation Act of 1990 (PL 101-508).

32. Richard Cravatts, *Wall Street Journal,* January 18, 1989, A16.

33. As an example, Edwin Feiler, a for-profit developer and president of the National Association of Home Builders, said he represented 157,000 builders in his testimony. "Affordability is the key word in housing today because prices have gone up, interest rates have gone up, costs have gone up, and incomes have not gone up to the same degree. I feel like the low-income housing credit is an effort to meet that problem head on" (House of Representatives, Low-Income Housing Tax Credit, 185).

34. A 1993 article in *Mortgage Banking* praised the move by Congress to make LIHTC permanent. "The program's permanency is encouraging corporate investors to now ante up big sums," according to Stuart Boesky (1995, 53). The investors were the most respected blue-chip corporations in the country: Bank of America, 3M, Campbell Soup, Nations-Bank, and Warren Buffet's investment company, Berkshire Hathaway.

35. Mitchell Pacelle, "An Expected Bush Veto of Tax Bill Poses Threat to Building Low-Income Rentals," *Wall Street Journal,* October 19, 1992, C17.

36. Federal Information Systems Corporation Federal News Service, "News Conference with Coalition of U.S. Mayors Who Are Urging Congress to Vote an Extension of Low-Income Housing Tax Credits," October 2, 1991.

37. Paul Grogan, "Points of Urban Light," *The Washington Post,* July 19, 1992, C3.

38. Author's interview with Janet Falk, vice president for real estate development, Mercy Housing California, January 13, 2003.

39. Fifteen years was the minimum period for compliance with rent restrictions. State tax credit allocation organizations had the option of extending the compliance period and over time most states raised it to 55 years.

40. Nick Ravo, "Tax-Credit Program on Borrowed Time," *The New York Times,* November 24, 1991, R3.

41. Ravo, "Tax-Credit Program," R3.

42. U.S. Congress, Senate, *Congressional Record* 102nd Congress 2nd sess., July 22, 1992, S10070.

43. *Los Angeles Times,* editorial, "Housing Credit Extension Is a Must—and Riots Tell Us Why," June 2, 1992, B6.

44. See Omnibus Budget Reconciliation Act of 1993 (PL 103-66). LIHTC became Section 42 of the Internal Revenue Code.

45. David Rogers and Bruce Ingersoll, "Two GOP Insurgents for House Seats in the South Cash in on Their Ties to Patrons in Washington," *Wall Street Journal,* Nov 1, 1996, A14.

46. The political tug-of-war led to the temporary shutdown of the U.S. government, a situation that voters largely blamed on Republicans in Congress. A CNN/USA Today/Gallup poll found that 48 percent of respondents blamed the Republican Congress as opposed to 26 percent who blamed Clinton (http://www.cnn.com/US/9511/debt_limit/11-15/poll/poll_gfx2.html).

47. David W. Chen, "Tax-Cut Plan May Endanger New Housing," *New York Times,* March 19, 2003, B1.

48. Charles Rangel (D-NY), ranking democrat on the House Ways and Means Committee, letter to Mel Martinez, dated January 9, 2003. It is also interesting in how the congressman raised the question of fairness: "The only credit exempt from this rule appears to be the foreign tax credit. You may wish to ask the Treasury Department why they took great care to protect a tax benefit available to corporations operating overseas, but chose to deny the benefit of domestic tax credits, such as the Low Income Housing Credit" (2).

49. Dana Milbank and Jim Vande Hei, "Bush Retreat Eased Bill's Advance," *Washington Post,* A05. See also 108th Congress, 1st Session, "H.R. 2: To Amend the Internal Revenue Code of 1986 to Provide Additional Tax Incentives to Encourage Economic Growth," February 27, 2003.

50. "Congress knew what they were doing—they were providing another brick in the wall toward the privatization of the welfare state, but this time they were also creating the opportunity for an unprecedented windfall for the corporate community" (Guthrie and McQuarrie 2005, 44).

51. For a detailed political history of the origins of this program, see Roberts (2005).

52. Kimura (2008) writes, "Fannie Mae leaders said they will look closely at the Housing and Economic Recovery Act of 2008 to see what the new bill might mean for their LIHTC business. The legislation includes several key changes to the LIHTC program, including repealing the alternative minimum tax limitations and other possible incentives for investors to return to the market. Signed by President Bush on July 30, the bill offers some hope for sparking renewed investor interest in the market."

53. Cisneros, along with his more conservative counterpart, embodied a more pragmatic approach to affordable housing policy—at least, it appeared to be more bipartisan, as evidenced by the publication of such reports as "Our Communities, Our Homes: Pathways to Housing and Homeownership in America's Cities and States," published by the Joint Center for Housing Studies of Harvard University (2007). This publication had contributions from former HUD secretaries Henry Cisneros and Jack Kemp and scholars Kent W. Colton and Nicolas P. Retsinas of Harvard's Joint Center for Housing Studies.

54. HOPE VI was created by HUD, the Department of Veterans Affairs, and the Independent Agencies Appropriations Act, 1993 (P.L. 102-389), approved on October 6, 1992. More information is available at http://www.hud.gov/offices/pih/programs/ph/hope6/about/.

55. A good overview of how HOPE VI fits into the larger efforts at improving public housing can be found in U.S. Congress (1997).

Chapter 4. Lessons Learned from What Was Built

1. See chapter 3 for a discussion of how Cincotta's activism made the Community Reinvestment Act a more effective incentive for lending in low-income communities.

2. Unless otherwise noted, all the information on Guyon Towers comes from a case study in Rohe et al. (1998, 139–45).

3. More information available at http://www.bethelnewlife.org/about.asp.

4. Like most banks, Harris lent mortgage financing only up to a certain fraction of the building's value—typically 70–80 percent of the building's appraised value.

5. The Chicago Equity Fund was an affiliate of the National Equity Fund (NEF) and a subsidiary of LISC.

6. "Stillman Community Development Program Proves a Great Asset to West Tuscaloosa," *Speakin' Out News,* March 7, 2000, 3.

7. Frank Sikora, "25-Year Odyssey of Change, Bill Edwards Now Driven by a 'Real Passion' for Better Housing," *The Birmingham News,* July 5, 1994, 101.

8. Sikora, "25-Year Odyssey," 101.

9. Information on housing services available at http://www.cspwal.com/housing. html#apartments.

10. Sikora, "25-Year Odyssey," 101.

11. Terner was a legendary figure in affordable housing development. In addition to founding BRIDGE, he made his mark as an academic at Harvard and Berkeley and, as a government official, as director of California's Housing and Community Development Department. He died in a 1996 plane crash with Commerce Secretary Ron Brown in Bosnia.

12. Details on EBALDC's real estate developments can be found at http://www.ebaldc. org/pg/7/real-estate-development. More information on BRIDGE is available athttp:// www.bridgehousing.com.

13. Jeffrey Spivak, "Group Cuts Back as Funding Withers: KC Neighborhood Alliance Sheds Staff Members and Considers Selling Rental Tracts," *Kansas City Star,* April, 14, 2007.

14. Joe Miller, "Here's How One Neighborhood Conquered White Flight, a Slumlord, Crack Wars, and City Neglect," *Kansas City Pitch,* January 17, 2002, 1.

15. The Low Income Housing Fund expanded dramatically during the 1990s and 2000s. Now known as the Low Income Investment Fund (LIIF), the organization has "provided more than $740 million in financing and technical assistance for projects benefiting low income communities in 26 states, leveraging additional private, public and philanthropic investments of over $5.0 billion: a six-to-one ratio."

16. Typically, a market-rate apartment building has one or two mortgages.

17. "According to the Hope VI blueprint, the federal government would provide financial assistance for the elimination of 100,000 apartments by the year 2000, construction on the same sites of smaller housing developments for mixed-income occupancy, and relocation of the uprooted tenants to privately owned buildings. As the 20th century drew to a close, policymakers in Washington had clearly repudiated the high-rise public housing experiment. The *New York Times* concluded: 'The federal govern-

ment is helping cities clear slums again, but this time they are slums it helped create'" (Bauman, Biles, and Szylvian 2000, 265).

18. All the NEF investor reports are available by request from NEF (120 South Riverside Plaza, 15th Fl., Chicago, Ill. 60606). The projects referenced in this chapter are from the author's files and are also available on request. ("NEF95" indicates that this project was syndicated by NEF in 1995.)

19. Michigan, for example, has combined its decentralized housing programs with a new initiative it calls "cool cities," in an effort to generate more interest in downtowns (see http://www.coolcities.com).

20. Jodie T. Allen, "South Bronx Cheer: A Miracle Grows amid the Rubble," *Washington Post*, July 19, 1992, C3.

21. Unless identified specifically, the following information comes the Urban Land Institute case studies.

22. The details for this case study come from Enlow (2007).

23. More information on Jamboree Housing is available on its web site http://www.jamboreehousing.com.

24. The details for this case study come from Newberg (2008).

25. The chemical was perchloroethylene, or PERC.

26. See the GreenPoint rating of Sara Conner Court on its web site http://www.builditgreen.org/greenpoint-rated/find-homes.

27. More sponsor information is available on its web site, http://www.eden housing.org.

28. The details for this case study come from Thoerig (2008).

29. The details for this case study come from Bach (2008).

30. Author interview with Michele Mozelsio, November 21, 2008.

Chapter 5. The Decentralized Housing Network and the Rise of a New Institution

1. The apartments summarized here are from the development programs. It excludes tenant-based Section 8 certificates and vouchers, which numbered 1,581,000 in 1999. I also include rural housing that is administered in partnership with the Department of Agriculture (410,000 units in 1999). This number is low compared to the affordable-housing construction boom in the 1970s, but many of those units were badly designed or constructed and had to be destroyed.

2. See U.S. Congress, Summary of Provisions Contained in H.R. 5662. The per capita amount went from $1.25 to $1.75.

3. "HOME Investment Partnerships Program," http://www.hud.gov/offices/cpd/affordablehousing/programs/home/index.cfm.

4. In all, there were 18 public and private funders. The initial group included the William and Flora Hewlett Foundation, John S. and James L. Knight Foundation, Lilly

Endowment, John D. and Catherine T. MacArthur Foundation, Pew Charitable Trusts, Prudential Insurance Company of America, Rockefeller Foundation, and Surdna Foundation. Additional subsequent funding came from the Annie E. Casey Foundation, Bankers Trust Company, Chase Manhattan Bank, McKnight Foundation, Metropolitan Life Foundation, J.P. Morgan & Company, HUD, Robert Wood Johnson Foundation, W.K. Kellogg Foundation, and Nationsbank.

5. The operating budget of CDCs also grew during the 1991–97 period. The Urban Institute's National Center for Nonprofit Statistics created a longitudinal database of the IRS Form 990 tax filings of all nonprofit groups in the country with incomes over $25,000 for the tax years 1990, 1992, 1993, and 1994. The Urban Institute study took a subgroup of nonprofits from the list that were likely to be CDCs and found that average annual CDC operating budgets in National Community Development Initiative cities rose from under $10 million to $16 million. Operating budgets more than doubled in Newark; Washington, D.C.; Denver; Indianapolis; Atlanta; and Portland (Walker and Weinheimer 1998, 32).

6. Nonprofits have certain built-in advantages in the decentralized funding programs. They are required by statute to receive 15 percent of their federal HOME, state LIHTC allocating agencies must set aside at least 10 percent of their annual allotment for nonprofits.

7. Author's interview with Barry Zigas, August 12, 2004.

8. The Community Reinvestment Act of 1977 (and its subsequent amendments) requires banks, thrifts, and other lending institutions to lend money in the communities where they accept deposits, including low-income and minority neighborhoods. For a fuller discussion of the CRA, see chapter 3.

9. This organization is now independent from LISC and is the country's only private real estate investment trust with a public purpose. For more information, see the company's web site at http://www.cdt.biz/.

10. Even though it lacked transparency, the decentralized housing network did not suffer from the high-profile corruption problems like the ones that HUD had in the 1980s and before.

11. On this aspect of CDC behavior, also see Goetz and Sidney (1995).

12. Jonathan Weisman, "Bush Plans Sharp Cuts in HUD Community Efforts," *The Washington Post*, January 14, 2005, A1.

13. The coalition included the United States Conference of Mayors, the National League of Cities, the National Association of Counties, the Association of Housing and Redevelopment Officials, the National Community Development Association, and the Local Initiatives Support Corporation (U.S. Newswire, "Mayors, County Officials, and Business Leaders Denounce Elimination of Community Development Block Grant (CDBG)," February 8, 2005).

14. Salamon (1995, 4–5) writes, the "Socialist government of Francois Mitterrand in France launched an ambitious program of decentralization and program reform in the early 1980s that featured heavy reliance on nonprofit organizations to deliver publicly financed services and similar developments are under way, or under consideration, elsewhere as well, most noticeably in the newly independent countries of central and eastern Europe."

Chapter 6. How Does Thinking Like a Network Change Our Approach to Public Policy?

1. There is controversy over whether some network aspects apply to economic production; see Polanyi (1944).

2. To give a sense of how big a player Fannie Mae was, it "committed over $1.18 billion for LIHTC equity investments that resulted in the development or rehabilitation of 17,426 affordable rental housing units" (Fannie Mae 2008).

3. H.R. 1—American Recovery and Reinvestment Act of 2009, 106. The full text of the bill is available at http://frwebgate.access.gpo.gov/cgi-bin/getdoc.cgi?dbname=111_cong_bills&docid=f:h1enr.pdf.

4. I think this organization could be something like an oversight board with representatives from many elements of the network—real estate development, finance, government, and other concerned parties.

5. For an overview, see Federal Reserve Bank of Chicago (2005).

6. There still may be value in promoting larger CDCs and CDFIs to become large corporations with wide geographic reach. The Housing Partnership Network (HPN), for example, represents many large CDCs and CDFIs. It has reached such scale and heft that it is able to pool resources in strategic ways. For more information on the Housing Partnership Network, see its web site at http://www.housingpartnership.net/. For example, as a group, HPN felt as though it was paying too high a premium for insuring its affordable housing apartment buildings because insurance companies did not acknowledge how well these properties were built and managed. As a result, the partners pooled their capital, lobbied for additional funds from Congress, and created their own internal insurance fund, which has yielded substantial savings to their members (Erickson 2006a, 21–22). Perhaps one solution to the quandary of small and local versus large and efficient is to focus on building a better network with both types of organizations. One example from the case studies is BRIDGE Housing, a big organization, partnering with a local CDC to build a complex housing and retail development as it did with the Frank G. Mar project in Oakland, California, described in chapter 4. Even among business leaders there is no consensus on whether large multidivision organizations (IBM), conglomerates (GE), or single-focused businesses (Intel) are the most innovative and competitive. See Skapinker (2001, 2).

7. Don Terner once talked about creating the U.S. Steel of affordable housing.

8. For more on this point, see Wei-Skillern and Marciano (2008).

9. For more background on the program, see GAO (2007).

10. One significant difference from the housing credit is that the CDFI Fund allots tax credits to intermediary organizations known as community development entities (CDEs) and not the states. Otherwise, the programs appear very similar in how they operate.

11. More information on the NMTC Coalition is available at http://www.newmarketstaxcreditcoalition.org/.

12. This is a difference from the LIHTC program, which provides projects with a deeper subsidy. The risks in a LIHTC project for an investor are usually concern getting the apartment building built and placed in service. There is no shortage of low-income

renters who could rent the apartments (in most areas of the country), so there is very little market risk in the projects.

13. Charles Babington, "Clinton Begins Tour of Poor Areas to Push Economic Incentives," *Washington Post*, July 5, 1999, A2.

14. For more background on the Riegle Community Development and Regulatory Improvement Act of 1994 (P.L. 103-325, 108 STAT. 2160), see Erickson (2006b, 29–30). The NMTC program started as a full-fledged program in 2000; however, it has still not achieved the same status of LIHTC with permanent funding.

15. For quotations and more details on the favorable opinions on the NMTC program across the political spectrum, see Benson F. Roberts (2005). Also, the program is still on a year-to-year authorization from Congress.

16. Office of the Press Secretary, "Interview of the President by Reverend Jesse Jackson," July 10, 1999.

17. To get a sense of an outstanding charter school and the challenges and opportunities it faces, see the *New York Times* series on Bronx Prep, available on the *New York Times* web site: http://www.nytimes.com/learning/general/specials/bronxprep/index.html.

18. See the Department of Education's web site on the credit enhancement program at: http://www.ed.gov/programs/charterfacilities/index.html.

19. The Center for Community Developments Investments is a part of the Federal Reserve Bank of San Francisco.

20. These statistics are available on the Department of Education's Credit Enhancement for Charter School Facilities web site: http://www.ed.gov/programs/charterfacilities/performance.html.

21. CMOs and intermediaries provide similar services to intermediaries (similar to LISC and Enterprise) and the construction of school facilities (similar to CDCs that build apartment buildings).

22. Other areas of public policy are also migrating in the decentralized network direction. One is emerging around environmental issues. There has been a long-standing tax credit program for environmental remediation with the Brownfields Tax Credit. (The Brownfields Tax Incentive was passed as part of the Taxpayer Relief Act of 1997 [Public Law 105-34], and codified through Section 198[a] of the Internal Revenue Code.) It is designed to encourage cleanup and redevelopment of land parcels that have been contaminated with hazardous materials. These sites are particularly common in older cities and contribute enough uncertainty about remediation costs that they discourage redevelopment even in the most desirable areas. According to EPA, "While this support is small relative to the number of brownfields and the investment often required to fully clean up contamination and redevelop properties, EPA's program has, in particular, helped communities address less desirable sites that might not be developed if left to the private real estate market" (U.S. Environmental Protection Agency n.d.). Since the program began in 1995, EPA has awarded 1,200 brownfield grants totaling about $400 million (GAO 2004, 9).

23. There is also a renewable energy tax credit that was created by the Energy Policy Act of 1992. Known as Section 45, this production credit subsidizes electricity produced from wind and biomass production. Additional tax incentives support the production of electricity from the following renewable sources: geothermal, solar, small irrigation

power facilities, landfill gas facilities, trash combustion facilities, refined coal production, and certain hydropower projects (GAO 2007).

24. For an excellent overview of the intersection of environmental and community development policy, see the Federal Reserve Bank of San Francisco's *Community Investments* (2008).

25. The National Association of Community Health Centers estimates that $18 billion is spent on unnecessary emergency room visits per year (National Association of Community Health Centers 2006).

26. For many community development problems, as many as 60 people know 1/60th of the answer; to make matters worse, these 60 people are usually housed in 40 separate institutions. Getting them to work together to solve problems efficiently and effectively is a problem.

27. This kind of development of communities of investors is already happening. See the *Economist* (2008).

28. Also see Lee Gomes, "More Firms Create Own Social Networks," *Wall Street Journal*, February 19, 2008.

29. The longest-running web-based information market is the Iowa Electronic Markets. For more information, see Berg et al. (2000).

30. For a quick overview on the concept of using information markets and dynamic polling to ascertain group opinions, see Surowieki (2004).

31. Jilian Mincer, "Principles and Principal: Socially Responsible Investing Is No Longer about Just What You Can't Buy. And That Makes It a Lot Easier to Make Money," *Wall Street Journal*, April 21, 2008, R5.

32. The recent calamity in the securitization process was driven largely by the weakness in the underlying asset, such as subprime mortgages, and a misunderstanding of the actual risk posed to investors (often the result of faulty analysis from credit rating agencies). It is likely that this technique will continue to be used but with greater transparency in the process.

33. I got this idea from a conversation with Chris Larsen, CEO of Prosper.com.

34. For an overview of 16 communities that fit this description, see Community Affairs Offices (2008).

35. According to its web site, "Coro is an organization begun in San Francisco in 1942 by W. Donald Fletcher, an attorney, and Van Duyn Dodge, an investment counselor, to train young veterans in the leadership skills necessary to assure that our [the U.S.] democratic system of government could more effectively meet the needs of its citizens. Since 1947, when the first program was delivered, Coro has grown to include Coro Centers in six cities, including San Francisco, Los Angeles (1957), St. Louis (1972), Kansas City (1975), New York (1980), Pittsburgh (1999), and a new Executive Fellows program in Cleveland, funded in partnership with The Cleveland Foundation (2005). At least 10,000 program alumni are currently serving as leaders in local, regional and national/ global businesses, nonprofit organizations, governmental agencies and elected public office." More information on the Coro Foundation can be found at http://www.coro.org. See also the Kellogg Foundation's web site: http://www.wkkf.org.

36. Tim Arango, "End of an Era on Wall Street: Goodbye to All That," *New York Times*, October 5, 2008.

References

Abrams, Richard. 2006. *America Transformed: Sixty Years of Revolutionary Change,* 1941–2001. New York: Cambridge University Press.

Agranoff, Robert, and Michael McGuire. 2003. *Collaborative Public Management: New Strategies for Local Governments.* Washington, DC: Georgetown University Press.

Alexander, Robert. 1973. "State Housing Finance Agencies Face Difficult Problems during Housing Freeze and Pending Federal Housing Re-Evaluation." *Journal of Housing* 30(3).

Apgar, William C., and Mark Duda. 2003. "The Twenty-Fifth Anniversary of the Community Reinvestment Act: Past Accomplishments and Future Regulatory Challenges." *Economic Policy Review* 9(2).

Bach, Alexa. 2008. "Plaza Apartments." Washington, DC: Urban Land Institute.

Barr, Michael S. 2005. "Credit Where It Counts: The Community Reinvestment Act and Its Critics." *New York University Law Review* 75:600.

Bartlett, Bruce. 2002. "Truth Be Told: Lamenting the Current State of Affairs of Congressional Economics." *National Review,* January 23. http://www.nationalreview.com/nrof_bartlett/bartlett012302.shtml.

Barton, Harvey. 1989. "A New Enterprise." *The Humanist* 49(3): 15.

Bauman, David. 2004. "Budget—Accounting for the Deficit." *National Journal Magazine,* June 12: 3.

Bauman, John. 2000. "Jimmy Carter, Patricia Roberts Harris, and Housing Policy in the Age of Limits." In *From Tenements to the Taylor Homes: In Search of an Urban Housing Policy in Twentieth-Century America,* edited by John F. Bauman, Roger Biles, and Kristin Szylvian. University Park: The Pennsylvania State University Press.

Bauman, John, Roger Biles, and Kristin Szylvian, eds. 2000. *From Tenements to the Taylor Homes: In Search of an Urban Housing Policy in Twentieth-Century America.* University Park: The Pennsylvania State University Press.

Benkler, Yochai. 2006. *The Wealth of Networks: How Social Production Transforms Markets and Freedoms.* New Haven, CT: Yale University Press.

Berg, Joyce, Robert Forsythe, Forrest Nelson, and Thomas Rietz. 2000. "Results from a Dozen Years of Election Futures Markets Research." In *Handbook of Experimental Economics Results,* edited by Charles R. Plott and Vernon L. Smith (742–51). Amsterdam: Elsevier Science Ltd.

Berger, Peter, and Richard Neuhaus. 1996. *To Empower People.* Washington, DC: The AEI Press.

Berkowitz, Edward, and Kim McQuaid. 1988. *Creating the Welfare State: The Political Economy of Twentieth-Century Reform,* 2nd ed. New York: Praeger.

Berndt, Harry Edward. 1977. *New Rulers of the Ghetto: The Community Development Corporation and Urban Poverty.* Westport, CT: Greenwood Press.

Berube, Alan, and Elizabeth Kneebone. 2006. "Two Steps Back: City and Suburban Poverty Trends, 1999–2005." Washington, DC: The Brookings Institution.

Biles, Roger. 2000. "Epilogue." In *From Tenements to the Taylor Homes: In Search of an Urban Housing Policy in Twentieth-Century America,* edited by John F. Bauman, Roger Biles, and Kristin M. Szylvian (265–70). Philadelphia: The Pennsylvania State University Press.

Bipartisan Millennial Housing Commission. 2002. "Meeting Our Nation's Housing Challenges: Report of the Bipartisan Millennial Housing Commission." Washington, DC: Bipartisan Millennial Housing Commission.

Bloom, Nicholas D. 2008. *Public Housing That Worked: New York in the Twentieth Century.* Philadelphia: University of Pennsylvania Press.

Boesky, Stuart. 1995. "Tax Credits at Work." *Mortgage Banking* 55 (12): 53–57.

Bratt, Rachel. 2007. "Financing Low- and Moderate-Income Housing." In *Financing Low-Income Communities,* edited by Julia Sass Rubin (183–226). New York: Russel Sage Foundation.

Brinkley, Alan. 1991. "Great Society." In *The Reader's Companion to American History,* edited by Eric Foner and John A. Garraty (470–72). Boston: Houghton Mifflin Company.

———. 2004. *The Unfinished Nation: A Concise History of the American People,* 4th ed. New York: McGraw Hill.

Brooks, Mary. 2002. "Housing Trust Fund Progress Report 2002: Local Responses to America's Housing Needs." Frazier Park, CA: Housing Trust Fund Project, Center for Community Change.

Bryan, Barbara. 1993. "The For-Profit Homebuilder's Perspective on Affordable Housing." In *Housing America: Mobilizing Bankers, Builders and Communities to Solve the Nation's Affordable Housing Crisis,* edited by Jess Lederman (119–26). Chicago: Probus Publishing Company.

California Legislative Analyst. 1979. "An Analysis of the Effect of Proposition 13 on Local Government." Sacramento, CA: Office of the Legislative Analyst.

Campbell, Ballard. 1995. *Growth of American Government: Governance from the Cleveland Era to the Present.* Bloomington: Indiana University Press.

Case, Karl E. 1991. "Investors, Developers, and Supply Side Subsidies: How Much Is Enough?" *Housing Policy Debate* 2(2): 341–56.

Case, Anne, and Lawrence Katz. 1991. "The Company You Keep: The Effects of Family and Neighborhood on Disadvantaged Youth." Working Paper 3705. Cambridge, MA: National Bureau of Economic Research.

Chafe, William H., and Harvard Sitkoff, eds. 1991. *A History of Our Time: Readings on Postwar America*, 3rd ed. New York: Oxford University Press.

Chandler, Jr., Alfred D. 1977. *The Visible Hand: The Managerial Revolution in American Business*. Cambridge, MA: Harvard University Press.

Chesbrough, Henry, and David Teece. 1996. "When Is Virtual Virtuous: Organizing for Innovation." *Harvard Business Review* January/February: 65–73.

Clancy, Patrick. 1988. "Tax Incentives and Federal Housing Programs: Proposed Principles for the 1990s." MIT Housing Policy Project. Cambridge, MA: MIT Center for Real Estate Development.

Clarke, Susan. 2000. "Governance Tasks and Nonprofit Organizations." In *Nonprofits in Urban America*, edited by Richard C. Hula and Cynthia Jackson-Elmoore (203–4). Westport, CT: Quorum Books.

Coase, Ronald H. 1937. "The Nature of the Firm." *Economica* 4:386–405.

Cohen, Deborah A., Karen Mason, Ariane Bedimo, Richard Scribner, Victoria Basolo, and Thomas Farley. 2003. "Neighborhood Physical Conditions and Health." *Journal of American Public Health* 93(3): 467–71.

Community Affairs Offices of the Federal Reserve System and Brookings Metropolitan Policy Program. 2008. "The Enduring Challenge of Concentrated Poverty in America." Washington, DC: The Federal Reserve and Brookings.

Consoletti, Alison, and Jeanne Allen, eds. 2007. "2007 Annual Survey of America's Charter Schools." Washington, DC: The Center for Education Reform.

Cross, Theodore. 1969. *Black Capitalism*. New York: Atheneum.

Cummings, Jean, and Denise DiPasquale. 1999. "The Low-Income Housing Tax Credit: An Analysis of the First Ten Years." *Housing Policy Debate* 10(2): 251–307.

"Current Topic Award: The Enterprise Foundation." 1989. *Planning* 55(3): 16.

Davidow, William H., and Michael S Malone. 1992. *The Virtual Corporation: Structuring and Revitalizing the Corporation for the 21st Century*. New York: Harper Collins.

Davis, Perry. 1986. "Public-Private Partnerships: Improving Urban Life." *Proceedings of the Academy of Political Science* 36(2): 35.

DeParle, Jason. 1996. "Slamming the Door." *New York Times Magazine*, October 20, 52.

DiPasquale, Denise, and Langley Keyes, eds. 1990. *Building Foundations: Housing and Federal Policy*. Philadelphia: University of Pennsylvania Press.

DiPasquale, Denise, and Jean L. Cummings. 1992. "Financing Multifamily Rental Housing: The Changing Role of Lenders and Investors." *Housing Policy Debate* 3(1): 71–116.

Donovan, Annie. 2008. "Charter School Facilities Finance: How CDFIs Created the Market and How to Stimulate Future Growth." Community Development Investment

Center Working Paper 2008-02. San Francisco: Federal Reserve Bank of San Francisco.

Downs, Anthony. 1972. "Federal Housing Subsidies: Their Nature and Effectiveness and What We Should Do About Them, Summary Report." Washington, DC: Real Estate Research Corporation.

Dreier, Peter. 1997. "Philanthropy and the Housing Crisis: The Dilemmas of Private Charity and Public Policy." *Housing Policy Debate* 8(1): 235–93.

Drucker, Peter. 1984. "Doing Good to Do Well: The New Opportunities for Business Enterprise." In *Public Private Partnerships: New Opportunities for Meeting Social Needs*, edited by Harvey Brooks, Lance Liebman, and Cornine Schelling. Cambridge, MA: Ballinger.

Economist. 2007. "Joined-up Thinking: Social-Networking Sites Are Not Just for Teenagers. They Have Business Uses Too." April 4.

———. 2008. "Beware Grannies on Facebook: Disgruntled Small Investors in Canada Flex Their Muscles." April 17.

Edsall, Thomas Byrne, with Mary Edsall. 1991. *Chain Reaction: The Impact of Race, Rights, and Taxes on American Politics.* New York: Norton.

Ellen, Ingrid Gould, and Margery Austin Turner. 1997. "Does Neighborhood Matter? Assessing Recent Evidence." *Housing Policy Debate* 8(4): 833–66.

Enlow, Clair. 2007. "Montecito Vista." Urban Land Institute Case Study. Washington, DC: Urban Land Institute.

Enterprise Foundation. 1983. "Annual Report." Columbia, MD: Enterprise Foundation.

———. 2003. "Annual Report." Columbia, MD: Enterprise Foundation.

Erickson, David J. 2006a. "The Secondary Market for Community Development Loans: Conference Proceedings." *Community Development Investment Review* 2(2): 5–20.

———. 2006b. "The Struggle to Establish a Vibrant Secondary Market for Community Development Loans." *Community Development Investment Review* 2(1): 17–34. http://www.frbsf.org/publications/community/review/062006/index.html.

Ernst & Young. 2003. "The Impact of the Dividend Exclusion Proposal on the Production of Affordable Housing." New York: Ernst & Young.

Esping-Andersen, Gøsta. 1990. *The Three Worlds of Welfare Capitalism.* Princeton: Princeton University Press.

Fannie Mae. 2008. "Fannie Mae's 2007 Annual Housing Activities Report." Washington, DC: Fannie Mae. http://www.hud.gov/offices/hsg/gse/reports/2007aharfnmanarrative.pdf.

Faux, Geoffrey. 1971. "CDCs: New Hope for the Inner City, Report of the Twentieth Century Fund Task Force on Community Development Corporations." New York: Twentieth Century Fund.

Federal Home Loan Mortgage Corporation. 2008. "Annual Housing Activities Report for 2007." Washington, DC: Federal Home Loan Mortgage Corporation. http://www.fhfa.gov/webfiles/386/HMG_MAC_-_2007_AHAR.pdf.

Federal Reserve Bank of Chicago. 2005. "An Informed Discussion: Achieving Sustainability, Scale, and Impact in Community Development Finance." Chicago: Federal Reserve Bank of Chicago.

Federal Reserve Bank of San Francisco. 2008. *Community Investments* 20(2). http://frbsf. org/publications/community/investments/0808/index.html.

Fellowes, Matt. 2006. "From Poverty, Opportunity: Putting the Market to Work for Low-Income Families." Washington, DC: Brookings Institution.

Ferguson, Thomas, and Joel Rogers. 1986. *Right Turn: The Decline of the Democrats and the Future of American Politics.* New York: Hill and Wang.

Finkel, Meryl, Charles Hanson, Richard Hilton, Ken Lam, and Melissa Vandawalker. 2006. *Multifamily Properties: Opting In, Opting Out, and Remaining Affordable.* Bethesda, MD, and Cambridge, MA: Econometrica, Inc., and Abt Associates.

Fishbein, Allen J. 1992. "The Ongoing Experiment with Regulation from Below: Expanded Reporting Requirements for HMDA and CRA." *Housing Policy Debate* 3(2): 609.

———. 2003. "What's Next for CRA?" *Journal of Housing and Community Development* 60(4): 18.

Fisher, Robert. 1994. *Let the People Decide: Neighborhood Organizing in America.* New York: Twayne Publishers.

Florida, Richard. 2004. *The Rise of the Creative Class: And How It's Transforming Work, Leisure, Community, and Everyday Life.* New York: Basic Books.

Ford Foundation. 1973. "Community Development Corporations: A Strategy for Depressed Urban and Rural Areas." New York: Ford Foundation.

———. 1991. "Annual Report." New York: Ford Foundation.

Fulton, William. 1993. "HUDdling with Henry Cisneros: An Interview with the Secretary of Housing and Urban Development." *Planning* 59(9): 18.

Gan, Carolyn. 1988. "Dang—Portrait of an Investor, Developer and Volunteer." *Asian Week* 10(1): 18.

Gerschenkron, Alexander. 1965. *Economic Backwardness in Historical Perspective.* New York: F. Praeger.

Gilbert, Neil. 2002. *Transformation of the Welfare State: The Silent Surrender of Public Responsibility.* New York: Oxford University Press.

Glyn, Andrew, Alan Hughes, Alain Lipietz, and Ajit Singh, eds. 1990. *The Rise and Fall of the Golden Age of Capitalism: Reinterpreting the Postwar Experience.* New York: Oxford University Press.

Goetz and Mara Sidney. 1995. "Community Development Corporations as Neighborhood Advocates: A Study of the Political Activism of Nonprofit Developers." *Applied Behavioral Science Review* 3(1): 1–20.

Goldsmith, Stephen, and William D. Eggers. 2004. *Governing by Network: The New Shape of the Public Sector.* Washington, DC: Brookings Institution Press.

Gorham, William, and Nathan Glazer. 1976. *The Urban Predicament.* Washington, DC: Urban Institute Press.

Gottschalk, Marie. 2000. *The Shadow Welfare State: Labor Business and the Politics of Welfare in the United States.* Ithaca, NY: Cornell University Press.

Gottschall, Bruce, and Francine Justa. 1997. "NeighborWorks Is Working." *Mortgage Banking* 57(12): 38.

Granovetter, Mark. 1985. "Economic Activity and Social Structure: The Problem of Embeddedness." *American Journal of Sociology* 91(3): 481–510.

Grant, Heather McLeod, and Leslie R. Crutchfield. 2007. "Creating High-Impact Non-profits." *Stanford Social Innovation Review.* Palo Alto, CA: Stanford University.

Grogan, Paul, and Benson Roberts. 1992. "Good Policy, Good Politics." *Shelterforce* 14(1): 12–15.

Guthrie, Doug, and Michael McQuarrie. 2005. "Privatization and Low-Income Housing in the United States since 1986." *Politics and the Corporation: Research in Political Sociology* 14: 15–51.

Haar, Charles. 1984a. "Foreword." In *Housing in the Eighties: Financial and Institutional Perspectives.* Cambridge, MA: Lincoln Institute of Land Policy.

———. 1984b. "The Joint Venture Approach to Urban Renewal: From Model Cities to Enterprise Zones." In *Public-Private Partnership: New Opportunities for Meeting Social Needs,* edited by Harvey Brooks, Lance Liebman, and Corinne S. Schelling (81–84). Cambridge, MA: Harper and Row.

Hacker, Jacob. 2002. *The Divided Welfare State: The Battle over Public and Private Social Benefits in the United States.* New York: Cambridge University Press.

Harrison, Bennett. 1995. *Building Bridges: Community Development Corporations and the World of Employment Training.* New York: Ford Foundation.

Hartman, Chester. 1992. "Feeding the Sparrows by Feeding the Horses." *Shelterforce* 14(1): 12–15.

Harvey, David. 2000. *The Conditions of Post Modernity: An Inquiry into the Origins of Cultural Change.* Malden, MA: Blackwell Publishers.

Hecht, Bennet. 1994. *Developing Affordable Housing: A Practical Guide for Nonprofit Organizations.* New York: John Wiley & Sons, Inc.

Henry, Shannon. 1994. "Arizona Community Development Group Is Showing the Others How It's Done." *American Banker* 159(110): 48.

Hershey, Stuart S. 1986. "Housing and Business Development through Community Development Corporations." *MIS Report* 18(8). Washington, DC: International City Management Association.

Hirsch, Arnold. 1998. *Making the Second Ghetto: Race and Housing in Chicago, 1940–1960.* Chicago: The University of Chicago Press.

Hirschman, Albert O. 2004. *Exit, Voice, and Loyalty: Responses to Decline in Firms, Organizations, and States.* Cambridge, MA: Harvard University Press.

Hise, Greg. 1997. *Magnetic Los Angeles: Planning the Twentieth-Century Metropolis.* Baltimore: Johns Hopkins University Press.

von Hoffman, Alexander. 2000. "A Study in Contradictions: The Origins and Legacy of the Housing Act of 1949." *Housing Policy Debate* 11(2): 299–327.

Hornung, Mark. 1991. "Activist Ousted from Bethel Role; Nelson's Losses Spur Directors to Hire Manager." *Crain's Chicago Business,* July 1.

Horwitt, Sanford D. 1989. *Let Them Call Me Rebel: Saul Alinksy, His Life and Legacy.* New York: Alfred A. Knopf.

Housing and Development Reporter. 1989. *Housing and Development Reporter* 17(14): 246.

Howard, Christopher. 1997. *The Hidden Welfare State: Tax Expenditures and Social Policy in the United States.* Princeton, NJ: Princeton University Press.

Huber, Evelyne, and John D. Stephens. 2001. *Development and Crisis of the Welfare State.* Chicago: University of Chicago Press.

HUD. See U.S. Department of Housing and Urban Development.

Hungerford, Thomas L. 2006. "Tax Expenditures: Trends and Critiques." Congressional Research Service, September 13.

Hunt, D. Bradford. 2006. "Review Essay: Rethinking the Retrenchment Narrative in U.S. Housing Policy." *Journal of Urban History* 32: 937.

Hunt, Valerie H. 2007. "Community Development Corporations and Public Participation: Lessons from a Case Study in the Arkansas Delta." *Journal of Sociology and Social Welfare* 34(3): 9–36.

Husock, Howard. 2003. *America's Trillion Dollar Housing Mistake: The Failure of American Housing Policy.* Chicago: Ivan R. Dee.

Isaacs, Julia B., Isabel V. Sawhill, and Ron Haskins. 2008. *Getting Ahead or Losing Ground: Economic Mobility in America.* Washington, DC: The Brookings Institution.

Jackson, Matthew O. 2008. *Social and Economic Networks.* Princeton, NJ: Princeton University Press.

Jacobs, Barry. 1997. "Washington Wire: Archer Abandons Plan to Sunset LIHTC." *National Real Estate Investor* 39(8): 30.

Johnston, Louis, and Samuel Williamson. 2002. "The Annual Real and Nominal GDP for the United States, 1789–Present." *Economic History Services,* April. http://www.eh.net/hmit/gdp/.

Joint Center for Housing Studies. 2002. "The 25th Anniversary of the Community Reinvestment Act: Access to Capital in an Evolving Financial Services System." Cambridge, MA: Harvard University.

Joint Center for Housing Studies of Harvard University. 2007. "Our Communities, Our Homes: Pathways to Housing and Homeownership in America's Cities and States." Cambridge MA: Joint Center for Housing Studies of Harvard University.

Journal of Housing. 1987. *Journal of Housing* 44(1).

Kaltenheuser, Skip. 1990. "Housing's Moment on Capitol Hill." *Mortgage Banking* March: 29.

Katz, Michael. 1986. *In the Shadow of the Poorhouse: A Social History of Welfare in America.* New York: Basic Books.

———. 2002. *The Price of Citizenship: Redefining the American Welfare State.* New York: Henry Holt.

Katznelson, Ira. 1989. "Was the Great Society a Lost Opportunity." In *The Rise and Fall of the New Deal Order, 1930–1980,* edited by Steve Fraser and Gary Gerstle (185–211). Princeton, NJ: Princeton University Press.

Kelly, Rita Mae. 1976. *Community Participation in Directing Economic Development.* Cambridge, MA: Center for Community Economic Development.

Kennedy, David M. 1999. *Freedom from Fear: The American People in Depression and War, 1929–1945.* New York: Oxford University Press.

Kickert, Walter J. M., Erik-Hans Klijn, and Joop F. M. Koppenjan, eds. 1997. *Managing Complex Networks: Strategies for the Public Sector.* London: Sage Publications.

Kimura, Donna. 2007. "Sara Conner Court Answers Urban Infill Challenge." *Affordable Housing Finance* August. http://www.housingfinance.com/ahf/articles/2007/aug/SARA-CONNER0807.htm.

———. 2008. "Syndicators Predict Better but Still Restrained Second Half." *Affordable Housing Finance* October. http://www.housingfinance.com/ahf/articles/2008/oct/1008-finance-tax-syndicators.htm.

Kivell, Jonathan. 2008. "Schools in Session: An Overview of Charter School Finance." Center for Community Development Investments, Working Paper 2008-03. San Francisco: Federal Reserve Bank of San Francisco. http://frbsf.org/publications/community/wpapers/index.html#july.

Klein, Jennifer. 2003. *For All These Rights: Business, Labor, and the Shaping of America's Public-Private Welfare State.* Princeton, NJ: Princeton University Press.

Kling, Jeffrey, Jeffrey Liebman, and Lawrence Katz. 2007. "Experimental Analysis of Neighborhood Effects." *Econometrica* 75(1): 83–119.

Knight, George. 1996. "A Solid Foundation for Affordable Lending." *Mortgage Banking* 56(1): 69–76.

Koo, Doris, and Jeffery Donaue. 2003. "Enterprise Foundation Annual Report." Columbia, MD: Enterprise Foundation.

Kotelchuck, Ronda. 2008. "Health Care Centers." *The Next American Opportunity: Good Policies for a Great America.* Philadelphia: Opportunity Finance Network.

Leifer, Loring. 1993. "Voice 'n the Hood: Colleen Hernandez Works to Make Kansas City's Inner-City Neighborhoods Viable Places to Live." *Ingram's For Successful Kansas Citians* 19(9): 44.

Leinberger, Christopher B. 2008. "The Subprime Crisis Is Just the Tip of the Iceberg. Fundamental Changes in American Life May Turn Today's McMansions into Tomorrow's Tenements." *Atlantic Monthly* March. http://www.theatlantic.com/doc/200803/subprime.

Leonard, Paul A., Cushing N. Dolbeare, and Edward Lazere. 1989. "A Place to Call Home: The Crisis in Housing for the Poor." Washington, DC: Center on Budget and Policy Priorities and Low-Income Housing Information Service.

Letts, Christine, Bill Ryan, and Allen Grossman. 1999. *High Performance Nonprofit Organizations: Managing Upstream for Greater Impact.* New York: John Wiley & Sons, Inc.

Levine, Daniel. 1988. *Poverty and Society: The Growth of the American Welfare State in International Comparison.* New Brunswick, NJ: Rutgers University Press.

LISC. See Local Initiatives Support Corporation.

Litan, Robert E., Nicolas P. Retsinas, Eric S. Belsky, and Susan White Haag. 2000. "The Community Reinvestment Act after Financial Modernization: A Baseline Report." Washington, DC: U.S. Department of the Treasury.

Local Initiatives Support Corporation (LISC). 1986. "Annual Report." New York: Local Initiatives Support Corporation.

————. 2002. "The Whole Agenda: The Past and Future of Community Development." New York: Local Initiatives Support Corporation.

Litan, Robert E., Nicolas P. Retsinas, Eric S. Belsky, and Susan White Haag. 2003. "The Community Reinvestment Act After Financial Modernization: A Baseline Report." Washington, DC: U.S. Department of the Treasury.

Mallach, Allan. 1984. *Inclusionary Housing Programs: Policies and Practices.* New Brunswick, NJ: Center for Urban Policy Research.

Mandell, Myrna P., ed. 2001. *Getting Results through Collaboration: Networks and Network Structures for Public Policy and Management.* Westport, CT: Quorum Books.

Marshall, Jeffrey. 1999. "Interview: A Redevelopment Pioneer Reflects." *U.S. Banker* 109(2): 62–68.

Marshall, T. H. 1950. *Citizenship and Social Class, and Other Essays.* Cambridge: Cambridge University Press.

Martin, Cathie. 1991. *Shifting the Burden: The Struggle over Growth and Corporate Taxation.* Chicago: University of Chicago Press.

Marwell, N. P. 2004. "Privatizing the Welfare State: Nonprofit Community-Based Organizations as Political Actors." *American Sociological Review* 69(April): 265–91.

Matasar, A. B., and D. D. Pavelka. 1998. "Federal Banking Regulators' Competition in Laxity: Evidence from CRA Audits." *International Advances in Economic Research* 4(1): 56–69.

Matulef, Mark. 1988. "Community Development: A National Perspective." *Journal of Housing* 45(5): 239–50.

Matusow, Alan J. 1984. *The Unraveling of America: A History of Liberalism in the 1960s.* New York: Harper and Row.

McCusker, John. 2001. "What Was the Inflation Rate Then?" Oxford, OH: Economic History Services. http://www.eh.net/hmit/inflation/.

McQuiston, Julian. 1996. "Tax Credits Fuel Growth of Affordable Housing." *Journal of Housing and Community Development* 53(6): 14–19.

Metzger, John. 1993. "Community Development: The Clinton Strategy." *Journal of Housing* 50(2): 83–88.

Mihm, J. Christopher. 2006. "Fernandez and Rainey: Managing Successful Organizational Change in the Public Sector: An Agenda for Research and Practice." *Public Administration Review* March/April: 36.

Mishra, Upendra. 1997. "Using Tax-Exempt Bonds to Finance Affordable Housing." *National Real Estate Investor* 39(6): 64.

Moss, Bob. 2008. "The LIHTC Correction of 2008 and How We Got Here." *Journal of Tax Credit Housing* 1(5): 1–2.

Multi-Housing News. 2002. "The Low-Income Housing Tax Credit: A Public/Private Partnership That Works." *Multi-Housing News* 37(4): 1.

Myles, J., and J. Quadagno. 2000. "Envisioning a Third Way: The Welfare State in the Twenty-First Century." *Contemporary Sociology* 29(1): 156–67.

National Association of Community Health Centers. 2006. "2006 Data on Community Health Centers—Summary of Findings." Bethesda, MD: National Association of Community Health Centers. http://www.nachc.com/client/documents/issues-advocacy/policy-library/research-data/research-reports/2006Datasummary.pdf.

National Congress for Community Economic Development (NCCED). 1997. "Coming of Age: Trends and Achievements of Community-Based Development Organizations." Washington, DC: NCCED.

———. 1988. "Tying It All Together: The Comprehensive Achievements of Community-Based Development Organizations." Washington, DC: NCCED.

———. 1991. "Changing the Odds: The Achievements of Community-Based Development Corporations." Washington, DC: NCCED.

———. 2005. "Reaching New Heights: Trends and Achievements of Community-Based Development Organizations—5th National Community Development Census." Washington, DC: NCCED.

National Council of State Housing Finance Agencies. 2008. *State HFA Factbook: 2006 NCSHA Annual Survey Results.* Washington, DC: National Council of State Housing Finance Agencies.

National Election Studies. 2000. "The NES Guide to Public Opinion and Electoral Behavior." Ann Arbor, MI: University of Michigan, Center for Political Studies. http://www.umich.edu/~nes/nesguide/nesguide.htm.

National Equity Fund. Various years. NEF Investor Reports. Chicago: National Equity Fund.

National Housing Forum. 1988. "Working Toward a Consensus, Final Report." Austin, TX: National Housing Forum.

National Housing Task Force. 1988. "A Decent Place to Live: The Report of the National Housing Task Force." Washington DC: Government Printing Office.

NCCED. See National Congress for Community Economic Development.

NCSHA. See National Council of State Housing Finance Agencies.

Neighborhood Reinvestment Corporation. 1979. "Annual Report." Washington, DC: Neighborhood Reinvestment Corporation.

Nelson, Kathryn P., Mark Treskon, and Danilo Pelletiere. 2004. "Losing Ground in the Best of Times: Low Income Renters in the 1990s." Washington, DC: National Low Income Housing Coalition.

Neumann, George R., and Ellen R. Rissman. 1984. "Where Have All the Union Members Gone?" *Journal of Labor Economics* 2(2): 175–92.

"New Republican Caucus Formed to Promote Affordable Housing." 1996. *National Real Estate Investor* 38(13): 74.

Newberg, Sam. 2008. "Sara Conner Court." Washington, DC: Urban Land Institute.

Nixon, Brian. 1994. "A New Model for Affordable Housing." *Savings and Community Banker* 3(10): 14–24.

Olsen, Johan. 2003. "Towards a European Administrative Space." *Journal of European Public Policy* 10(4): 506–31.

Olsen, Joshua. 2003. *Better Places, Better Lives: A Biography of James Rouse.* Washington, DC: Urban Land Institute.

OMB. See U.S. Office of Management and Budget.

Orlebeke, Charles J. 2000. "The Evolution of Low-Income Housing Policy, 1949 to 1999." *Housing Policy Debate* 11(2): 489–520.

Osborne, David, and Ted Gaebler. 1992. *Reinventing Government: How the Entrepreneurial Spirit Is Transforming the Public Sector.* Reading, MA: Addison-Wesley.

Patterson, James T. 1981. *American's Struggle Against Poverty, 1900–1985.* Cambridge, MA: Harvard University Press.

———. 1996. *Grand Expectations: The United States, 1945–1974.* New York: Oxford University Press.

Peterson, George, and Dana Sundblad. 1994. "Corporations as Partners in Strengthening Urban Communities." New York: The Conference Board.

Peterson, Wallace. 1995. *Silent Depression: Fate of the American Dream.* New York: W.W. Norton.

Pierce, Neal, and Carol Steinbach. 1990. "Enterprising Communities: Community-Based Development in America." Washington, DC: National Council for Community-Based Development.

Pierce, Neal, and Carol Steinbach. 1987. *Corrective Capitalism: The Rise of America's Community Development Corporations.* New York: Ford Foundation.

Pierson, Paul. 2004. *Politics in Time: History, Institutions, and Social Analysis.* Princeton, NJ: Princeton University Press.

Piore, Michael, and Charles Sabel. 1984. *The Second Industrial Divide: Possibilities for Prosperity.* New York: Basic Books.

Pitcoff, Winton. 2002. *Shelterforce Online* 122 (March/April). http://www.nhi.org/online/issues/122/Dolbeare.html.

Piven, Frances Fox, and Richard Cloward. 1993. *Regulating the Poor: The Functions of Public Welfare.* New York: Vintage Books.

Polanyi, Karl. 1944. *The Great Transformation: The Political and Economic Origins of Our Time.* Boston: Beacon Press.

Pomar, Edgar. 1986. "New Housing Complex in Oakland Chinatown: Rev. Frank Mar to Attend Dedication." *Asian Week* 8(11): 15.

Popkin, Susan J. 2002. "The HOPE VI Program: What about the Residents?" Washington, DC: Urban Institute.

Popkin, Susan J., Bruce Katz, Mary K. Cunningham, Karen D. Brown, Jeremy Gustafson, and Margery A. Turner. 2004. "A Decade of HOPE VI: Research Findings and Policy Challenges." Washington, DC: Urban Institute.

Powell, Walter W., and Laurel Smith-Doerr. 1994. "Networks and Economic Life." In *The Handbook of Economic Sociology,* edited by Neil Smelser and Richard Swedberg (368–402). Princeton, NJ: Princeton University Press.

Powell, Walter. 1990. "Neither Market nor Hierarchy: Network Forms of Organization." In *Research in Organizational Behavior,* edited by L. L. Cummins and B. M. Staw (295–336). Greenwhich, CT: JAI Press.

Putnam, Robert. 2000. *Bowling Alone: The Collapse and Revival of American Community.* New York: Simon & Schuster.

Quadagno, Jill. 1988. "From Old-Age Assistance to Supplemental Security Income: The Political Economy of Relief in the South, 1935–1972." In *The Politics of Social Policy in the United States,* edited by Margaret Weir, Ana Shola Orloff, and Theda Skocpol (235–264). Princeton, NJ: Princeton University Press.

Radford, Gail. 1996. *Modern Housing for America: Policy Struggles in the New Deal Era.* Chicago: University of Chicago Press.

Reed, Robert. 1988. "Neighborhood Lending Pacts." *Crain's Chicago Business,* October 10: 31.

Richardson, Todd. 2005. "CDBG Formula Targeting to Community Development Need." Washington, DC: Office of Policy Development and Research, U.S. Department of Housing and Urban Development.

Roberts, Benson F. 2005. "The Political History of and Prospects for Reauthorizing New Markets." *Community Development Investment Review* 1(1): 21–32. http://frbsf.org/publications/community/review/122005/article3.pdf.

———. 2008a. "Beyond Section 42: How the New Housing Bill Affects LIHTC Projects." *Journal of Tax Credit Housing* 1(8).

———. 2008b. "Using Federal Funding to Mobilize Private Capital." *The Next American Opportunity: Good Policies for a Great America.* Philadelphia, PA: Opportunity Finance Network.

Rohe, William M., Roberto G. Quercia, Diane K. Levy, and Protip Biswas. 1998. *Sustainable Nonprofit Housing Development: An Analysis of the Maxwell Award Winners.* Washington, DC: Fannie Mae Foundation.

Rovner, Julie, Macon Morehouse, and Phil Kuntz. 1988. "Bush's Social Policy: Big Ideas, Little Money." *Congressional Quarterly,* December 10: 3459.

Rubin, Julia Sass, and Gregory M. Stankiewicz. 2005. "The New Markets Tax Credit Program: A Midcourse Assessment." *Community Development Investment Review* 1(1): 1–11.

Salamon, Lester M. 1995. *Partners in Public Service: Government-Nonprofit Relations in the Modern Welfare State.* Baltimore, MD: The Johns Hopkins University Press.

———, ed. 2002. *The Tools of Government: A Guide to the New Governance.* New York: Oxford University Press.

Sanbonmatsu, Lisa, Jeffrey R. Kling, Greg J. Duncan, and Jeanne Brooks-Gunn. 2006. "Neighborhoods and Academic Achievement: Results from the Moving to Opportunity Experiment." Working Paper 11909. Cambridge, MA: National Bureau of Economic Research.

Sanders, Marion. 1970. *The Professional Radical: Conversations with Saul Alinsky.* New York: Harper & Row.

Sard, Barbara, and Will Fischer. 2008. "Preserving Safe, High Quality Pubic Housing Should Be a Priority of Federal Housing Policy." Washington, DC: Center on Budget and Policy Priorities.

Schnare, Ann B. 2001. "The Impact of Changes in Multifamily Housing Finance in Older Urban Areas." Washington, DC, and Cambridge, MA: The Brookings Institution Center on Urban and Metropolitan Policy and the Joint Center for Housing Studies of Harvard University.

Schwartz, Alex. 1999. "New York City and Subsidized Housing: Impacts and Lessons of the City's $5 Billion Capital Budget Housing Plan." *Housing Policy Debate* (10)4: 843.

Sears, David, and Jack Citrin. 1982. *Tax Revolt: Something for Nothing in California.* Cambridge, MA: Harvard University Press.

Seiberg, Jaret. 1995. "Bankers Join in Bid to Rescue Low-Income-Housing Credits Series: 1" *American Banker* 160(243): 1.

Shabecoff, Alice. 1987. "Neighborhood Housing: Development Innovations." *Journal of Housing* 44(4): 105–18.

Shashaty, A. R. 1997. "Archer vs. Clinton: The Rematch." *Affordable Housing Finance* 5: 4. Quoted in Steven Rathgeb Smith, "Government Funding of Nonprofit Activity," in *Nonprofits and Government: Collaboration and Conflict,* edited by Elizabeth Boris and C. Eugene Steuerle (Washington, DC: The Urban Institute Press, 1999), 202–3.

Shaw, Janice Simsohn. 2007. "Leveraging Your Assets with Loans and Other Program Related Investments (PRIs)." Washington, DC: Association of Small Foundations.

Sidney, Mara S. 2003. *Unfair Housing: How National Policy Shapes Community Action.* Lawrence, KS: University Press of Kansas.

Simon, William. 2001. *The Community Economic Development Movement.* Durham, NC: Duke University Press.

Sirianni, Carmen, and Lewis Friedland. 2001. *Civic Innovation in America: Community Empowerment, Public Policy, and the Movement for Civic Renewal.* Berkeley: University of California Press.

Skocpol, Theda. 1992. *Protecting Soldiers and Mothers: The Political Origins of Social Policy in the United States.* Cambridge, MA: Harvard University Press.

Smith, Steven Rathgeb. 1999. "Government Funding of Nonprofit Activity." In *Nonprofits and Government: Collaboration and Conflict,* edited by Elizabeth T. Boris and C. Eugene Steuerle. Washington, DC: Urban Institute Press.

Smith, Steven Rathgeb, and Michael Lipsky. 1993. *Nonprofits for Hire: The Welfare State in the Age of Contracting.* Cambridge, MA: Harvard University Press.

Solomon, Rod. 2005. "Public Housing Reform and Voucher Success: Progress and Challenges." Washington, DC: Brookings Metropolitan Program.

Stegman, Michael. 1974. "Housing Finance Agencies: Are They Crucial Instruments of Government?" *Journal of the American Institute of Planners* 40(5): 307.

———. 1981. "Housing Finance Agencies: Technicians as Policy Makers." *Journal of Housing* 38(9): 478–81.

———. 2002. "The Fall and Rise of Public Housing." *Regulation* 25(2): 68.

Steinmo, Sven, Kathleen Ann Thelen, and Frank Longstreth, eds. 1992. *Structuring Politics: Historical Institutionalism in Comparative Analysis.* New York: Cambridge University Press.

Stinchcombe, Arthur. 1990. *Information and Organizations.* Berkeley: University of California Press.

Stockman, David. 1986. *The Triumph of Politics: How the Reagan Revolution Failed.* New York: Harper & Row.

Stoecker, Randy. 1997. "The CDC Model of Urban Redevelopment: A Critique and an Alternative." *Journal of Urban Affairs* 19(1): 5.

Struyk, Raymond J., Margery A. Turner, and Makiko Ueno. 1987. *Future U.S. Housing Policy: Meeting the Demographic Challenge.* Washington, DC: Urban Institute Press.

Sun Reporter. 1995. "Housing Program Redesigned in Response to Families with HIV." *Sun Reporter* 51(26): S5.

Suchman, Diane. 1990. *Public/Private Housing Partnerships.* Washington, DC: The Urban Land Institute.

Sugrue, Thomas. 1996. *The Origins of the Urban Crisis: Race and Inequality in Postwar Detroit.* Princeton, NJ: Princeton University Press.

Surowieki, James. 2004. *The Wisdom of Crowds: Why the Many Are Smarter Than the Few and How Collective Wisdom Shapes Business, Economies, Societies and Nations.* New York: Random House.

Tapscott, Don, and Anthony D. Williams. 2006. *Wikinomics: How Mass Collaboration Changes Everything.* New York: Penguin Books.

Terner, Ian Donald, and Thomas B. Cook. 1990. "New Directions for Federal Housing Policy: The Role of the States." In *Building Foundations: Housing and Federal Policy,* edited by Denise DiPasquale and Langley Keyes. Philadelphia: University of Pennsylvania Press.

Thoerig, Ted. 2008. "Solara." Washington, DC: Urban Land Institute.

Tingerthal, Mary. 2009. "Community Development Financial Expertise Put in Service of Neighborhood Stabilization." *Community Development Investment Review* 5(1): 53–64.

Trattner, Walter I. 1989. *From Poor Law to Welfare State: A History of Social Welfare in America,* 4th ed. New York: Free Press.

Trilling, Lionell. 1950. *The Liberal Imagination.* New York: Anchor-Doubleday.

Turner, Margery Austin, and Veronica M. Reed. 1990. *Housing America: Learning from the Past, Planning for the Future.* Washington, DC: Urban Institute Press.

Turnham, Jennifer, and Jill Khadduri. 2004. *Integrating School Reform and Neighborhood Revitalization: Opportunities and Challenges.* Cambridge, MA: Abt Associates, Inc.

U.S. Census Bureau. 2006. "2006 American Community Survey." Washington, DC: U.S. Census Bureau.

U.S. Congress. 1969. House Committee on Banking and Currency. "First Annual Report on National Housing Goals, Pursuant to the Provisions of the Housing and Urban Development Act of 1968." Washington, DC: U.S. House of Representatives.

———. 1970. House Committee on Banking and Currency. "The Second Annual Report on National Housing Goals, Pursuant to the Provisions of Section 1603 of the Housing and Urban Development Act of 1968." Washington, DC: U.S. House of Representatives.

———. 1971. House Committee on Banking and Currency. "The Third Annual Report on National Housing Goals, Pursuant to the Provisions of Section 1603 of the Housing and Urban Development Act of 1968." Washington, DC: U.S. House of Representatives.

———. 1972. House Committee on Banking and Currency. "The Fourth Annual Report on National Housing Goals, Pursuant to the Provisions of Section 1603 of the Housing and Urban Development Act of 1968." Washington, DC: U.S. House of Representatives.

———. 1973. House Committee on Banking and Currency, Subcommittee on Housing, "Housing and Community Development Legislation—1973." Washington, DC: U.S. House of Representatives.

———. 1974. House Committee on Banking and Currency, Subcommittee on Housing. "The Administration's Housing and Community Development Proposals." Washington, DC: U.S. House of Representatives.

———. 1977. Senate Committee on Banking, Housing, and Urban Affairs. "Community Credit Needs." Washington, DC: U.S. Senate.

———. 1983. "Federal Subsidies for Public Housing: Issues and Options." Washington, DC: U.S. Government Printing Office.

———. 1988a. Senate Committee on Banking, Housing, and Urban Affairs. "Report of the National Housing Task Force." Washington, DC: U.S. Senate.

———. 1988b. Senate Subcommittee on Housing and Urban Affairs. "Hearings on the National Affordable Housing Act." Washington, DC: U.S. Senate.

———. 1988c. Senate Subcommittee on Housing and Urban Affairs. "Hearings on the Goal to Implement an Effective New National Housing Policy." Washington, DC: U.S. Senate.

———. 1989. House Committee on Ways and Means. "Low Income Housing Tax Credit: Hearing before the Subcommittee on Select Revenue Measures of the Committee on Ways and Means." Washington, DC: U.S. House of Representatives.

———. 1990. Committee on Banking, Housing, and Urban Affairs. "The Homeownership and Opportunity for People Everywhere (HOPE) Initiatives: Joint Hearings before the Committee on Banking, Housing, and Urban Affairs and the Subcommittee on Housing and Urban Affairs." Washington, DC: U.S. Congress.

———. 1991. "Extension of Remarks (November 1)." Congressional Record, E3640. Washington, DC: U.S. House of Representatives.

———. 1992. "Hearings on the Housing and Community Development Program Reauthorization Act (September 10)." Congressional Record S8198. Washington, DC: U.S. Government Printing Office.

———. 1997. "The Public Housing Reform and Responsibility Act of 1997: Report of the Committee on Banking, Housing, and Urban Affairs, United States Senate, to Accompany S. 462 Together with Additional Views." Washington, DC: U.S. Government Printing Office.

———. 2000. Joint Committee on Taxation. "Summary of Provisions Contained in H.R. 5662, The Community Renewal Tax Relief Act of 2000." Washington, DC: U.S Congress.

U.S. Congressional Budget Office. 1983. "Federal Subsidies for Public Housing: Issues and Options." Washington, DC: U.S. Government Printing Office.

———. 2002. "The Budget and Economic Outlook: Fiscal Years 2003–2012." Washington, DC: Government Printing Office.

U.S. Department of Housing and Urban Development. 1974. "Housing in the Seventies: A Report of the National Housing Policy Review." Washington, DC: HUD.

———. 1995. "A Place to Live Is the Place to Start: A Statement of Principles for Changing HUD to Meet America's Housing and Community Priorities." Washington, DC: HUD.

———. 1996. "Building Public-Private Partnerships to Develop Affordable Housing." Washington DC: HUD.

———. 1997. "A New HUD: Opportunity for All." Washington, DC: HUD.

———. 2000. "Section 8 Tenant-Based Housing Assistance: A Look Back after 30 Years." Washington, DC: HUD. http://www.huduser.org/publications/pubasst/look.html.

———. 2003. "Trends in Worst Case Housing Needs for Housing, 1978–1999." Washington, DC: HUD. http://www.huduser.org/Publications/PDF/trends.pdf.

———. 2006. "Multifamily Properties: Opting In, Opting Out, and Remaining Affordable." Washington, DC: HUD.

———. 2007. "Hope VI Program Authority and Funding History." Washington, DC: HUD. http://www.hud.gov/offices/pih/programs/ph/hope6/about/fundinghistory.pdf.

———. 2008. "HOME Program National Production Report." Washington, DC: HUD. http://www.hud.gov/offices/cpd/affordablehousing/reports/production/073108.pdf.

U.S. Environmental Protection Agency. n.d. "Brownfields Tax Credit: Frequently Asked Questions." Washington, DC: U.S. Environmental Protection Agency. http://www.epa.gov/swerosps/bf/bftaxinc.htm

U.S. General Accounting Office. 1997. "Tax Credits: Opportunities to Improve Oversight of the Low Income Housing Program." Washington, DC: U.S. Government Printing Office.

U.S. Government Accountability Office. 2004. "Brownfield Redevelopment: Stakeholders Report That EPA's Program Helps to Redevelop Sites, but Additional Measures Could Complement Agency Efforts." Washington, DC: U.S. Government Accountability Office.

———. 2006. "Community Development Block Grants: Program Offers Recipients Flexibility but Oversight Can Be Improved." GAO-06-732. Washington, DC: Government Accountability Office.

———. 2007a. "Federal Electricity Subsidies: Information on Research Funding, Tax Expenditures, and Other Activities That Support Electricity Production." GAO-08-102. Washington, DC: Government Accountability Office.

———. 2007b. "Tax Policy: New Markets Tax Credit Appears to Increase Investment by Investors in Low-Income Communities, but Opportunities Exist to Better Monitor Compliance." GAO-07-296. Washington, DC: Government Accountability Office.

U.S. Housing and Home Finance Agency. 1950. "A Handbook of Information on Provisions of the Housing Act of 1949 and Operations under the Various Programs." Washington DC: Housing and Home Finance Agency, Office of the Administrator.

U.S. Millennial Housing Commission. "Meeting Our Nation's Housing Challenges." Washington, DC: U.S. Millennial Housing Commission.

U.S. Office of Economic Development. 1975. "Special Impact Program Policies and Priorities." Washington, DC: Community Services Administration.

———. 1976. "Guidelines for Community Development Corporation Planning Grants under Title VII, Special Impact Programs, of the Community Services Act of 1974." Washington, DC: Community Services Administration.

U.S. Office of Management and Budget. 2006. "Analytical Perspectives: Budget of the United States Government, Fiscal Year 2007." Washington, DC: U.S. Government Printing Office.

———. 2008. "Budget of the United States Government: Fiscal Year 2008." Washington, DC: U.S. Government Printing Office.

U.S. President's Commission on Housing. 1982. "Report of the President's Commission on Housing, Chaired by William F. McKenna." Washington, DC: Government Printing Office.

U.S. President's Committee on Urban Housing. 1969. "A Decent Home: The Report of the President's Committee on Urban Housing, Chaired by Edgar F. Kaiser." Washington, DC: U.S. Government Printing Office.

U.S. President's Urban and Regional Policy Group. 1978. "A New Partnership to Conserve America's Communities: A Status Report on the President's Urban Policy." Washington, DC: HUD.

Urban Institute. 1996. "Implementing Block Grants for Housing: An Evaluation of the First Year of HOME." Washington, DC: U.S. Department of Housing and Urban Development.

———. 1999. "Expanding the Nation's Supply of Affordable Housing: An Evaluation of the HOME Investment Partnership Program." Washington, DC: Urban Institute.

Vale, Lawrence. 2000. *From the Puritans to the Projects: Public Housing and Public Neighborhoods.* Cambridge, MA: Harvard University Press.

———. 2000. *Reclaiming Public Housing: A Half Century of Struggle in Three Public Housing Neighborhoods.* Cambridge, MA: Harvard University Press.

Verba, Sidney, Kay Lehman Sholzman, and Henry E. Brady. 1995. *Voice and Equality: Civic Voluntarism in American Politics.* Cambridge, MA: Harvard University Press.

Vidal, Avis. 1992. *Rebuilding Communities: A National Study of Urban Community Development Corporations.* New York: New School for Social Research.

———. 1997. "Can Community Development Re-Invent Itself?" *Journal of the American Planning Association* 63(4): 429–38.

Walker, Christopher. 1993. "Nonprofit Housing Development: Status, Trends, and Prospects." *Housing Policy Debate* 4(3): 369–414.

Walker, Christopher, and Mark Weinheimer. 1998. *Community Development in the 1990s.* Washington, DC: Urban Institute Press.

Walker, Christopher, Paul Dommel, Harry P. Hatry, Amy Bogdon, and Patrick Boxall. 1994. "Federal Funds, Local Choices." Washington, DC: Urban Institute.

Walker, Jeffrey. 1986. "Privatization of Housing Programs: Policy and Implications." *Journal of Housing* 43(6): 241–50.

Weaver, Robert. 1996. "Address to a Convention of the National League of Cities by HUD Secretary Robert Weaver, March 30." Record Group 207, Federal Archives, College Park, MD.

Wei-Skillern, Jane, and Sonia Marciano. 2008. "The Networked Nonprofit." Stanford *Social Innovation Review*. Palo Alto, CA: Stanford University.

Wildavsky, Aaron. 1996. "Government and the People." In *The Essential Neoconservative Reader*, edited by Mark Gerson. Menlo Park, CA: Addison-Wesley Publishing Company, Inc..

Wilensky, Harold. 2002. *Rich Democracies: Political Economy, Public Policy, and Performance*. Berkeley: University of California Press.

Williamson, Oliver E. 2000. "The New Institutional Economics: Taking Stock, Looking Ahead." *Journal of Economic Literature* 38(3): 595–613.

———. 2005. "The Economics of Governance." *American Economic Association* 95(2): 1–18.

Wood, Robert. 1984. "HUD in the Eighties: Doubt—Ability and Do-Ability." In *Housing in the Eighties: Financial and Institutional Perspectives*, edited by Charles M. Haar. Cambridge, MA: Lincoln Institute of Land Policy.

Wright, David J. 2001. *It Takes a Neighborhood: Strategies to Prevent Urban Decline*. New York: Rockefeller Institute Press.

Yellen, Janet L. 2006. Speech to the Center for the Study of Democracy, University of California, Irvine, November 6. http://www.frbsf.org/news/speeches/2006/1106.html.

Zelizer, Julian E. 1998. *Taxing America: Wilbur Mills, Congress, and the State, 1945–1975*. New York: Cambridge University Press.

Zielenbach, Sean. 2000. *The Art of Revitalization: Improving Conditions in Distressed Neighborhoods*. New York: Garland Publishing.

Zoglin, Richard. 1996. "The Urban Renewer: James W. Rouse: 1914–1996." *Time*, April 22: 97.

Zuckman, Jill. 1990. "Provisions: Housing Authorizations." *Congressional Quarterly*, December 8: 4091.

About the Author

David Erickson is director of the Center for Community Development Investments at the Federal Reserve Bank of San Francisco and edits the Federal Reserve journal *Community Development Investment Review*. His research areas in the community development department of the Federal Reserve include community development finance, affordable housing, economic development, and institutional changes that benefit low-income communities. He recently served as an editor of a joint research project with the Brookings Metropolitan Policy Program studying areas of concentrated poverty in the United States and was also an editor of a recently released collection of research papers and essays on the Community Reinvestment Act.

He has five years of experience in the affordable housing industry working for government, nonprofit, and private-sector employers. He has a Ph.D. in history from the University of California, Berkeley, with a focus on economic history and public policy. He also holds a master's degree in public policy from the Goldman School of Public Policy at Berkeley.

Index